THE INVENTION OF
PRIMITIVE SOCIETY

THE INVENTION
OF PRIMITIVE
SOCIETY

Transformations of an Illusion

ADAM KUPER

ROUTLEDGE
London and New York

For Simon, Jeremy and Hannah

On fait de la science – et surtout de la sociologie – contre sa formation autant qu'avec sa formation. Et seule l'histoire peut nous débarrasser de l'histoire.

Pierre Boudieu (1982), *Leçon sur le leçon*, Paris, Les Editions de Minuit

First published in 1988 by Routledge
11 New Fetter Lane, London EC4P 4EE

Published in the USA by Routledge
a division of Routledge, Chapman and Hall, Inc.
29 West 35th Street, New York, NY 10001

Set in 10 on 11 point Plantin Light
and printed in Great Britain
by Butler & Tanner Ltd,
Frome and London

Library of Congress Cataloging in Publication Data

Kuper, Adam.
    The invention of primitive society : transformations of an
    illusion/Adam Kuper
        p.   cm.
    Bibliography: p.
    Includes index.
    1. Ethnology—History.   2. Society, Primitive.   I. Title.
    GN308.K87 1988
    306'.09—dc 19   88-12201

British Library CIP Data also available
ISBN 0–415–00902–2 (c)
        0–415–00903–0 (p)

CONTENTS

PREFACE   vii

1   *The idea of primitive society*   1

PART I   The constitution of primitive society   15

2   *Patriarchal theory*   17
3   *Lewis Henry Morgan and ancient society*   42
4   *The question of totemism*   76
5   *Australian totemism*   92
6   *Totem and taboo*   105

PART II   Academic anthropologists and primitive society   123

7   *The Boasians and the critique of evolutionism*   125
8   *Rivers and Melanesian society*   152
9   *The reaction to Rivers*   171
10   *Descent theory: a phoenix from the ashes*   190
11   *A short history of alliance theory*   210
12   *Conclusion*   231

BIBLIOGRAPHY   245
INDEX   262

PREFACE

In 1981 I was commissioned to write a retrospective essay on lineage theory for the *Annual Review of Anthropology*. Faced with a politely but firmly enforced deadline, I duly completed the essay within a couple of months. Even more than most exercises of this kind, however, it deposited a residue of curiosity and dissatisfaction. I had done enough work to realize that I knew very little even about how kinship theory had developed, but I was left with a strong suspicion that the history of anthropological theory had disturbing implications for a practitioner of the discipline. There was also the promise of a bizarre but potentially significant case-study in the history of the social sciences. Clearly I had to read on and work out the implications. This book is the result.

Earlier versions of the passages on Maine, Morgan and Durkheim were published in *Anthropology and History*, the *Journal of the History of the Behavioral Sciences* and the *British Journal of Sociology* respectively. Other sections of the book were presented in the form of seminar papers at Leiden University, Brunel University, the London School of Economics and Cambridge University. Much of the chapter on the early theory of totemism was first worked up for a Henry Myers lecture at Edinburgh University. I am grateful to my colleagues, and the editors of the journals concerned, for giving me some encouragement and assistance during the long period in which I was struggling with the material for this book.

When I thought that the book was almost ready I showed it to Alan A. Stone, who indicated very forcefully that it still needed a lot of work. Some time later an improved version was read by Gerhard Baumann, who contributed many perceptive suggestions, and by Isaac Schapera, whose meticulous attention to detail cleared up numerous errors and confusions. Nell Blane carefully proof-read the manuscript.

Leiden and London, 1982–7

CHAPTER 1

The idea of primitive society

This book is a history of the ways in which anthropologists have thought about primitive society. Speculations about primitive society have a long and complicated ancestry, but I am concerned with the distinctive and novel version of this idea which crystallized, with anthropology itself, in the 1860s and 1870s and which persisted until very recently (indeed, still survives, if no longer within mainstream anthropology). The idea of primitive society is intimately related to other potent and beguiling notions concerning primitive mentality, primitive religion, primitive art, primitive money, and so on. Nevertheless, the sociological thread in this discourse can be separated out quite easily, and I hope it will become apparent that it does make sense to treat it as a distinct topic.

The rapidity with which the anthropological idea of primitive society was worked out is very striking, but its persistence is perhaps yet more extraordinary. Conventional histories of anthropology describe a succession of quasi-philosophical theories – evolutionism, diffusionism, functionalism, structuralism, etc. Each reigned briefly and then was rudely overthrown. Yet all these theoretical traditions addressed the same idea of primitive society. The persistence of this prototype for well over a hundred years is the more remarkable since empirical investigation of tropical 'primitive' societies only began in a systematic way and on any scale in the last decade of the nineteenth century.

Darwin and Maine

The moment at which the new idea took shape can be fixed only roughly. Darwin's *The Origin of Species* appeared in 1859. During the following two decades a series of 'sociological' monographs appeared dealing with primitive society. These included classic studies by Bachofen, Maine, Fustel de Coulanges, Lubbock, McLennan, Morgan and Tylor. All shared a concern with the nature of 'primitive' society and religion. Virtually all assumed a direct progression from primitive society through various intermediate stages to modern society. Nevertheless, although these writers would all be lumped together as 'evolutionists' by later generations, Darwin's theory was not their common inspiration.[1]

There is a paradox here, for Darwin's triumph stimulated a very un-Darwinian anthropology. As Darwinism won ground in Britain, broadly evolutionist kinds of thought gained fresh currency. Associates of Darwin like Huxley, Galton and Lubbock established a new space for evolutionary anthropological investigations within the field of the natural sciences and even in the humanities. Nevertheless, those untrained in biology were very likely to prefer a Lamarckian to a Darwinian view of evolution, if, indeed, they recognized the differences. Herbert Spencer – a crude Lamarckian – had at least as much impact on Maine or even Tylor and Durkheim as did Darwin.

Perhaps the main difficulty which Darwin's theory presented was his idea that evolution did not imply direction or progress, that it did not follow any plan. Darwin argued that natural selection worked upon more or less random individual variations. And while environmental changes were of decisive importance, they were unpredictable. Natural selection was an ineluctable process, but particular adaptations were the product of chance. It followed that history was not unilinear. Groups with the same origin would develop in different ways if they were isolated in different environments. One could accordingly trace the history of a species backwards in time, but there was no way of predicting its future path. It was also very difficult, if not impossible, to assess 'progress'.

These were new and radical ideas which were not in general shared by those contemporaries of Darwin who wrote about primitive culture or primitive society. They were much more likely to believe with Spencer that human history was a history of progress, and that all living societies could be ranked on a single evolutionary

---

1 This argument was made powerfully – but perhaps with some rhetorical exaggeration – in J. W. Burrow's *Evolution and Society* (1966).

scale. They also generally accepted the classic Lamarckian ideas: that evolutionary change took the form of revolutionary leaps between one stage of development and another; that the impulse for these changes was internal rather than external; and that acquired traits were transmitted by heredity.

I would not wish to overstate the case. Some early anthropologists were indeed directly influenced by Darwin. Rather more were inspired (perhaps at second-hand) to adopt broadly evolutionist frameworks of argument. Only a few – including Henry Maine – took very little notice of Darwin or even of Spencer. But it is certainly correct that the early anthropologists were seldom ✓ Darwinians in the strict sense.

Nor is this altogether surprising, since the study of primitive society was not generally regarded as a branch of natural history. Rather it was treated initially as a branch of legal studies. Many of the key authors were lawyers, including Bachofen, Köhler, Maine, McLennan and Morgan. The issues which they investigated – the development of marriage, the family, private property and the state – were conceived of as legal questions. The initial source – the common case-study – was provided by Roman law. This shared legal background also distinguished the lawyer-sociologists from other contemporary 'anthropologists' such as Tylor or Darwin's friend Lubbock, whose primary concerns were with material culture and the development of religion. It was Tylor indeed who commented in 1865 that the study of such an issue as exogamy 'belongs properly to that interesting, but difficult and almost unworked subject, the Comparative Jurisprudence of the lower races, and no one not versed in Civil Law could do it justice'.[2]

When I come to discuss individual authors, the diversity of their intellectual sources will be evident. There were obvious continuities with writers of the Scottish and French Enlightenment, and more immediately with Herbert Spencer and the Utilitarians in England, and with Comte and the Positivists in France. Victorian constitutional historians like Macaulay, Stubbs, Freeman and Froude were transforming the tradition of universal histories associated with the Scottish Enlightenment. This new historiography particularly influenced Maine, but its impact can be traced upon other social evolutionists of the 1860s and 1870s.[3] Some of the new

2 Tylor (1865), *Researches into the Early History of Mankind*, p. 277.
3 See Burrow (1981), *A Liberal Descent: Victorian Historians and the English Past.*

anthropologists were also stirred by the findings and the methods of German philology, mediated in Britain by Max Müller.[4] And each particular author had his own idiosyncratic intellectual interests and drew on distinctive specialities – Maine on Roman law, Robertson Smith on Biblical scholarship, Frazer on the classics, and so forth.

Nor were the anthropologists responding to a single political concern. The Morant Bay rebellion in Jamaica and the Civil War in the United States revived earlier European debates on slavery. The development of the Indian Empire and the colonization of Africa raised fundamental questions about the nature of government and of civilization itself. Intellectuals were also concerned – some almost obsessively – with the consequences of extending the franchise to new social classes. Particularly in continental Europe, there was great interest in the vitality of nationalist movements. All these political questions seemed apt for anthropological commentary, but they did not impinge upon every anthropologist to the same degree or in the same sort of way. For many, religious questions seemed still more urgent, as intellectuals began to come to terms with the challenge of Lyell and Darwin to the authorized Biblical account of history. One can in fact identify a transition in the 1870s from a central concern with political issues to a greater interest in religion.

In the end, however, it may be that something yet more fundamental than political and religious concerns informed the new wave of interest in human origins. In the second half of the nineteenth century, Europeans believed themselves to be witnessing a revolutionary transition in the type of their society. Marx defined a capitalist society emerging from a feudal society; Weber was to write about the rationalization, the bureaucratization, the disenchantment of the old world; Tönnies about the move from community to association; Durkheim about the change from mechanical to organic forms of solidarity. Each conceived of the new world in contrast to 'traditional society'; and behind this 'traditional society' they discerned a primitive or primeval society.

---

4 Max Müller gave a distinctly evolutionist cast to his historical reconstructions. Moreover, Darwin drew on theories of language development in *The Origin of Species* (1859). Nevertheless, the philological tradition was generally speaking evolutionist, if at all, only in a vague and old-fashioned way.

[The anthropologists took this primitive society as their special subject, but in practice primitive society proved to be their own society (as they understood it) seen in a distorting mirror. For them modern society was defined above all by the territorial state, the monogamous family and private property. Primitive society therefore must have been nomadic, ordered by blood ties, sexually promiscuous and communist. There had also been a progression in mentality. Primitive man was illogical and given to magic.] In time he had developed more sophisticated religious ideas. Modern man, however, had invented science. Like their most reflective contemporaries, in short, the pioneer anthropologists believed that their own was an age of massive transition. They looked back in order to understand the nature of the present, on the assumption that modern society had evolved from its antithesis.

The prototype of primitive society

The inspiration behind the new wave of books on primitive society was therefore very diverse. Darwin's theory was by no means the common source of the pioneer anthropologists. If one book is to be placed at the head of what became a new series, it is perhaps more appropriate to begin two years after the publication of *The Origin of Species*, with the appearance in 1861 of Henry Maine's *Ancient Law*. Although most of Maine's specific ideas were soon discarded, he placed on the agenda most of the central questions which were to preoccupy his rivals and successors for the next half-century. His contribution was not at the level of theory. Rather, he re-established and embellished a classic notion of the original human condition, and he made it seem directly relevant to the intellectual concerns of his contemporaries.

Maine's history (like the Old Testament and many classical sources) assumed that man was originally a member of a corporate family group ruled by a despotic patriarch. Later, patriarchal power provided the basis for larger associations. Later still, waifs and strays were brought in by adoption. The principle of patriarchal authority was diluted. Local association became increasingly important. Ultimately, societies based on kinship were replaced by societies based upon the state. This transition from blood to soil, from status to contract, was the greatest revolution in human history.

In the very year in which *Ancient Law* was published, a Swiss professor of Roman Law, Johannes Bachofen, had appealed to some of the same sources – particularly Greek myth and Roman law – but he had concluded that man's original family structure was matriarchal. Bachofen's strange book had little impact, however. In 1864 the French scholar Fustel de Coulanges published *La Cité Antique*, which neglected both Maine and Bachofen, but gave an account of mankind's social and political history similar to Maine's, while introducing a new determinant, religious progress. In 1865 a Scottish lawyer, J. F. McLennan, reached a similar conclusion to Bachofen, but in ignorance of his work and directly in reaction to Maine. The publication of his *Primitive Marriage*, in turn, inspired an American lawyer, Lewis Henry Morgan, to develop the most influential of these new images of early society. His best-known book, *Ancient Society*, appeared sixteen years after *Ancient Law*. It echoed Maine's title and belonged to the same universe of discourse.

By the late nineteenth century two authorities had established themselves in Anglo-American anthropology, E. B. Tylor and J. G. Frazer. They sifted the arguments in every branch of the new discipline and asserted an orthodoxy. Together they adjudicated the disputes between Maine and his rivals, and settled the broad characteristics of primeval human societies. Primitive society was originally an organic whole. It then split into two or more identical building blocks. (This idea went back to Spencer.) The component units of society were exogamous, corporate descent groups. By the 1880s it was generally agreed (despite Maine's continued dissent) that these groups were 'matriarchal', tracing descent in the female line. Women and goods were held communally by the men of each group. Marriage took the form of regular exchanges between them. These social forms, no longer extant, were preserved in the languages (especially in kinship terminologies), and in the ceremonies of contemporary 'primitive' peoples.

It is striking how much agreement there soon was even on matters of detail. By the last decade of the nineteenth century, almost all the new specialists would have agreed with the following propositions.

1   The most primitive societies were ordered on the basis of kinship relations.
2   Their kinship organization was based on descent groups.
3   These descent groups were exogamous and were related by a series of marriage exchanges.

4 Like extinct species, these primeval institutions were preserved in fossil form, ceremonies and kinship terminologies bearing witness to long-dead practices.

5 Finally, with the development of private property, the descent groups withered away and a territorial state emerged. This was the most revolutionary change in the history of humanity. It marked the transition from ancient to modern society.

These ideas were also linked to the theory of primitive religion. The original religion was 'animism', a belief that natural species and objects had souls and should be worshipped. In the most primitive societies each descent group believed that it was descended from an animal or vegetable god, which it revered.

The persistence of an illusion

The rapid establishment and the endurance of a theory is not particularly remarkable if the theory is substantially correct. But hardly any anthropologist today would accept that this classic account of primitive society can be sustained. On the contrary, the orthodox modern view is that there never was such a thing as 'primitive society'. Certainly, no such thing can be reconstructed now. There is not even a sensible way in which one can specify what a 'primitive society' is. The term implies some historical point of reference. It presumably defines a type of society ancestral to more advanced forms, on the analogy of an evolutionary history of some natural species. But human societies cannot be traced back to a single point of origin, and there is no way of reconstituting prehistoric social forms, classifying them, and aligning them in a time series. There are no fossils of social organization.

Even if some very ancient social order could be reconstituted, one could not generalize it. If it is useful to apply evolutionary theory to social history, then it must direct attention to variation, to adaptation to all sorts of local circumstances, and so to diversification. And it does seem likely that early human societies were indeed rather diverse. Surviving hunter-gatherers certainly do not conform to a single organizational type.[5] Since ecological variations constrain social organization, especially where technology is

---

5 However, this diversity is arguably a consequence (at least in part) of the relationships which have formed over recent centuries with settled agricultural populations.

simple, there must have been considerable differences in social structure between the earliest human societies. Not to put too fine a point upon it, the history of the theory of primitive society is the history of an illusion. It is our phlogiston, our aether; or, less grandly, our equivalent to the notion of hysteria. This conclusion, commonplace enough amongst modern anthropologists, raises all sorts of problems for the historian.

If there is a current orthodoxy in the humanities and social sciences, then it is perhaps relativism. It is indeed from within the social sciences that the present wave of unjudging and relativistic history of science is being attempted. The model is often the anthropological treatment of other cultures. The aim is to avoid culture-bound misapprehensions, to achieve phenomenological validity. It may even be suggested that to understand all is to forgive all.

However, it is one thing to set an argument in its context; it is quite another to pretend that it cannot be rejected. I start, on the contrary, from the supremely unrelativist assumption that the theory of primitive society is on a par with the history of the theory of aether. The theory of primitive society is about something which does not and never has existed. One of my reasons for writing this book is to remove the constitution of primitive society from the agenda of anthropology and political theory once and for all. (This is quite unashamedly a story with a moral.)

At the same time, criticism is not my main concern. I am more interested in accounting for the genesis of the illusion, and more particularly for its persistence. The persistence of the model is peculiarly problematic since various of its basic assumptions were quite directly contradicted by ethnographic evidence and by the logic of evolutionary theory itself. The difficulties were clearly stated by some of the leading scholars in the field (notably Westermarck, Boas and Malinowski). Notwithstanding, social anthropologists busied themselves for over a hundred years with the manipulation of a fantasy – a fantasy which had been constructed by speculative lawyers in the late nineteenth century. This is a fact which must provoke thought, and not among anthropologists alone.

There are basically two ways of accounting for the persistence of the old styles of thinking. One would appeal to continuing features of the political environment. The idea of primitive society could and did feed a variety of ideological positions. Among its most celebrated protagonists were Engels, Freud, Durkheim and

Kropotkin. Its birth may be related to the late Victorian surge of imperialism, and its perhaps terminal decline in the last two decades may be related to the end of the Empire. The rise and fall of nationalism is probably equally relevant. The idea of primitive society fed the common belief that societies were based either on blood or on soil, and that these principles of descent and territoriality may be equated with race and citizenship, the contrasting components of every imperialism and every nationalism. Yet the idea of primitive society was never merely an imperial myth, or a charter for nationalism. Nor, at the other extreme, was it ever exclusively identified with Marxism, despite the adoption of Morgan's theories by Engels. The evolutionist framework did offer both communists and colonialists the hope that although social institutions varied from society to society, they formed a single hierarchy, through which all would eventually progress. Yet while it could serve so many ideological purposes, it could at times also serve none.

Moreover, as anthropology became increasingly academic, so ideological factors became less decisive (though they were seldom insignificant). Increasingly the idea of primitive society was sustained by forces internal to the discipline of anthropology. Maine and his contemporaries established primitive society as the object of social anthropology. They posed strategic questions about the origin of the family, the state and religion. They also prepared a specialized set of tools. Primitive society then became the preserve of a new discipline, which soon developed a sophisticated, quasi-mathematical set of techniques for kinship studies. When this happened, the survival of the idea of primitive society was ensured.

As an initial rough approximation, the classic idea of primitive society persisted within anthropology – or with anthropology – because it was 'good to think'. It referred to ultimate social concerns, the state, citizenship, the family and so on. And it generated a specialized tradition of puzzle-solving.

The idea of primitive society probably could not have persisted within anthropology if it had remained static. But it did not. On the contrary, it lent itself to the most dazzling play of variations. This capacity for renewal facilitated accommodation to virtually any theoretical or political discourse, a process which allowed generations of scholars to feel that they were making genuinely novel contributions to their science.

Transformations

How best to conceive this combination of conservatism and innovation? The most famous modern characterization of scientific change is that of Thomas Kuhn. For Kuhn, significant changes are sudden and radical. The switch from one 'paradigm' to another involves a sharp break in continuity.

Scientific development depends in part on a process of non-incremental or revolutionary change. Some revolutions are large, like those associated with the names of Copernicus, Newton, or Darwin, but most are much smaller, like the discovery of oxygen or the planet Uranus. The usual prelude to changes of this sort is ... the awareness of anomaly, of an occurrence or set of occurrences that does not fit existing ways of ordering phenomena. The changes that result therefore require 'putting on a different kind of thinking-cap', one that renders the anomalous lawlike but that, in the process, also transforms the order exhibited by some other phenomena, previously unproblematic.[6]

A number of historians of science have questioned the Kuhnian idea that science changes by way of radical changes of paradigm, or epistemological breaks (to use the continental phrase). They point to the continuities and demonstrate that many famous discoveries were anticipated, at least in part. A more original reaction is that of I. Bernard Cohen. While emphasizing the striking conservatism of even the most celebrated 'scientific revolutions', he is not tempted by those at the other extreme who are content to trace the sources of a new theory and then to describe it as a 'synthesis'. Instead he suggests that great instances of creativity – literary as much as scientific – may best be described as 'transformations'.[7] He argues that Newton, for instance, 'certainly did not merely combine in a synthetic "stew" the principles of Copernicus, Kepler and Galileo, Descartes, Hooke and Huygens. Rather, he carefully selected certain ideas ... and *transformed* them, giving each of them a new form which only then was useful to him'.[8] Another example Cohen chooses is Darwin's 'transformation' of ideas which had been developed by Lyell and by Malthus. Darwin had been per-

---

6 Kuhn (1977), *The Essential Tension*, p. xvii. Critics had pointed out the difficulties in his use of the terms 'paradigm' and 'paradigm shift', and Kuhn here adopted Butterfield's homely allusion to putting on another thinking-cap.

7 Cohen (1980), *The Newtonian Revolution*, especially Chapter 4.

8 *Op. cit.*, p. 158.

suaded by Lyell's idea that whole species were in historic competition for a place in the sun. Then he read Malthus and realized that he had to consider rather the chances of individual survival.

An observation of special relevance to the present book is that some ideas are especially apt for transformation, and that this particular quality may increase the chances of their survival, even if they turn out to be quite wrong. Cohen instances some of the crucial ideas which 'undergo successive transformations and continue to live on for a long time in science, such as atom, energy and impetus', but refers also to ideas like aether ('transformed into the imponderable fluids of heat, electricity and magnetism') which 'have a measured but fruitful existence and survive only as archeological remains in the scientific language'.[9]

Precisely what Cohen means by a transformation is not entirely clear. Some of his examples seem to involve no more than a revision, more or less radical, of a specific idea; a scientist incorporates an older idea, but changes it slightly, or applies it in a new context. At other times Cohen invokes the notion of a mathematical transformation. This suggests a different kind of process, involving systematic shifts in a whole conceptual structure. In this sense, transformations might be as radical and complete as Kuhnian paradigm changes. Cohen also refers to the work of both Mach and Foucault, who certainly envisaged something in the nature of structural shifts in the development of scientific ideas.[10]

I am persuaded that the notion of transformations is a powerful tool in the history of science, but I would like to introduce the specific idea of transformation which has been developed by Lévi-Strauss, most systematically in his writings on myth. Lévi-Strauss argues that in mythology the mind

operates essentially through a process of transformation. A myth no sooner comes into being than it is modified through a change of narrator ... some elements drop out and are replaced by others, sequences change places, and the modified structure moves through a series of states, the variations of which nevertheless still belong to the same set.

9 *Op. cit.*, p. 197.
10 Cohen, *op. cit.*, pp. 280–9. Cf. Foucault (1972), *The Archaeology of Knowledge*; Mach (1898), *Popular Scientific Lectures*.

Moreover, these transformations of a myth do not simply result in minor changes, differences which can be reduced to 'small positive or negative increments'. Rather the transformations are accomplished by systematic manipulations of the myth as a whole, yielding 'clear-cut relationships such as contrariness, contradiction, inversion or symmetry'.[11]

Lévi-Strauss believes that the human mind acts upon its raw materials in a highly constrained manner. It establishes structures and then manipulates them, almost mechanically. Moreover he insists that the kind of thinking which anthropologists have identified in exotic mythologies – what he calls mytho-logic – or in the ethno-science of hunters and gatherers is no different in principle from the most sophisticated scientific thought.[12]

Like Cohen, Lévi-Strauss also believes that similar kinds of innovation can be found in the arts and in the sciences. He refers approvingly to the remarkable first chapter of D'Arcy Thompson's masterpiece, *On Growth and Form* (1917), which cited the use of transformations in mathematics and in natural history, and equally in the botany of Goethe and the art of Dürer.[13]

If Lévi-Strauss is right, then scientists think rather like artists, and perhaps we all think, at least at times, like Amazonian Indians. Moreover, scientific theories may have a great deal in common with Amazonian myths. Yet there is one evident difference between the established ideal of scientific thought and what Lévi-Stauss calls 'the logic of the concrete', which operates by transforming structures. Scientific thought is ideally progressive. Each stage of understanding should be an advance on its predecessor. One does not go

11 Lévi-Strauss (1981), *The Naked Man*, p. 675.

12 In a famous passage he wrote that:

the kind of logic in mythical thought is as rigorous as that of modern science, and that the difference lies, not in the quality of the intellectual process, but in the nature of things to which it is applied ... man has always been thinking equally well; the improvement lies, not in an alleged progress of man's mind, but in the discovery of new areas to which it may apply its unchanged and unchanging powers. (Lévi-Strauss (1963), *Structural Anthropology*, p. 230)

13 At this stage the notion of transformations may seem a little mystifying. I hope that it will be clarified by examples, but in the meantime it may be helpful to recall something that the distinguished anthropologist Meyer Fortes used to tell me, to put me on my guard against the dodges of the English. The public-school types, he said, were trained to take the accepted arguments and to turn them upside-down; a purely mechanical trick, but one which produced the appearance of originality.

backwards in science. But if an argument proceeds – to put it crudely – by turning a previous argument on its head, then at some stage someone will effect a further transformation by setting it back in its former position. In short, a series of structural transformations is quite likely to end up where it began.[14]

I think that this is true, at least for much of anthropological discourse. It cannot be denied that formal transformations of the Lévi-Straussian kind abound in the history of the idea of primitive society. The various models of primitive society are typically straightforward, even mechanical, transformations of their predecessors. Indeed, this book is very largely an account of the transformations of an illusion within an increasingly hermetic professional discourse.

But that is not the whole story. There are also syntheses on the lines of Cohen's transformations. Different ideas are yoked together, sets of data placed in fresh juxtapositions. And some of the most influential figures did not effect significant transformations of any kind. Rather they gave current ideas an authoritative form. At the other extreme, a few individuals attempted to step outside the bounds of the established discourse. The recurrent characteristic mode of the innovators is, however, the structural transformation.

I concede that this book is not a good advertisement for the creative value of structural transformations. It is very largely a record of intellectual failures by famous anthropologists. My colleagues may in consequence accuse me of spreading despondency and gloom, or of wasting my time on ideas which have in any case been abandoned.

At this stage I would enter three defences. First of all, the ideas I deal with have not by any means been universally discredited. They may be unfashionable in mainstream anthropology, but they still flourish in the backwaters and are paraded in too many lecture

---

14 In an interview with me, Edmund Leach insisted that 'the sequence is always dialectical'. He illustrated this thesis from his own experience:

There was ... a point in my anthropological development when Malinowski could do no wrong. In the next phase Malinowski could do no right. But with maturity I came to see that there was merit on both sides. I see this as a Hegelian process, a very fundamental element in the way that thinking in the humanities develops over time. But when this sequence leads you round in a circle, you are not just back where you started. You have moved on a bit, or you have moved somewhere else. But always the process involves the initial rejection of your immediate ancestors, the teachers to whom you are most directly indebted. (Kuper (1986), 'An interview with Edmund Leach', p. 380)

courses before the wondering eyes of undergraduates. Secondly, the idea of primitive society was never the exclusive preserve of social anthropology. It infused the political and historical consciousness of several generations. Its history must be of consequence, even for many who are otherwise content to remain quite ignorant of anthropology. Finally, although the history I shall trace is rather deplorable, similar accounts could be given of many other intellectual traditions. We need to consider the ways in which we delude ourselves. If this book helps to explain the persistence of an illusion, then perhaps it may even hold out the promise of an escape from illusion.[15]

This book, then, is a critical history of an idea, its crystallization, transformations and persistence. I have not attempted to be exhaustive, to track down its every expression, to document every variant form it took. I am dealing with the central orthodoxy of social anthropology, and so it has been possible to focus on some central writers. They were especially influential, both in their own time and after. By and large they also produced the most powerful variants of the central model. Each of the writers with whom I shall be dealing can also stand for many others, since each refracted the concerns and influences which defined the study of 'primitive society' within a particular intellectual arena.

15 This may even be taken as a defence of anthropology, or at least of a sort of anthropology.

PART I

The constitution of primitive society

CHAPTER 2

Patriarchal theory

Henry Maine's *Ancient Law* (1861) could almost have been designed to illustrate the differences between Cohen's idea of transformation and Lévi-Strauss's. Maine drew upon various sources, most particularly the German traditions of Roman legal history and of philology. He made his own synthesis of these, not simply by welding them together but by selecting certain themes, combining them in new ways, and giving them a fresh application. This would certainly constitute a transformation in Cohen's sense; but Maine's synthesis was really only a means to an end. His real purpose was political. Broadly, he wanted to refute the radical theory of government and of law which was associated with Rousseau and – in Maine's generation – particularly with Bentham and the Utilitarians. Specifically, he was out to discredit the application of this theory to the Indian Empire. His strategy was to take Bentham's theory and stand it on its head. In consequence, *Ancient Law* also exemplifies transformation in Lévi-Strauss's sense.

Henry Maine (1822–88)[1]

Raised in conditions of shabby gentility, Henry Maine went up to

---

1 Biographical information on Maine has been drawn largely from George Feaver (1969), *From Status to Contract: A Biography of Sir Henry Maine, 1822–1888.* J. W. Burrow discussed Maine's intellectual development in (1966) *Evolution and Society*, pp. 137–78. Maine's life is actually rather poorly documented. One reason is that Lady Maine did not preserve her husband's papers. She threw away his letters from famous writers after cutting off their signatures for sale. There was no typical Victorian 'Life and Letters'. W. Stokes' *Life and Speeches of Sir Henry Maine* contains only a brief memoir as a preface to long extracts from Maine's speeches.

Cambridge in 1840 where he enjoyed a brilliant undergraduate career, marked by such Cambridge triumphs as the award of the Chancellor's medal for English verse (for a poem on the birth of the Prince of Wales), and election to the Apostles. In 1844 he became Senior Classic and accepted a fellowship at Trinity Hall, a law college, where he began to specialize in Roman Law. In 1847 (a friend's father having the decisive voice) he was appointed Regius Professor of Civil Law at Cambridge, at the age of twenty-five. According to a friend, James Fitzjames Stephen, the professorship was an 'ill-paid sinecure', and in 1852 Maine took a Readership in Roman Law in the Middle Temple, resigning his Cambridge chair two years later.

On moving to London in the early 1850s, Maine became an active political journalist. A Peelite Whig, and one of the founders of *The Saturday Review*, he championed aristocratic forms of government and set himself against the extension of the suffrage and the erosion of established authority. He also defended the traditional form of the Indian Empire, then in a state of upheaval.[2]

The Utilitarians and India

The future of India, perhaps the central political question of the mid-1850s, raised legal and philosophical issues of intense interest.[3] The Indian government was committed to respect indigenous law and custom by the theory of dual rule, and officials of a Burkean persuasion genuinely wished to conserve customary legal arrangements. Yet the Permanent Settlement of Bengal in 1793 had already introduced Whig principles of government, above all the principle that individual rights in land should be established and maintained by law. The extension of these policies was advocated by the 'anglicizing' party, a coalition of evangelists, free traders, *dirigiste* bureaucrats and philosophical radicals.

The Utilitarians were prominent members of this party. Jeremy Bentham, the prophet of Utilitarianism, had long taken an interest

---

2 'That wonderful succession of events which has brought the youngest civilization in the world to instruct and correct the oldest, which has reunited those wings of the Indo-European race which separated in the far infancy of time to work out their strangely different missions, which has avenged the miscarriages of the Crusades.' (W. Stokes (1892), *Life and Speeches of Sir Henry Maine*, p. 16)

3 The outstanding source for the debate on India, and the ideas of the Utilitarians, is E. Stokes (1959), *English Utilitarians and India*. I have drawn heavily on it.

in Indian affairs. He had even hoped that India might provide the laboratory for his system of law. This was derived from a 'calculus' of individual interests, which was designed to promote the rational pursuit of happiness. The purpose of law was to prevent individuals from impinging upon the liberty of others and to foster the common good. This doctrine was related to the traditional radical belief in the social contract, particularly to Hume's formulation of this doctrine. Individual adherence to contracts and the attachment to a state flowed independently from a rational perception of self-interest. The state, represented by the sovereign, enacted the laws which protected the individual in his pursuit of private happiness.

Bentham and his disciple John Austin developed elaborate legal codes which were designed to promote communal happiness and rational individual freedom. These remained largely theoretical, but Bentham died in the hope that his theories might be applied in India. One of the most powerful men in the India Office, James Mill, was a Utilitarian, committed to reform. 'Mill will be the living executive,' Bentham declared, 'I shall be the dead legislative of British India.'[4]

Fortunately there seemed to be no practical or moral hindrance. Mill's study of Indian history had convinced him that India was in terrible shape, and with no internal resources for reform. On the contrary, 'despotism and priestcraft taken together, the Hindus, in mind and body, were the most enslaved portion of the human race'.[5] Consequently the Indian government had both a duty and an opportunity to institute radical changes. Mill wrote:

As I believe that India stands more in need of a code than any other country in the world, I believe also that there is no country on which that great benefit can more easily be conferred. A Code is almost the only blessing – perhaps it is the only blessing – which absolute governments are better fitted to confer on a nation than popular governments.[6]

As he became more powerful in the India Office, Mill was able to promote his policies. His protegé, Macaulay, who became legal member of the Viceroy's Council, designed a penal code on pure Benthamite principles in 1835. But despite this promising start,

---

4 Stokes (1959) uses this striking remark as the motto of his *English Utilitarians and India*.
5 James Mill (1817), *The History of British India*, vol. 2, p. 167.
6 Cited by E. Stokes (1959), *English Utilitarians and India*, p. 219.

the Indian reform movement lost its impetus. Mill died, and Macaulay's plans were shelved.

In the 1850s there was a mild revival of the reform programme, and in 1856 a law commission recommended the preparation of a code of civil law, which was to be based on simplified English law, modified to suit Indian conditions. In 1857 the Sepoy Mutiny occurred, giving a new impetus to plans for reform and Macaulay's penal code was finally enacted in 1860.

Maine had no interest in the penal code, commenting dismissively that 'nobody cares about criminal law except theorists and habitual criminals'.[7] But civil law was a different matter entirely. He was fiercely opposed to the radical programme for the reform of Indian administration and civil law and published a series of articles in *The Saturday Review* urging the maintenance of the dual system in India. He then proceeded to write *Ancient Law* (1861), which was constructed as a weightier vehicle for similar arguments.

However the book was not just about India. It was a broad ideological statement, a general assault on radical *a priori* social philosophy as represented especially by Bentham. The radicals believed that government was based on a social contract, entered into by individuals for the protection of property. Maine proposed to demonstrate that on the contrary the original societies were based on families, not individuals, related by status, not contract, and held property in common. The radicals also believed that in a state of nature man had been free, the master of his own fate. Maine insisted that in primitive communities man was subject to the whims of a 'patriarchal despot'. Finally, he rejected the radical conviction that popular demand would impose progressive reforms. History – in Maine's hands – demonstrated that progress was rare. Where things did improve, this was probably thanks to an élite of lawyers (though occasionally Maine credited it rather to the force of the Greek spirit).

Sources for a conservative critique

Maine taught Roman law, which was dominated in his day by German scholars. His familiarity with the work of Savigny and Jhering must immediately have suggested parallels between the

7 Cited by G. Feaver (1969), *From Status to Contract*, pp. 102–3.

Indian debate and the learned controversy about the reception of Roman law in early German societies. The German debate had raised precisely the same issue. How could codification and legal reform be reconciled with a respect for tradition?[8]

Savigny, a conservative Prussian nobleman, had achieved early fame with a pamphlet published in 1814 attacking a proposal to codify the civil law. Codification was associated with French domination and generally with radical plans for rationalization and change. Savigny put the case against codification in both theoretical and nationalist terms; in terms, indeed, that provided a theoretical foundation for a nationalist law policy. He argued that a legal system, like a language, grows out of the historical experience of a nation; it expresses what came to be called a *Volksgeist*. Such a complex historical growth should not be subjected to radical reform, though there might be a case for carefully judged amendments which would bring the law into line with modern conditions.

The great example of successful conservative legal reform was the reception of Roman law in medieval Germany. Savigny argued that the German *doctores juris* had made innovations which were in the spirit of the national law, permitting the *Volksgeist* to manifest itself even through Roman borrowings. This was the central theme of his life-work, the multi-volume (1834–50) *Die Geschichte des Römischen Rechts in Mittelalter*, sections of which continued to be published until 1850.

The so-called 'Germanists' disputed the value Savigny attached to the reception of Roman law. There were also 'Romanists', notably Jhering, who developed a less nationalistic and altogether more pragmatic version of the argument. Maine appears to have been influenced particularly by Jhering, but the internal differences of the German scholars were not critical to his own enterprise. What he took from them, above all, was a substantive description of how Roman law influenced Germanic societies.

---

8 See Kantorowicz (1937), 'Savigny and the historical school of law' for a lucid English account of his career and theories. M. Smith (1895), 'Four German jurists' is also useful, particularly on Jhering's contribution. An assessment of Maine's debt to these writers can be found in Vinogradoff's (1904) *The Teaching of Sir Henry Maine*. For modern assessments of some central arguments see Peter Stein (1980), *Legal Evolution: The Story of an Idea*, and P. Atiyah (1979), *The Rise and Fall of Freedom of Contract*.

Savigny and many of his followers were concerned not only with legal history but more generally with national culture. This broader concern drew them particularly to the study of language and folklore, in the belief that language and myth crystallized the anonymous genius of a people. Moreover, philologists had demonstrated that the Germanic languages were ultimately related to classical Greek and Latin and even to Sanskrit, so furnishing an immense historical perspective within which the development of the *Volksgeist* could be traced.

The existence and extent of the Indo-European language family had been firmly established by the time Maine began to write *Ancient Law*. A central figure in this great triumph of nineteenth-century linguistics had been a student of Savigny, Jacob Grimm. Grimm had identified regular consonant-shifts in Proto-Indo-European (Grimm's Law), and reduced to simple rules the processes involved in sound shifts between languages as different as German, Greek and Sanskrit. He had also, even more famously, with his brother Wilhelm, collected Germanic folktales as documents of popular wisdom.

It was quite widely assumed that the Indo-European family of languages coincided with a cultural tradition. Contemporaries examined parallels between German folklore and the mythology of ancient Rome and Greece, and even India. Grimm believed that there had been a very widespread ancient type of Indo-European folk community, which he identified with the old German *mark*. This *mark* was the original village unit, patriarchal and democratic, in which land was held and worked in common; and it was the forge of the political virtues of the race.

In the second half of the nineteenth century this German philological and folkloristic enterprise was represented in Britain by Max Müller, who became professor of Sanskrit at Oxford. A superb intellectual publicist, he helped to build up support for the German theories in Britain. At the same time, the theory of the *mark* was developed by a school of Anglo-Saxon historians. John Kemble, a student of Grimm, introduced the model into English historiography, arguing that the Saxons had brought the *mark*-community with them to England. His book *The Saxons in England*, published in 1849, inspired a school of British constitutional historians who dominated the field for the next quarter of a century. Stubbs, Freeman and Green treated the *mark* as the basis of medieval English politics and the direct ancestor of Westminster government.[9]

In *Ancient Law*, drawing on these German models, Maine offered a solution to the apparent conflict between Indian and British legal ideas. There was, he suggested, a path which could be traced in the legal history of the Indo-European family of nations. It led from India and ancient Germany through Rome to Britain. British law was, as it were, a mature and civilized outgrowth from Indian law. He could therefore reconcile his conservatism with a touch of reformist optimism. India might move forward under British guidance, as Germany had done by grace of Rome. And so, while Victorian historians were writing constitutional histories of Britain, Maine wrote a comparable constitutional history of India in *Ancient Law*. It was a prospective constitutional history – at once Whig and Burkean – of the India he hoped to see.

'Ancient Law'

When he came to write *Ancient Law*, Maine therefore had a primarily political agenda. His book is best read as a two-pronged attack on his radical opponents. He was after them root and branch – the root being their belief that modern society was wicked, natural society good; and the branch being the conclusion that modern societies (India, for instance) should be reformed by the application of reason.

Maine associates Bentham, rather unfairly, with the traditional radical postulate that there had been an original state of nature, in which free men agreed to a social contract, electing a leader to govern them and to pass laws in the common interest. Unfortunately leaders had eventually arisen who had betrayed this trust, pulled the wool over the eyes of their followers. Government everywhere had become a conspiracy of the rich.[10] Born free, man was

---

9 See J. W. Burrow (1981), *A Liberal Descent: Victorian Historians and the English Past.* In his essay on the 'German school of history' published in 1886, Acton linked Maine and Fustel de Coulanges with Humboldt, Savigny, Grimm and Ritter. 'They trifled for a time with fancy, but they doubled the horizons of Europe. They admitted India to an equality with Greece, mediaeval Rome with classical.' Reprinted in Acton (1907), *Historical Essays and Studies*, quotation from p. 346.

10 Nor was this point of view restricted to radicals. In Adam Smith's uncompromising formulation,

now everywhere in chains. It was necessary to start over again from scratch. The philosopher should imagine himself back in a state of nature, and apply his reason to working out a rational and just system of government.

Maine regarded this kind of thinking with scorn, and traced it right back to the ancient theory of Natural Law. This was a Greek notion, but the Romans had adopted it when faced with the problem of administering foreigners whose customs were very different from their own. Trusting to the Greek assumption that certain legal principles were universal, the Romans had developed rules based upon abstract principles of justice. There was an implicit notion that somewhere, once, these universal abstract principles had ruled. Justice might therefore be identified with some former natural condition. The theory obviously provided an open invitation to speculation. The Romans had, however, used this licence in a sober fashion, and so had been spared the worst excesses of a philosophy which Maine called 'the ancient counterpart of Benthamism'.[11]

The radical philosophers, however, had made precisely this leap from the idea of natural justice to the vision of an original state of grace. They even believed that this original state of nature provided a model for a future society based on just principles. 'Rousseau's belief was that a perfect social order could be evolved from the unassisted consideration of the natural state, a social order wholly irrespective of the actual condition of the world and wholly unlike it.'[12] Nor was this speculation an innocent intellectual sport. The theory had

helped most powerfully to bring about the grosser disappointments of which the first French revolution was fertile. It gave birth, or intense stimulus, to the vices of mental habit all but universal at the time, disdain

---

Laws and government may be considered ... in every case as a combination of the rich to oppress the poor, and preserve to themselves the inequality of the goods which would otherwise be soon destroyed by the attacks of the poor, who if not hindered by the government would soon reduce the others to an equality with themselves by open violence.

This quotation is taken from Ronald Meek's (1975) *Social Science and the Ignoble Savage* (p. 123), Chapter 4 of which provides an excellent account of the 'anthropological' theories of the Scottish school, with which Maine and McLennan were familiar.

11 Maine (1861), *Ancient Law*, p. 76.
12 *Op. cit.*, p. 85.

of positive law, impatience of experience, and the preference of *a priori* to all other reasoning.[13]

The foolish belief in the state of nature could only be countered by applying the historical method. The origin of social forms must be reconstructed scientifically. This imperative should be evident to all. Indeed, Maine insisted that

whenever (religious objections apart) any mind is seen to resist or contemn that mode of investigation, it will generally be found under the influence of a prejudice or vicious bias traceable to a conscious or unconscious reliance on a non-historic, natural, condition of society or the individual.[14]

The evidence from which the 'rudiments of the social state' could be reliably reconstructed was of three kinds – 'accounts by contemporary observers of civilisations less advanced than their own, the records which particular races have preserved concerning their primitive history, and ancient law'.[15] ('It will at least be acknowledged that, if the materials for this process are sufficient, and if the comparisons be accurately executed, the methods followed are as little objectionable as those which have led to such surprising results in comparative philology.'[16])

The conclusion of these investigations was very different from Rousseau's. There was no original Eden, but instead a primordial patriarchal despotism. 'The effect of the evidence derived from comparative jurisprudence is to establish that view of the primeval condition of the human race which is known as the Patriarchal Theory.'[17]

Patriarchal theory is in fact a direct inversion of Rousseau's state of nature. In Rousseau's construct, free and equal individuals had decided to band together, entering into a contract for their better government. This ancient state of liberty and equality was contrasted with the degenerate despotism of the modern world. In Maine's ancient world, on the contrary, man was originally confined in societies which completely suppressed individual interests.

13 *Op. cit.*, p. 88.
14 *Op. cit.*, p. 87.
15 *Op. cit.*, p. 116.
16 *Op. cit.*; p. 118.
17 *Op. cit.*, p. 116.

This was a world not of free individuals but of solidary family corporations, ruled by totalitarian patriarchs.

Men are first seen distributed in perfectly insulated groups held together by obedience to the parent. Law is the parent's word ... society in primitive times was not what it is assumed to be at present, a collection of *individuals*. In fact, and in the view of the men who composed it, it was *an aggregation of families*. The contrast may be most forcibly expressed by saying that the *unit* of an ancient society was the Family, of a modern society the Individual.[18]

Intriguing evidence for an original state of despotism came from the Roman doctrine of agnation. In Roman law 'agnates' are kin who are related to each other exclusively through male links. Maine argued that this was the original category of relatives. In the primeval human society the patriarch ruled. Daughters moved away on marriage, and their children came under the rule of their fathers-in-law. Consequently they were no longer counted as relatives. Only the children of sons remained members of the original patriarchal corporation.[19]

How was this ancient patriarchal despotism reformed? The first step was to draw waifs and strays into family groups by means of the first and greatest of the legal fictions, adoption (ritually consecrated by shared sacrifices). Soon it must have been evident that the theory of *patria potestas* was being stretched to accommodate a very different reality, that agnation no longer described the relationship between members of the corporation. 'The composition of the state, uniformly assumed to be natural, was nevertheless known to be in great measure artificial.'[20] Initially the new accretions had been welcomed as strengthening the group, but gradually the hereditary members of the inner core began to discriminate against the individuals who became attached to them through weakness. As these second-class citizens came to constitute a majority, they developed an alternative ideology of civil rights.

18 *Op. cit.*, p. 121.
19 The foundation of Agnation is not the marriage of Father and Mother, but the authority of the Father. All persons are Agnatically connected together who are under the same Paternal Power, or who have been under it or who might have been under it if their lineal ancestor had lived long enough to exercise his empire. In truth, in the primitive view, Relationship is exactly limited to Patria Potestas. (*Op. cit.*, p. 144)
20 *Op. cit.*, p. 125.

Their sternness in maintaining the central principle of a system under which political rights were attainable on no terms whatever except connexion in blood, real or artificial, taught their inferiors another principle, which proved to be endowed with a far greater measure of vitality. This was the principle of local contiguity, now recognized everywhere as the condition of community in political functions.[21]

As the corporation had loosened its grip, so individuals became more independent. Finally, at the end of many aeons of development, the social contract had been introduced. Individualism and contract were the fruits of the highest civilization.

The movement of the progressive societies has been uniform in one respect. Through all its course it has been distinguished by the gradual dissolution of family dependency and the growth of individual obligation in its place. The individual is steadily substituted for the Family, as the unit of which civil laws take account ... Nor is it difficult to see what is the tie between man and man which replaces by degrees those forms of reciprocity in rights and duties which have their origin in the Family. It is Contract. Starting, as from one terminus of history, from a condition of society in which all the relations of Persons are summed up in the relations of Family, we seem to have steadily moved towards a phase of social order in which all these relations arise from the free agreement of individuals.[22]

Maine used the term 'status' to refer to ascribed rights and duties, which derived particularly from the family. In that sense 'status' was the opposite to 'contract' (which was the mark of liberty and the clarion call of the radicals). Relationships of status characterized early societies, while free contractual relationships characterized modern societies. Contract marked the liberation of the individual from the primordial constraints of status. As Maine summed it up in his most famous generalization, 'we may say that the movement of the progressive societies has hitherto been a movement *from Status to Contract*'.[23]

Ancient sources commonly assumed that families were the original units of society. These had gradually aggregated to form a gens or house. Houses had then joined together to form a tribe. Finally, tribes had associated in a commonwealth. This picture had been endorsed by writers from Aristotle to Grote. In the tradition of

21 *Op. cit.*, pp. 127–8.
22 *Op. cit.*, p. 163.
23 *Op. cit.*, p. 165.

Lamarck, however, Maine argued that history had not progressed gradually by small reforms from one stage to another. Political progress had been punctuated by a great revolution. This was the change from societies based upon family relations – upon blood – to societies based upon territory and the state.

The history of political ideas begins, in fact, with the assumption that kinship in blood is the sole possible ground of community in political functions; nor is there any of those subversions of feeling, which we term emphatically revolutions, so startling and so complete as the change which is accomplished when some other principle – such as that, for instance of *local contiguity* – establishes itself for the first time as the basis of common political action.[24]

Maine noted that his image of ancient society corresponded closely to the society of the patriarchs as described in the Bible. It was also rather similar to Aristotle's idea of early society. Similar ideas were taken for granted by the writers of the Scottish Enlightenment. More recently, James Mill (1817) in his *History of British India* had traced an evolution, from scattered family groups to divinely-inspired authorities and so to monarchy, which clearly anticipates Maine. His image of the village community, especially, was very like that adopted by Maine:

it was the usual arrangement in early stages of society, for the different members of a family to live together; and to possess the property in common. The father was rather the head of a number of partners, than the sole proprietor ... The laws of inheritance among the Hindus are almost entirely founded upon this patriarchal arranagement.[25]

Maine added little to this idealized picture of the Indian village,[26] but he linked it to the German notion of the *mark* community, which had been introduced into British historiography by Kemble (1849) in *The Saxons in England*. Kemble described the *mark* communities as 'great family unions ... some, in direct descent

24 *Op. cit.*, p. 124.
25 Mill (1817), *History of British India*, vol. 1, p. 146.
26 Maine played down the complexities of Indian land tenure and the internal hierarchy of the village, and he did not locate the village in the broader political system. As Dumont commented, he 'hardly ever looked at the Indian village in itself, but only as a counterpart to Teutonic, Slavonic or other institutions' (Dumont (1966), 'The "village community" from Munro to Maine', p. 85). Cf. Dewey (1972), 'Images of the village community' and Srinivas (1975), 'The Indian village: myth and reality'.

from the common ancestors ... others, more distantly connected ... some admitted into communion by marriage, others by adoption ... but all recognising a brotherhood, a kinsmanship'.[27] In his second book, *Village Communities in the East and West* (1871), Maine made these sources more explicit, and developed the parallels between the German *mark* and the Hindu village.[28]

The origin of law

Maine's account of the origin of society controverted the classic radical version on every point. That was to strike at the root of radical political philosophy. In dealing with the branch – the theory of law developed by Bentham and Austin – his tactic was the same. He presented a version of Bentham's construct, and then turned it upside down.

Bentham believed that law should be made consciously and by the political authority. Not precedent but legislation should form the basis of the legal system. Maine remarked that Bentham and Austin 'resolve every law into a *command* of the lawgiver, an *obligation* imposed thereby on the citizen, and a *sanction* threatened in the event of disobedience'. This was a fairly accurate description of the conditions of 'mature jurisprudence', but

it is curious that the farther we penetrate into the primitive history of thought, the farther we find ourselves from a conception of law which at all resembles a compound of the elements which Bentham determined. It is certain that, in the infancy of mankind, no sort of legislature, not even a distinct author of law, is contemplated or conceived of.

On the contrary, in ancient times 'every man, living during the greater part of his life under patriarchal despotism, was practically controlled in all his actions by a regime not of law but of caprice'.[29]

The first laws took the form of judgments which were believed to derive from divine inspiration. In time an aristocracy displaced the divinely-inspired leaders; in the west a political oligarchy, in the east a priestly caste. The new élite took over the judicial role of the king, but did not pretend to divine inspiration. Instead the élite claimed a monopoly of knowledge of custom. With the

27 Kemble (1849), *The Saxons in England*, pp. 56–7.
28 See, e.g., Dewey (1972), 'Images of the village community: a study in Anglo-Indian ideology'.
29 Maine (1861), *Ancient Law*, pp. 7–8.

invention of writing the oligarchy lost its monopoly of knowledge; the customs were set down in codes. This was of course the great Benthamite moment, for Bentham favoured not only legislation but the creation of complete legal codes. Maine objected that codes really restated custom, although he complicated matters by suggesting that somehow there was a moment when a legal system was ripe for codification. The Roman code, the Twelve Tables, had been compiled at a stage when usage was still wholesome, though further delay might have been fatal. The Hindu codes, however, had been corrupted. The masses had got their hands on the law and contaminated it with irrational superstitions.

But if codes simply ordered custom, how could rational and useful changes be introduced in the law? Maine believed that there were a few progressive societies in which educated opinion had seen the necessity for improvements, and where appropriate legal reforms had been introduced. The Roman system was the best documented of these, and Roman legal history demonstrated that three mechanisms operated successively to bring about legal change. These were legal fictions, equity, and legislation.

This may seem a curious trinity of instruments of reform. To grasp the logic of the argument one must once again consider its relevance to the theories of Bentham and Austin. They had given all the credit for legal progress to legislation. Maine argued that legislation had not been a significant factor until recent times. The Utilitarian theorists had also emphasized the significance of equity, with its appeal to natural principles of law. Maine debunked the logic of equity, and played down its historical importance.

On the other hand, Bentham and Austin had heaped scorn on the use of 'irrational' legal fictions. According to Bentham, legal fictions were amongst the mystifications upon which despots relied to retard progress. A legal fiction was 'a wilful falsehood, having for its object the stealing of legislative power, by and for hands which could not, or durst not, openly claim it, and but for the delusion thus produced could not exercise it'. 'Fiction of use to justice? Exactly as swindling is to trade.'[30] Maine accordingly chose legal fictions as his favoured mode of reform.

Following Savigny and Jhering,[31] Maine argued that legal fict-

---

30 L. Fuller's *Legal Fictions* (1967) includes an account of Bentham's and Maine's theories. The citations from Bentham are taken from Fuller.

31 Fuller (1967), pp. 59–63.

ions were not originally instruments of reaction. On the contrary, they were mechanisms of progressive reform. Under the cover of fictions the élite introduced reforms, while maintaining the illusion, so much cherished by the conservative majority, that nothing had really been altered. They 'satisfy the desire for improvement at the same time that they do not offend the superstitious disrelish for change'.[32]

After a period of reform by way of legal fictions, the Romans had briefly adopted the principle of equity (initially in dealing only with foreigners). Finally, as the laws became more and more unwieldy and complex, the imperial constitutions attempted to codify them.

This view of legal history (presented in the first three chapters of *Ancient Law*) controverted the Benthamite *a priori* by the creation of an 'historical' sequence. Legislation and codification marked the peak of legal evolution, not its origin.

It would be wrong to treat *Ancient Law* as a work of high scholarship. The history is very compressed and reveals little evidence of original research. There is in fact nothing in Maine's history which could not have been gleaned from Gibbon's famous forty-fourth chapter, in which he reviewed the development of Roman law. According to his friend J. F. Stephen, 'Neither Maine himself, nor I suppose, anyone else in England, knew anything whatever about Roman Law at that time.'[33] ('I suppose he knew the Institutes, but I doubt if he ever knew much of the Pandects.') But this did not imply that *Ancient Law* was worthless. Stephen conceded that 'being a man of talent and originality, coming close to Genesis, Maine transfigured one of the driest of subjects into all sorts of beautiful things, without knowing or caring much of its details'. However, Maine's use of legal history was primarily rhetorical; he was out to trounce the radicals. As Stephen concluded, 'He was enabled to sniff at Bentham for knowing nothing about it, & writing in consequence about English law, in a merely revolutionary manner'.[34]

The origins of the law having been traced, Chapters 6 to 9 of *Ancient Law* gave an account of its development to modern times. The thesis was that primitive society had been based upon communal

---

32 Maine (1861), *Ancient Law*, p. 25.
33 Quoted in Feaver (1969), *From Status to Contract*, p. 25.
34 *Ibid.*

family groups. Consequently private property as well as contract and testaments were the product of an historical evolution.

The early family was a corporation which survived its members ('Corporations never die'[35]). Succession to the patriarch's position passed by seniority among those subject to the same *patria potestas*. But sometimes there were no obvious heirs, and contingency arrangements had to be developed. Wills introduced flexibility. The Roman invention of the will created 'the institution which, next to Contract, has exercised the greatest influence in transforming human society'.[36]

The comparative method

Maine insisted that in contrast to Bentham he employed a scientific 'historical method'. On many points, however, he was obliged to deny the evidence of his own sources. For example, he was confronted by the difficulty that even the earliest Roman sources unambiguously recognized individual rights, or placed great emphasis upon cognatic relationships. His response was that Roman jurisprudence had been transformed by the theory of natural law. The lawyers had then applied themselves to rewriting the past.

Fortunately, however, Maine was equipped to reconstruct the authentic origins of Roman law because he was armed with the comparative method. The Indo-European peoples formed a family, but some members of the family had done very much better than others. The poor relations still lived in the way we had once lived ourselves. Therefore the customs of backward branches of the family could be used to provide evidence for the ancient practices of its more progressive members. It was not necessary to rely on Roman sources which had systematically rewritten history. Maine could appeal to India, for Hindu law seldom 'cast aside the shell in which it was originally reared'.[37]

The Roman sources might talk in terms of individual property rights, but

among the Hindoos, we do find a form of ownership which ought at once to rivet our attention from its exactly fitting in with the ideas which our studies in the Law of Persons would lead us to entertain respecting the

35 Maine (1861), *Ancient Law*, p. 180.
36 *Op. cit.*, p. 188.
37 *Op. cit.*, p. 252.

original condition of property. The Village Community of India is at once an organized patriarchal society and an assemblage of co-proprietors.[38]

Yet however riveting, the Indian evidence was still by no means always unambiguous. Maine was obliged to be selective. On the question of ancient community of property, for instance, he cited a rather murky passage from Elphinstone in his favour, but he ignored the testimony of George Campbell, whose *Modern India*, published by John Murray in 1852, must have been known to him. Campbell admitted the existence of village communities 'comprised of a number of families, claiming to be of the same brotherhood or clan', but insisted that

they do by no means 'enjoy to a great degree the community of goods', as Mill supposes. I never knew an instance in which the cultivaton was carried on in common, or in which any of the private concerns of the villagers were in any way in common, and I very much doubt the existence of any such state of things.[39]

On the matter of contract Maine found himself on still weaker ground. He disparaged the Roman sources but here Indian sources, however selectively used, were also of no help. Maine was now obliged to appeal to German sources, on the argument that although the Romans had introduced their principles of contract to the German tribes, feudal laws otherwise differed little from primitive usages.

Maine in India

Ancient Law was obviously relevant to the debate on Indian legal reform. It sent a straightforward message to the politicians. India had initially been like ancient Germany, a society based on communal ownership and the patriarchal family. However, while the German societies had been civilized by the reception of Roman Law (and especially by the introduction of contract law) and by the development of private property, India had stagnated, a prey to obscurantism and despotism. The Indian Empire should now introduce British legal principles to some of the most backward of the Indo-European peoples, just as the Roman lawyers had reformed German societies.

38 *Op. cit.*, p. 252.
39 G. Campbell (1852), *Modern India: A Sketch of the System of Civil Government*, p. 86.

In 1861, shortly after the publication of *Ancient Law*, Maine was appointed legal member in the Viceroy's Council, effectively becoming the head of the Indian legal system. In India he distinguished himself by a hectic legislative activity. He remained legal member from 1862 to 1869, longer than any other nineteenth-century incumbent of the office, and as his biographer remarked, he 'strove to make the major theses of his *Ancient Law* a self-fulfilling prophecy'.[40] He passed laws which extended freedom of contract, and promoted individual land rights. In speeches to the Council he cited his own theories, and drew parallels between the imposition of British law in India and the reception of Roman law by the Germans.[41] In the field of education he also advocated the progressive introduction of European scholarship (as had his predecessor, Macaulay). In 1866, as Vice-Chancellor, he told the graduating class of Calcutta University that 'their real affinities are with Europe and the Future, not with India and the Past'.[42]

It is conceivable that Maine wrote *Ancient Law* in order to become legal member. He was certainly enough of a pragmatist to have done so. Lord Acton, who as a young Whig MP had put Maine's name forward for the position after his book appeared, later wrote in disillusion to Mary Gladstone that Maine's nature was 'to exercise power, and to find good reasons for adopted policy'.[43]

In 1871, shortly after he returned from India, Maine was appointed to the newly-created Chair of Jurisprudence at Oxford, but although he was to be an academic for the rest of his life he retained political interests and ambitions. He sought the Permanent Under-Secretaryship at the India Office and was the first person to be appointed a life member of the Council of India. When he resigned his Oxford chair in 1878, he received offers from the Indian government and the Foreign Secretary. Although he chose rather to accept the position of Master of Trinity Hall, Cambridge, he later toyed with other possible government appointments. Nor did he lose his political interests. His penultimate book, *Popular*

---

40 Feaver (1969), *From Status to Contract*, p. 73.
41 *Op. cit.*, pp. 87–8.
42 *Op. cit.*, p. 90.
43 *Op. cit.*, p. 179.

Government, published in 1885, was a tract against the Reform Bill and democracy.

All this time his academic career continued to prosper. In 1887, the year before his death, he was named to the Whewell Professorship of International Law at Cambridge. And yet his most famous scholarly contribution, his patriarchal theory, had by then been almost universally abandoned.

Matriarchy: the critique

In 1861, the year in which *Ancient Law* appeared, a Swiss jurist, Johannes Bachofen, had published a book entitled *Das Mutterrecht*. Himself a product of the German school of Roman historical legal studies, Bachofen took classical myths as his main source, in the manner of Grimm. These suggested to him an original condition in which societies were controlled by women rather than by patriarchs.

Maine paid virtually no attention to Bachofen, and his ideas had little direct influence in Britain or America. Soon, however, the 'matriarchy' thesis was to be propounded in Britain by a formidable polemicist, J. F. McLennan.

John Ferguson McLennan was born in Inverness in 1827, the son of an insurance agent.[44] He was educated at King's College, Aberdeen, and at Trinity College, Cambridge. Going down from Cambridge without a degree, he spent two years on Grub Street, writing for *The Leader* and other periodicals. In 1857 he was called to the bar in Edinburgh. At the same time he contributed the entry on 'Law' to the *Encyclopaedia Britannica*, in which he sketched the conventional theory of political development, from the patriarchal family to the tribe to the state.

McLennan's legal career was unspectacular, though he was for a while secretary of the Scottish Society for Promoting the Amendment of the Law. Then (as Tylor remarked in an obituary of McLennan in *The Academy*) 'in 1865 he published a law-book which had the natural and immediate effect of losing him half his briefs. This was *Primitive Marriage*, the work by which he made his mark in the scientific study of man.'[45]

---

44 Rivière provides a biography of McLennan in his introduction to the 1970 reprint of *Primitive Marriage* published by the University of Chicago Press.
45 Tylor's obituary appeared in *The Academy* in 1881. *Primitive Marriage* was

McLennan admitted that he had been in some measure anticipated by Bachofen, but claimed that he had read *Das Mutterrecht*
for the first time only in 1866, and certainly the structure of his
argument is very different.[46] A much more significant influence on
Primitive Marriage is Malthus. In Chapter 3 of his *Essay on the
Principle of Population* Malthus had speculated on the ways in
which primitive communities had restricted their populations to a
number which could be supported by their resources. He pointed
to the great 'vices' of famine, epidemic and war, and also to abortion
and infanticide, writing of a 'prodigious waste of human life
occasioned by this perpetual struggle for room and food'.

Female infanticide was actually discovered by British admin-
istrators among some high-caste groups in North India. In 1857
Cave-Browne published a detailed account, *Indian Infanticide: Its
Origin, Progress and Suppression*, and his book aroused considerable
controversy. Like many contemporaries, McLennan assumed that
primitive peoples had been driven to kill female children in their
struggle to survive.

Foremost among the results of this early struggle for food and security,
must have been an effect upon the balance of the sexes. As braves and
hunters were required and valued, it would be in the interest of every
horde to rear, when possible, its healthy male children. It would be less in
its interest to rear females, as they would be less capable of self-support,
and of contributing, by their exertions, to the common good. In this lies

---

published in 1865. McLennan reprinted this monograph together with some
subsequent essays under the title of *Studies in Ancient History* in 1876. (That is
the edition used here.) In 1885 his brother edited and completed some further
writings by McLennan and published them under the title *Patriarchal Theory*.
McLennan's ideas on the evolution of marriage and the family remained essentially unchanged from 1865, but in 1869–70 he published an influential essay on
totemism, in which he linked this early state of the family to early religious
forms. This theory will be discussed in a later chapter.

46 In a chapter on Bachofen in his *Studies in Ancient History* (1876), McLennan
commented, and with reason, that Bachofen's book was 'mystic' and difficult to
read, counselling readers rather to consult Giraud-Teulon's French summary,
which appeared in 1867 (*La mère chez certains peuples de l'antiquité*). Giraud-
Teulon for his part cited Baron Eckstein as his own immediate authority and as
a predecessor of Bachofen. Ferdinand Eckstein (1790–1861) studied philology
and Sanskrit in Germany early in the nineteenth century and worked mainly as
a journalist but wrote books about German and Indian cultures.

the only explanation which can be accepted of those systems of female infanticide still existing.[47]

Primitive Marriage was also directly and obviously inspired by Maine's *Ancient Law* – but Maine stirred McLennan to opposition rather than emulation. 'Maine is McLennan's chief antagonist', Rivière has commented, adding that 'besides his theories Maine was also an ideal representation of everything to which McLennan was either antagonistic or to which he had aspired and had failed to achieve', for Maine was a successful jurist, a prominent journalist, and an uncompromising reactionary.[48]

The notion that primitive peoples went in for wholesale female infanticide suggested to McLennan a way in which to attack patriarchal theory. The practice of large-scale female infanticide must have obliged them to look for wives elsewhere, leading to a measure of outmarriage (for which McLennan coined the term 'exogamy'). Since a perpetual struggle was going on between different communities, exogamy could not have been organized in a peaceful fashion; men would have had to capture wives. Wives would nevertheless have remained in short supply, and so men shared the wives captured by their group. (McLennan called this arrangement 'rude polyandry'. 'Rude polyandry' evidently stood to polyandry proper much as coarse fishing stands to fishing.) In such conditions it would have been difficult to establish who a person's father was. Consequently the first kinship systems would have been based on blood relationships traced through women only.

In time, the 'ruder' forms of wife-sharing would have given way to a more refined arrangement, in which uterine brothers, recognizing a degree of solidarity, held a wife in common. This was the type of 'Tibetan polyandry' which McLennan posited as a general stage of the development of marriage. 'Tibetan polyandry' implied that a woman's children also shared common descent from a set of brothers. This was a step in the direction of the recognition of fatherhood. Polyandry might then yield to a more advanced system, the levirate. The idea of fatherhood would become firmly established. Its development would be stimulated by a parallel growth in economic well-being, which would create a need for

47 McLennan (1876), *Studies in Ancient History*, p 132.
48 Rivière, Introduction to 1970 edition of McLennan's *Primitive Marriage*, pp. xxxiii and xxxv.

rules to govern the transmission of property between generations. The way was now open for the development of agnation.

Paternity having become certain, a system of kinship through males would arise with the growth of property, and a practice of sons succeeding, as heirs direct, to the estates of fathers; and as the system of kinship through males arose, that through females would – and chiefly under the influence of property – die away.[49]

In essence, McLennan inverted Maine's patriarchal theory. The classical assumption had been that the family was the original social group, that it had gradually yielded the gens, which developed into the tribe, and that eventually tribes had coalesced to form the state. Maine had amended this familiar story in two crucial ways. First of all, he had stressed the 'patriarchal' nature of the original family group. Secondly, instead of a gentle progression from family through tribe to state, Maine had introduced the idea of a radical break in human history, a revolution, as the principle of blood gave way to the principle of territory. In McLennan's version, the first kin-based systems were matrilineal. Moreover, the whole traditional series of developmental stages was inverted, and the family was placed at the end instead of the beginning of the story. 'The order of social development ... is then, that the tribe stands first; the gens or house next; and last of all the family.'[50]

McLennan's sources were very various. He cited Indian examples of infanticide and polyandry but did not limit himself to Indo-European comparisons. Unlike Maine, he was prepared to draw on any descriptions of 'primitive' behaviour to support his speculations.[51] This was because he assumed, in the traditional Scottish philosophical way, that the development of social institutions had everywhere followed a similar path.[52]

There was also a more directly 'evolutionist' element in his

---

49 McLennan (1865), *Primitive Marriage*, p. 196.

50 *Op. cit.*, p. 333.

51 This feature of McLennan's writings has led some commentators to make quite unwarranted claims on his behalf. Evans-Pritchard (1981) even asserted that McLennan 'was the first to make a comprehensive analysis of everything known about primitive people' (*A History of Anthropological Thought*, p. 66). However, Waitz's encyclopaedic compilation of comparative ethnography had begun to appear in 1859, and an English translation of the first volume was published in 1863. Tylor, a contemporary of McLennan, also drew on a much wider range of ethnographic materials.

52 McLennan (1876), *Studies in Ancient History*, pp. xiv–xv.

procedures. Like Lubbock and Tylor he was looking for fossils, for what Tylor termed 'survivals'. Here the indirect influence of Lyell and Darwin is evident. There might be no material relics of ancient social institutions, but McLennan believed that the equivalent of fossils was to be found in 'the symbols employed by advanced nations in the constitution or exercise of civil rights'. These symbols reflected earlier institutional forms – 'wherever we discover symbolical forms, we are justified in inferring that in the past life of the people employing them, there were corresponding realities'.[53] The symbol which McLennan used as his point of departure in *Primitive Marriage* was the pretence, which so often cropped up in marriage ceremonies, that the bride was being forcibly abducted. This referred back to a state of affairs in which men really had gone out and captured their wives.

Maine's defence

At first Maine tried to minimize the threat posed to his theory by McLennan and his supporters, who soon included the influential Lubbock. Whatever such critics might say to the contrary, Indian villages were firmly based on *patria potestas*. There was little evidence that India, as least, had passed through a 'matriarchal' phase.[54] Furthermore, *patria potestas* turned out to be the original condition not only of the Indo-Europeans, but of all civilized peoples including the Semites and the 'Uralians' (the Turks, Hungarians and Finns). The arguments of McLennan might or might not apply to less civilized races, but they 'do not concern us till the Kinship of the higher races can be distinctly shown to have grown out of the Kinship now known only to the lower, and even then they concern us only remotely'.[55]

However, in 1871 a more elaborate version of McLennan's thesis was published by an American lawyer, Lewis Henry Morgan. Morgan followed this up in 1877 with a book, *Ancient Society*, which provided another bold account of social and political evolution which, like McLennan's, started with a matriarchal group and ended with the simultaneous apotheosis of the state and the family. These competing models won over many of the leading

53 *Op. cit.*, p. 7.
54 Maine (1871), *Village Communities in the East and West*.
55 Maine (1875), *Lectures on the Early History of Institutions*, p. 67.

authors of the day, but it was only in 1833, two years after both Morgan and McLennan had died, that Maine published an all-out attack on their work, in a section of his *Dissertations on Early Law and Custom* entitled 'Theories of primitive society'.

Maine could not content himself any longer with the simple assertion that his rivals were talking about something else entirely, that their model might apply to savages but had nothing to do with the higher races. By now the Darwinians had won a crucial battle, and it was no longer respectable to assume that different human races had quite distinct origins. This issue – which split the anthropological world in the 1860s – had been broadly resolved by the 1880s in favour of the 'Monogenistic School', who took the Darwinian view that the various human races shared a common ancestry.

Maine therefore had to accept that the arguments of McLennan and Morgan represented an alternative to his own – indeed, as he pointed out, they were a direct inversion of it.[56] However, he drew attention to the contradictions and lacunae in the models, and showed that McLennan and Morgan differed with one another in their view of the stages through which horde-societies passed before reaching the patriarchal stage. Moreover their evidence for the original horde was based chiefly on dubious reports of contemporary 'savage societies' which traced relationships for some purposes through women only. Yet even in these societies ignorance of paternity was not general.[57]

But Maine's central arguments were drawn – for the first time in his work – from Darwin. In *The Descent of Man*, published in 1871, Darwin had taken issue with McLennan, arguing that sexual jealousy was a fundamental emotion, and that it must have contributed to the early establishment of orderly mating arrangements amongst men. Promiscuous hordes were counter to man's sexual

56 The other theory which is now opposed to that long called Patriarchal is the theory of the origin of society, not in the Family but in the horde... It derives the smaller from the larger group, not the larger from the smaller. Founded, as was the Patriarchal theory, on observation, but on observation of the ideas and practices of the now savage races, it deduces all later social order from the miscellaneous unorganised horde. (1883, *Dissertations on Early Law and Custom*, pp. 199–200)

57 Maine cited Fustel de Coulanges' remark that 'the problem of procreation' was to the ancients 'very much what the problem of creation is to the moderns'. (1883, *Dissertations on Early Law and Custom*, p. 203)

nature. Maine concluded that 'sexual jealousy, indulged through power, might serve as a definition of the Patriarchal Family'.[58]

Maine also appealed to another tenet of Darwinian theory, which denied the likelihood of parallel evolutionary developments.

So far as I am aware, there is nothing in the recorded history of society to justify the belief that, during the vast chapter of its growth which is wholly unwritten, the same transformations of social constitution succeeded one another everywhere, uniformly if not simultaneously. A strong force lying deep in human nature, and never at rest, might no doubt in the long run produce an uniform result, in spite of the vast varieties accompanying the stern struggle for existence; but it is in the highest degree incredible that the action of this force would be uniform from beginning to end.[59]

It was a powerful counter-attack, but when Maine published this final denunciation of his rivals, his reputation was already past its peak. Moreover, the German model upon which he had relied was itself under attack. The romantic image of the *mark* began to erode under the pressure of conflicting evidence. A revisionist school of writers introduced a new interpretation of the *mark* community, stressing the existence of private property, serfdom, the relationship of the *mark* to the feudal manor, the transmission of property through women, and even the ownership of property by women.[60]

For their part, the new evolutionist models of McLennan and Morgan had drawn more powerfully and persuasively on ethnographic materials, and their models incorporated the ideas of technological and intellectual evolution which were advocated by Tylor and Lubbock. It is hardly surprising that the matriarchal thesis came to dominate the anthropology of the next generation; above all, in the version of Lewis Henry Morgan.

---

58 *Op. cit.*, p. 209.
59 *Op. cit.*, pp. 218–19.
60 See Vinogradoff (1892), *Villainage in England*. Cf. Meinhard (1975), 'The patrilineal principle in early Teutonic kinship'. Soon Vinogradoff could remark – in a public lecture on Maine – 'It is not unusual nowadays to talk in a rather supercilious manner of the lack of erudition and accuracy, of the allusiveness and vagueness of Maine's writings'. (1904, *The Teaching of Sir Henry Maine*, p. 2)

CHAPTER 3

Lewis Henry Morgan and ancient society

An American, Lewis Henry Morgan, was to prove the most influential of those who developed the anthropological idea of primitive society. His influence on his immediate successors was so great, indeed, that it forms a serious barrier to a fresh reading of his work today. His theory was appropriated early on by Engels, whose particular interpretation still has committed supporters. Later, Boas made Morgan the special target of his critique of evolutionism. In consequence, Morgan's theses became the battleground for two generations of American anthropologists. Precisely on account of this intense controversy, Morgan's ideas have very often been misrepresented and misunderstood.[1]

In order to recapture the intended meaning of what Morgan wrote, one must try to ignore what was to come, and to concentrate upon the immediate sources and contexts of his thinking; to recreate his intellectual milieu, which he assumed his readers would share. This is an intriguing exercise in itself, and it is an essential preliminary if one wishes to specify the kinds of transformation which characterize his work. Morgan reacted to his contemporaries, but not in the radical way which led Maine and McLennan to select particular adversaries and then to turn their ideas on their heads. He collected enormous quantities of data and drew with considerable expertise upon a variety of theories (including McLennan's); but in the end he reworked his materials to fit the models which had become current among the British scholars in his field.

---

1 Cf. E. Service (1985), *A Century of Controversy*, Chapter 3.

Yankees, Presbyterians and Darwinism

Morgan's immediate intellectual circle is perhaps best approached by way of his closest friend during his early adult years in Rochester, New York, the Rev. J. S. McIlvaine, who was the Presbyterian minister of Rochester from 1848 until 1860. McIlvaine was intimately associated with Morgan's research, and he was instrumental in securing the eventual publication of Morgan's *Systems of Consanguinity* (1871). A formidable intellectual, he was a philologist, and a recognized authority on Sanskrit. McIlvaine was associated with the Smithsonian Institution, and when he left Rochester it was to take up an academic appointment at Princeton.

He was also a minister of religion. He did his best – with the support of Morgan's wife – to ignite Morgan's Christian faith, but with only partial success, though he claimed that Morgan's heart lay in the end with the Christian religion; and Morgan was certainly at the least a Deist, and was prepared to respect McIlvaine's faith. An earlier generation sometimes represented McIlvaine as a censor, who checked the free expression of Morgan's Darwinian beliefs for theological reasons. This interpretation derived some plausibility from McIlvaine's own claim:

that whilst his great work on 'Ancient Society' was passing through the press, I called his attention to a passage which inadvertently might have found its place there, and which might be construed as an endorsement of these materialistic speculations in connection with evolution; and he immediately cancelled the whole page, although it had already been stereotyped.[2]

This view of McIlvaine's role altered as the context of the evolutionist debate in the United States was better appreciated. Indeed Morgan's second biographer, Carl Resek, concluded that on the contrary McIlvaine had inspired Morgan's evolutionist hypothesis.[3]

Morgan and McIlvaine's branch of the Presbyterian church participated in a markedly liberal movement within New England-Calvinism in the second half of the nineteenth century.[4] It repudi-

---

2 McIlvaine (1923), 'The life and works of Lewis H. Morgan, LL.D.: an address at his funeral', p. 57

3 Resek (1980), *Lewis Henry Morgan: American Scholar*.

4 For discussions of contemporary American Calvinism, its attitudes to slavery and to Darwinian theory, see: Winthrop Hudson (1965), *Religion in America*; James

ated slavery and affirmed a faith in democracy and Utilitarian political ideas. On scientific matters, it was equally determined to accommodate the most enlightened modern theories. Nor was the theory of evolution a special problem. Evolution might even be reconciled with Calvinist ideas of predestination – 'Evolution', as one divine explained, 'is God's way of doing things'.[5] The new chronology could also be taken on board. 'I cannot find sufficient data in the Scriptures for a revealed chronology', McIlvaine commented. 'Neither, as I read the first chapters of Genesis, does it appear that man was created in a high state of development, though certainly in a state of innocence.'[6]

The northern Presbyterians in fact welcomed Darwin's witness with respect to one very sensitive political issue. This was the question of the unity of origin of the human species. They were up in arms against their southern Presbyterian brethren, who justified slavery on the grounds that God had created several distinct species of man, each with a particular destiny. During the Civil War an 'American school of anthropology' developed in the South which propagated this view. It drew the support even of Agassiz, the eccentric Lamarckian biologist of Harvard.[7]

According to the northern Presbyterians, this 'polygenist' thesis was a denial of the truth, to which both the Bible and the Declaration of Independence bore witness, that all men were created equal. Darwin unequivocally supported the view that all the races were simply varieties of one species, with a common origin. This aspect of Darwinian theory was particularly stressed by Asa Gray, Agassiz's rival at Harvard, and the leader of the American Darwinians.

On one vital matter, however, Darwin's views were unacceptable to many, indeed most, Christians. He posited the mutability of species and – despite his inital caution – it became evident that he believed man had evolved from non-human primate forebears. This theory of the transmutation of species was clearly irreconcilable with the Book of Genesis, but there were many respect-

Moore (1979), *The Post-Darwinian Controversies*; H. Smith *et. al.* (1963), *American Christianity*; and R. Wilson (1967), *Darwin and the American Intellectuals*.

5 Quoted in Hudson (1965), *Religion in America*, p. 267.

6 McIlvaine (1923), 'The life and works of Lewis H. Morgan', p. 56.

7 See especially William Stanton (1960), *The Leopard's Spots: Scientific Attitudes toward Race in America 1815–1859*.

able scholars who believed that it was also at odds with biological facts. A great number of mainstream biologists in the 1860s believed that the species were fixed. Agassiz's version of Cuvier's typology even allowed for the separate creation of each individual species. Morgan, a competent amateur biologist, sided with Agassiz on this issue. He wrote a naturalist's study of the American beaver (which won Agassiz's admiration) in which he strongly affirmed his faith in Cuvier and in the separate creation of the human species.[8]

One could, however, believe that the species were fixed without having to believe that they were changeless. Agassiz and many of his colleagues might rule out 'transmutation', the change of one species into another; but they still believed that a species could develop along appropriate lines. Each species might realize an inner potential, which gradually unfolded. Those who thought in this way commonly conceived of the development of species on the analogy of the evolution of the embryo. The tadpole might become a frog, but that did not amount to a change of species. Indeed, ontogeny, the development of an individual, might recapitulate phylogeny, the history of a species. The term 'evolution' itself was generally used in this embryological sense until about 1880, and neither Darwin in *The Origin of Species* (1859) nor Morgan in *Systems* (1871) or *Ancient Society* (1877), used the word 'evolution' at all.[9]

Agassiz's version of evolution assumed that the world had been designed by God. Particular species had been created in order to fit into particular ecological relations. They were, moreover, programmed to develop as the whole cosmological order itself progressed. Adaptation was a sign of planning rather than of selection. Agassiz was quite explicit that evolution was comprehensible only as the gradual unfolding of a divine plan. Species were incarnations of a divine idea. 'Natural History must, in good time,

---

8 Morgan (1868a), *The American Beaver and His Works*.
9 See Bowler (1975), 'The changing meaning of "evolution"'. Morgan's first biographer, Stern, wrote:

> It was undoubtedly out of deference to the pressure of McIlvaine ... that Morgan nowhere in his books uses the word 'evolution' or has a word of praise for the writers on this subject, although his works are permeated by their influence'. (1931, *Lewis Henry Morgan: Social Evolutionist*, p. 23)

> This was a complete misrepresentation of the true situation.

become the analysis of the thoughts of the Creator of the Universe, as manifested in the animal and vegetable kingdoms.'[10]

Agassiz's theory of development was the biological equivalent of a common New England Calvinist belief that human history, since Christ, was a record of progress and moral improvement inspired by God, in which every group had its preordained rôle. This idealistic view was in stark contrast to the scepticism of Darwin or the pessimism of Malthus. 'I believe in no fixed law of development', Darwin had written in *Origin*, and when Christian intellectuals attacked his 'materialist' theory they meant in particular his view that history is contingent, unplanned, without a goal, the product simply of random mutation and natural selection. McIlvaine, similarly, objected to the thesis of Malthus because it left no place for divine planning.[11]

This belief in progress according to a divine plan had a political counterpart in American political thought, which commonly represented political 'development' as a series of progressive approximations to the principles of government which had been set out in the Declaration of Independence. This was perhaps Morgan's most important theme. McIlvaine rightly emphasized it in his funeral oration, praising Morgan's

demonstration that progress is a fundamental law of human society, and one which has always prevailed – progress in thought and knowledge, in industry, in morality, in social organization, in institutions, and in all things tending to, or advancing, civilization and general well-being.[12]

But these were only the broadest considerations which informed Morgan's thinking. His more immediate concern was with questions of American ethnology, and his initial inspiration was drawn from philology and history rather than biology. These intellectual roots of the early Morgan are similar to those which sustained Maine.

10 See Mayr (1959), 'Agassiz, Darwin and evolution'. The passage from Agassiz is cited on p. 171.
11 McIlvaine (1867), 'Malthusianism'.
12 McIlvaine (1923), 'The life and works of Lewis H. Morgan'.

'The League of the Iroquois'

Lewis Henry Morgan, the ninth of thirteen children, was born in 1818 in Aurora, New York (then 'still a wilderness surrounded by Indians'[13]). His father, a wealthy farmer, a state senator, and a devout Presbyterian, died when Morgan was a boy of eight. In 1838 he went to Union College, a school distinguished for its Whig politics, which found fashionable expression in the idealization of the democratic civilization of Athens.[14] In 1844 he received a licence to practise law, and established himself in practice in Rochester, New York.

In Rochester, Morgan set up a fraternity. There was an Iroquois reservation nearby, and the fraternity took the name Iroquois and considered organizing itself on the lines of the Iroquois League. Morgan began to visit the nearby reservation and to collect ethnographic information. He also intervened successfully with Washington on behalf of an Iroquois group on a land question.[15] Eventually he wrote up his ethnographic findings, so discharging an undertaking which, he thought, had now come to an end.

With the publication [of *The League of the Iroquois*] in January 1851 I laid aside the Indian subject to devote my time to my profession. My principal object in writing this work, which exhibits abundant evidence of hasty execution, was to free myself of the subject.[16]

Although primarily a descriptive work, *The League of the Iroquois* is informed by a progressive spirit. Like Maine, Morgan was impressed by a model of ancient history, and his particular inspiration was Grote's vastly influential Utilitarian study of Greece. The Greeks, according to Grote, had evolved from a family-based polity to city-states. Initially there were separate, independent families. These then joined together in groups, the gens, phratry and tribe. The gens was particularly significant, and Grote described it as a kinship and political unit, democratic in nature, and with religious

---

13 Stern (1931), *Lewis Henry Morgan*, p. 3.

14 See Resek (1960), *Lewis Henry Morgan*, p. 9.

15 See R. Bieder (1980), 'The Grand Order of the Iroquois: influences on Lewis Henry Morgan's ethnology', and E. Tooker (1983), 'The structure of the Iroquois League: Lewis H. Morgan's research and observations'.

16 Quoted in White (1957), 'How Morgan came to write *Systems of Consanguinity and Affinity*', p. 257.

functions. In their political evolution the Greeks passed from a democracy based on kinship groups to a stage of monarchy and despotism, eventually in the case of Athens achieving a higher democratic form.

In *Ancient Society* (1877) Morgan was to reject the priority of the family over the gens and phratry. He also came to deny that all societies had to endure a stage of monarchy and despotism. In *The League of the Iroquois* (1851), however, he accepted Grote's argument. Echoing Grote, Morgan asserted that:

there is a regular progression of political institutions, from the monarchical, which are the earliest in time, on to the democratical, which are the last, noblest, and the most intellectual. This position can be established by the rise and development of the Grecian institutions, and may be further illustrated by the progressive change in the spirit and nature of other governments.[17]

Despotic monarchy was a form of government 'natural to a people when in an uncivilized state, or when just emerging from barbarism'.

The Iroquois represented a yet earlier condition, in which 'Family Relationships' still provided the fundamental scheme of government.

These relations are older than the notions of society or government, and are consistent alike with the hunter, the pastoral and the civilized state. The several nations of the Iroquois, united, constituted one Family, dwelling together in one Long House; and those ties of family relationship were carried throughout their civil and social system, from individuals to tribes, from tribes to nations, and from the nations to the League itself, and bound them together in one common, indissoluble brotherhood.[18]

Morgan also described the unfamiliar Iroquois terminology for kin, which was 'unlike that of the civil or canon law; but was yet a clear and definite system. No distinction was made between the lineal and collateral lines, either in the ascending or descending series'.[19] He linked this system with the use of consanguineal relationships to build up large political units. There is no suggestion of his later theory that the kinship terminology reflected exotic

17   Morgan (1851), *League of the Iroquois*, p. 122.
18   *Op. cit.*, pp. 56–7.
19   *Op. cit.*, p. 81.

forms of marriage or family relationships. Indeed, Morgan clearly described the Iroquois marriage forms, remarking mainly on the absence of affection between man and wife. Marriage was in essence a contract arranged between the mothers of the couple, who acted for larger family units.

The American Indian

With the publication of his book, Morgan believed that he had put Indian ethnography behind him. He now concentrated on business, and prospered. In 1855 he became a director of the Iron Mountain Rail Road Co., and he soon extended his interest to other railway companies. 'From the close of 1850 until the summer of 1857,' he recorded in his Journal, 'Indian affairs were laid entirely aside'.[20]

As he became rich, Morgan was able to devote more time to outside interests. He took up politics, serving as Republican congressman and then senator in the state assembly between 1861 and 1869, and became chairman of the Indian affairs committee of the assembly. He also angled for federal preferment, but it never came. At the same time, he maintained his intellectual interests. With McIlvaine he founded the Pundit Club in Rochester, at which papers were read dealing with such matters as Lyell's geology, Sanskrit, and ethnology.

In 1856 Morgan was elected to the Association for the Advancement of Science. This encouraged him to return at last to his Iroquois notes in order to prepare a paper for the following annual meeting. The paper he wrote, entitled 'Laws of descent of the Iroquois', dealt mainly with their system of classifying kin, which he considered a unique invention of the tribe. Soon, however, a fresh discovery was to change his mind.

In the summer of 1858 Morgan found that the Ojibwa, who spoke a different language from the Iroquois, nevertheless had essentially the same system of classifying kin.

Every term of relationship was radically different from the corresponding term in the Iroquois; but the classification of kindred was the same. It

---

20 White (1957), 'How Morgan came to write *Systems of Consanguinity and Affinity*', p. 262.

was manifest that the two systems were identical in their fundamental characteristics.[21]

In the following year he recorded in his journal the extraordinary hypothesis which this discovery suggested to him.

From this time I began to be sensible to the important uses which such a primary institution as this must have in its bearing upon the question of the genetic connection of the American Indian nation, not only, but also on the still more important question of their Asiatic origin.[22]

It was now – at the age of forty – that his most important research began.

To appreciate what Morgan had in mind, it is necessary first to consider the state of play in American ethnology at the time. This had just been thoroughly and critically reviewed by Samuel Haven, in his *Archaeology of the United States*, which was published by the Smithsonian Institution in 1856, precisely at the moment when Morgan's interest in American ethnology was quickened once again.

The central issue raised in Haven's summary was familiar and of vital importance. This was the polygenist–monogenist controversy. Haven conceded with some reluctance that 'The subject of American ethnology passes ... insensibly into the general question of the original unity or diversity of mankind.'[23] He reviewed in detail the linguistic studies of American languages, emphasizing Gallatin's conclusion that the Indian languages shared a common and distinct character, probably resulting from a very long period of isolation. This unity existed despite wide variations in vocabulary: 'however differing in their words, the most striking uniformity in their grammatical forms and structure appears to exist in all the American languages'.[24] According to Gallatin, the most characteristic structural feature of the Indian languages was what Von Humboldt had called 'agglutination', i.e. glueing together; 'a tendency to accumulate a multitude of ideas in a single word', as Haven defined it.[25]

---

21 Morgan (1871), *Systems of Consanguinity and Affinity of the Human Family*, p. 3.
22 Quoted Stern (1931), *Lewis Henry Morgan*, p. 73.
23 Haven (1856), p. 81.
24 *Op. cit.*, p. 65.
25 *Op. cit.*, p. 67. This was a simplification of the then current technical linguistic

Haven then covered the physiological studies which had been carried out, dealing very fairly with the polygenist school, though finally rejecting their conclusions. He also surveyed the discoveries of the archaeologists. His final conclusion was that:

The deductions from scientific investigations, philological and physiological, tend to prove that American races are of great antiquity. Their religious doctrines, their superstitions ... and their arts, accord with those of the most primitive age of mankind. With all their characteristics affinities are found in the early condition of Asiatic races.[26]

The evidence therefore apparently supported the monogenist argument, while (in Haven's view) not necessarily contradicting the received chronology.

Haven's most striking data came from philology, and this was a field which Morgan must have learnt from McIlvaine. McIlvaine was a Sanskritist, but this meant that he was an Indo-European man, and the models of Gallatin and other American linguists had been taken over directly from the Indo-Europeanists.

The Indo-European philologists had established relationships between languages hitherto regarded as completely distinct. They agreed that most of the European languages were distantly related to Sanskrit, and that their point of origin was in India. The Semitic languages were similarly interrelated, and they too had an Asian point of origin. In the 1860s some scholars mooted the possibility that the Indo-European and Semitic language stocks were also ultimately related to each other.

The Professor of Sanskrit at Oxford, Max Müller, propagated the view that there was a third stock, which he called 'Turanian'. It was divided into a European, northern branch (Turkish, Finnish, Mongolian, Basque, etc.) and a southern, tropical branch. This tropical language family included most if not all of the other languages in the world, including Tamil (the main Indian language which is not related to Sanskrit) and the languages of the American Indians.

It seemed a very diverse group. Superficially at least, its members

---

notion of agglutination, but Morgan was at best an amateur philologist, and his own semantics of 'classificatory systems' fit in well with Haven's definition of agglutination. For a sophisticated (essentially grammatical) definition of agglutination by a contemporary, see Max Müller's (1861) *Lectures on the Science of Language*, especially Chapter 8.

26 Haven, *op. cit.*, pp. 158–9.

had few linguistic features in common. But then Müller did not expect these languages to be very similar. He believed that the people who spoke Turanian languages were typically nomads, with the consequence that their languages were liable to rapid change and much dialectical variation. He instanced the terms for kin, explaining that these were stable in Aryan languages but not in Turanian. Yet although words themselves changed, underlying concepts might be constant. At this level the Turanian languages

share much in common, and show that before their divergency a certain nucleus of language was formed, in which some parts of language, the first to crystallize and the most difficult to be analysed, had become fixed and stationary. Numerals, pronouns, and some of the simplest applied verbal roots belong to this class of words.[27]

They had something else in common, too, for Müller believed that they all exhibited Von Humboldt's 'agglutinating' tendency.

Were these three linguistic stocks – all, probably, ultimately of Asian origin – independent? Were there any traces of an original language spoken by a once-united human race? (If this, too, was located in Asia, perhaps the Book of Genesis was accurate after all!) Müller could find no philological basis for such a conclusion, but he proposed an alternative resolution of the issue. Using Von Humboldt's typology, which classified languages according to grammatical principles that he termed 'isolation, agglutination and inflexion', Müller argued – as indeed Schleicher had argued before him – that language stocks could be ordered on a scale of progressive development. The most primitive languages were 'isolating'. Each word consisted of a single, stable root. At a more advanced level they were characterized by 'agglutination' – roots were 'glued together' to form new words. The most developed languages went in for 'amalgamation', developing inflected forms in which the original roots, once simply glued together, merged to form quite new words.

There were difficulties with this scheme. Chinese, for instance, was classified as an 'isolating language' (i.e. each word consists of a single, stable root). Yet it was hard to believe that Chinese was exceptionally primitive. Müller tried to resolve this particular difficulty by providing Chinese with its own private evolutionary

27 Müller in Bunsen (1854), *Outlines of the Philosophy of Universal History Applied to Language and Religion*, vol. 1, p. 478.

track. But for the rest, the southern Turanian languages could be classified as 'agglutinating', while the northern (or European) Turanian languages could be classified with the Semitic and Indo-European languages as 'amalgamating'. They had, however, once been 'agglutinating' themselves. 'Amalgamation' was a direct advance on 'agglutination'. The classification therefore cross-cut the established boundaries of language families and yielded a new classification, in which the languages of Europe, the Middle East and North India were associated together and opposed to most of the languages spoken in the tropics. But this did not contradict the idea that all men – and all languages – had a common origin. The languages of Europe were certainly more advanced, but they had once been 'agglutinating', and even 'isolating' themselves.

Müller also linked this scheme of linguistic development with the models of technical and social progress constructed by the writers of the Scottish Enlightenment, borrowing their famous four-stage model. ('The four stages of society are hunting, pasturing, farming and commerce' to quote Adam Smith's classic formulation.) These economic stages had from the first been associated with a model of political development from anarchic communism to private property and the state.[28] Müller now added a theory of linguistic progress.

Some Indo-European scholars had tried to find philological clues to the early condition of the Indo-Europeans. Had they been nomads or agriculturalists? At what stage might they have shifted from nomadism to agriculture? Müller's synthetic model opposed a category of primitive, anarchic, dispersed nomads, speaking agglutinating languages in a state of continual dialectical flux, and civilized, centralized, agricultural societies, with literate élites and, consequently, more stable and advanced languages characterized by 'amalgamation'. In the long essay on these issues, which he contributed to a book by his patron, Bunsen, he summarized his ideas (see Figure 3.1).

The beauty of Müller's model was that it both divided and united humanity. Müller endorsed the division of humanity into 'higher' Aryan and Semitic and 'lower' southern Turanian people. At the same time, his model assumed that all men had a single origin.

---

28 See Meek (1975), *Social Science and Ignoble Savage*. These ideas were becoming very fashionable at the time in America. See Stevens (1975), 'Adam Smith and the colonial disturbances'.

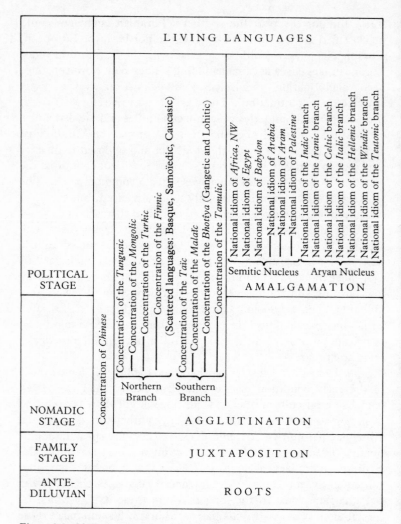

Figure 3.1 Müller's summary of linguistic progress (from Max Müller's contribution to C. C. J. Bunsen (1854), *Outlines of the Philosophy of University History applied to Language and Religion,* 2 vols, London, Longman).

This was the paradigm which Morgan referred to most often in his 1871 *Systems.*

Asian origins

After stumbling upon the fact that the Ojibwa had substantially the same system of classifying relatives as the Iroquois, Morgan checked with Rigg's lexicon of the Dakota language and found that they lumped relatives together in the same 'classificatory' manner as the Iroquois and Ojibwa. The question now arose: How widely was the system distributed? In December 1858 he sent schedules out to Indian areas to be filled in by missionaries and Indian agents. The results were disappointing, perhaps not surprisingly, since the questionnaire ran to eight printed pages and its completion demanded considerable time and effort. But a few satisfactory schedules were returned, and Morgan carried out his enquiries in person in reservations in Kansas and Nebraska. By mid-1859 he was convinced that the system of classifying relatives was fundamentally uniform throughout North America. This he took as evidence that the North American Indians had a common origin.

But if the Indians were ultimately one group, where had they come from? Morgan was inclined to accept the hypothesis of School-craft and other specialists, supported by Haven, that they were ultimately of Asian origin. Obviously they were not 'Aryan', and so Morgan looked for connections among Müller's prototypical Asian Turanians, the Tamils. Accordingly, he invited an American missionary, Dr Scudder, to prepare a schedule for Tamil and Telugu.

McIlvaine testified that at this time Morgan:

lived and worked often in a state of great mental excitement, and the answers he received, as they came in, sometimes nearly overpowered him. I well remember one occasion when he came into my study, saying, 'I shall find it, I shall find it among the Tamil people and Dravidian tribes of Southern India'. At that time I had no expectation of any such result; and I said to him, 'My friend, you have enough to do in working out your discovery in connection with the tribes of the American continent – let the peoples of the old world go'. He replied, 'I cannot do it – I must go on, for I am sure I shall find it all there'.[29]

29 McIlvaine (1923), 'The life and works of Lewis H. Morgan', pp. 50–1.

When the Tamil-Telegu schedule came back, Morgan laid it side by side with the Seneca-Iroquois system and concluded that it had the same structure. He wrote to Scudder 'that we had now been able to put our hands upon decisive evidence of the Asiatic origin of the American Indian race'.[30] In *Systems* he expressed the same conclusion more grandiloquently:

When the discoverers of the New World bestowed upon its inhabitants the name of *Indians*, under the impression that they had reached the Indies, they little suspected that children of the same original family, although upon a different continent, stood before them. By a singular coincidence error was truth.[31]

Classificatory and descriptive systems of consanguinity

Morgan concluded that all the members of Müller's southern Turanian family had what he called 'classificatory' kinship systems. The Aryans, Semites and northern Turanians all had 'descriptive' systems. These two types of systems were quite distinct. Indeed, they were virtually inversions of each other.

In descriptive systems there are different terms for father and mother, husband and wife, brother and sister, and son and daughter, and none of these terms is applied outside the nuclear family. Morgan argued that such systems mirror the reality of biological kinship, clearly marking the degrees of blood relationship.

Classificatory systems, in contrast, did not reflect the natural degrees of kinship. They lumped relationships of different kinds together under one term. The same word might refer, for example, to father, father's brother, father's father's brother's son, and also perhaps to other relatives, confusing different kinds and degrees of biological relatedness. 'It thus confounds relationships, which, under the descriptive system, are distinct, and enlarges the signification both of the primary and secondary terms beyond their seemingly appropriate sense.'[32] The classificatory principle immediately suggested the mechanism of 'agglutination'. Moreover, the languages which according to Morgan applied one kin term to

30 Stern (1931), *Lewis Henry Morgan*, p. 27.
31 Morgan (1871), *Systems of Consanguinity and Affinity*, p. 508.
32 *Op. cit.*, p. 12.

various degrees of relationships were precisely those which Müller regarded as 'agglutinating'.

But if classificatory systems did not properly describe biological relationships, they were by no means incoherent. Like the man who thought he was Napoleon, the systems made perfect sense if their underlying axioms were granted. If, for example, father's brother was 'father', then, quite properly, father's brother's wife was 'mother', father's brother's son 'brother', etc. Morgan concluded that

a system has been created which must be regarded as a domestic institution in the highest sense of this expression. No other can properly characterize a structure the framework of which is so complete, and the details of which are so rigorously adjusted.[33]

The opposition between descriptive and classificatory systems was not always clear-cut. Morgan was aware that the 'descriptive' systems often had 'classificatory' elements. For example, discussing the Dutch kinship terminology, he commented that 'The terms *neef* and *nicht* are applied indiscriminately to a nephew and niece, to a grandson and granddaughter, and to each of the four classes of cousins.'[34] This was the sort of lumping together one might expect to find in a classificatory system. But Morgan argued that the history of the Germanic systems showed that they were originally purely descriptive in form, as some of the Scandinavian systems have remained. The introduction of classificatory terms for 'uncle' and 'aunt', subsequently for 'nephew' and 'niece', and finally for 'cousin', were later rationalizations, which simplified the system while not transgressing its fundamental opposition between lineal and collateral kin. In this particular instance the argument was made more difficult by the fact that the Dutch classified nephews, male cousins and also grandsons together, so indeed confusing lineals and collaterals. Morgan's comment was that the Dutch system 'is defective in arrangement, and imprecise in the discrimination of relationships', which placed the error firmly with the Dutch rather than in his theory.[35]

Nor did the classificatory systems constitute a uniform set.

33 *Op. cit.*, p. 472.
34 *Op. cit.*, p. 35.
35 *Op. cit.*, p. 35. It is perhaps worth remarking that the use of the terms *neef* and *nicht* for grandchildren is now obsolete in Dutch.

Morgan divided Müller's southern Turanian group into three, on the basis of a typology of classificatory systems. The three types were termed respectively the Turanian, the Malayan, and the Ganowanian (the American Indian group). He was, of course, particularly interested in the Ganowanian, and his discussion of the American systems is the longest and most detailed, running to 135 pages of text plus 100 pages of tables, or almost 40 per cent of the whole of *Systems of Consanguinity and Affinity*. But he was convinced that the Ganowanian system was closely related to the Turanian, of which the Tamil and Dravidian systems were typical. Chinese and Japanese were also 'Turanian'. The 'Malayan' systems were, however, very different from them.

In both the Turanian and Ganowanian systems, only one set of cousins was identified with siblings and termed 'brother' and 'sister'. These were children of father's brothers or mother's sisters. Other cousins (children of father's sisters or mother's brothers) were distinguished from siblings. The Malayan systems, in contrast, classed all cousins together with siblings, and all parents' siblings together with parents. This category included not only the peoples of the Pacific but a number of far-flung peoples, and even the Zulu, Morgan's only African group.

'Systems of Consanguinity and Affinity of the Human Family'

When his argument had reached this stage, Morgan believed that he had successfully completed a type of philological study. It demonstrated the unity and the ultimately Asian origin of the American Indian languages, and suggested the existence of two great linguistic stocks, one European and north-west Asian, and the other southern, tropical and firmly non-European. Within this framework Morgan wrote up his massive materials, tabulating and analysing 139 kinship schedules from all the over the world, listing over 260 kin-types for each.

In 1865 he submitted the manuscript for publication to the Smithsonian Institution. Joseph Henry, the director of the Smithsonian, was reluctant to accept it, writing to Morgan that 'the first impression of one who has been engaged in physical research is that, in proportion to the conclusions arrived at, the quantity of your material is very large'[36]; but he sent it for consideration to two philologists and Sanskritists – Whitney at Yale, and McIlvaine.

36 Quoted by Resek (1960), *Lewis Henry Morgan*, pp. 96–7.

McIlvaine was prepared to accept that the analysis was incomplete. Morgan had demonstrated the inner coherence of classificatory systems, but their meaning remained a mystery. He remarked that at this stage:

> our friend had not perceived any material significance or explanation of the immense body of entirely new facts which he had discovered and collected. He could not at all acount for them. In fact, he regarded this system, or these slightly different forms of one system, as invented and wholly artificial, so different was it from that which now prevails in civilized society, and which evidently follows the flow of the blood. During all these years, he had not the least conception of any process of thought in which it could have originated, or of anything which could have caused it so universally to prevail. He treated it as something which must throw great light upon pre-historic man, but what light he had not discovered.[37]

And yet, a year before the submission of the manuscript, McIlvaine had discussed with Morgan a plausible explanation of the classificatory systems. In a letter dated March 1864, he wrote:

> I have just lighted upon certain references which throw some light upon the origin of your Tamilian or Indian system of relationships; at least on some parts of it. You remember we were talking about whether it did not point back to a state of promiscuous intercourse. You will find in Aristotle's politics Book II chapter 3 where he is refuting Plato's doctrine of a community of wives this sentence, 'Some tribes in upper Africa have their wives in common', and in a note in Bonn's translation of it the following references, 'For example the Masimanes (Herodotus IV, 172) and the Ayseuses (ib. IV, 180)'...
>
> I am inclined to think that this state of society might, upon a full and minute investigation of the remains of antiquity, be found more extensively to have prevailed than is commonly supposed.[38]

The hypothesis was, then, that the mysterious 'classificatory' designation of kin was based on real parent-child relationships, as was the descriptive system. Both described a consanguineal reality, but the realities were differently ordered. In societies with 'classificatory' terminologies, wives were held in common. A child would therefore not know who its father was. Accordingly, all potential fathers were 'father', all their children 'brother' or 'sister',

---

37 McIlvaine (1923), 'The life and works of Lewis H. Morgan', pp. 51–2.
38 Quoted in Resek (1960), *Lewis Henry Morgan*, p. 94.

etc. Similarly, all the women who were actually or potentially the mates of a 'father' were termed 'mother'.

Morgan did not immediately develop this suggestion. It was only after Joseph Henry's rejection of his manuscript that he returned to the idea, and then only after studying, with some jealousy, McLennan's new theory.[39] McLennan's *Primitive Marriage*, which appeared just at this moment, in 1865, described an initial state in which fatherhood was uncertain, since women were held in common. An original condition of promiscuity was later replaced by polyandry, which at least fixed motherhood, and so allowed the tracing of kin ties in the female line. In a higher form, a group of brothers held one wife in common, so permitting the tracing of kinships through men also. Gradually 'gentes' of related men emerged. 'Most probably contiguous tribes would be composed of precisely the same stocks – would contain gentes of precisely the same names, and thus be in the strictest sense akin – kindred', McLennan wrote. These units would eventually unite in a state. 'The order of social development, in our view, is then, that the tribe stands first; the gens or house next; and last of all, the family.' (As he pointed out, this inverted Maine's and Grote's postulated line of development.) Gradually clan property appeared; finally, in the wake of Barbarism, individual property, and consequently the family. As the family became the vital social unit, so modern forms of marriage emerged. The crucial factor in this shift was the emergence of private property:

the laws of succession which had sprung up with family property – which were springing up with individual property – were training the people to consider a few persons only as their kinsmen in any special sense ... However strongly implanted the principle of exogamy may have originally been it must have succumbed to the influences which thus disintegrated the old bonds of kinship.[40]

In May 1867 Morgan wrote a paper in which he linked the types of kinship classification with specific modes of marriage, and the following February he presented it to a meeting of the American Academy of Art and Sciences, under the title 'A conjectural solution to the origin of the classificatory system of relationship'.

39 *Op. cit.*, p. 92.
40 Citations can be found in McLennan (1876), *Studies in Ancient History*, pp. 221, 222 and 225.

His audience included Agassiz and Asa Gray, and Morgan was evidently tense. He left hurriedly after the lecture, convinced he had failed, and wrote to a friend that 'Agassiz does not know, nor could the other members present fully appreciate the remarkable character of the system ... I was afraid to show more lest they would not bear it.'[41] But in the event the Academy requested the text of his lecture for publication and elected him to its membership. This paper provided the basis for a new final chapter for *Systems*. Morgan added a lengthy review of the possibility that diffusion and borrowing might account for common elements of classification, but concluded that the facts pointed to the common origin of structurally similar systems. With the addition of this chapter *Systems* was at last accepted for publication by the Smithsonian, although problems of format and expense delayed its appearance until 1871. It was the most expensive book which the Smithsonian had published up to that time.

The argument Morgan developed was a variant of that sketched by McLennan. McLennan had posited an original condition of promiscuity, which had evolved into polyandry. Morgan rejected McLennan's emphasis upon polyandry. He lighted rather on an institution which had been briefly described by some missionaries in Hawaii, and which he called the 'Hawaiian custom'. This was 'a compound form of polyginia and polyandria', whereby a set of brothers was married collectively to their own sisters. Within this group, husbands and wives were held in common. Such a form of marriage would logically generate a 'Malayan' system of classificatory kinship terminology. For example:

All the children of my several brothers, myself a male, are my sons and daughters, Reason: I cohabit with all my brothers' wives, who are my own wives as well (using the terms *husband* and *wife* in the sense of the custom). As it would be impossible for me to distinguish my own children from those of my brothers, if I call any one my child, I must call them all my children. One is as likely to be mine as another.[42]

Similarly, a man's sisters were his wives, and so their children were counted as his own; and so forth.

The next step was the prohibition of intermarriage between

41 Quoted in Resek (1960), *Lewis Henry Morgan*, p. 98.
42 Morgan (1868b), 'A conjectural solution of the origin of the classificatory system of relationship', p. 465.

siblings – in other words, McLennan's 'exogamy'. This abolition of marriage between brothers and sisters did not necessarily imply the total abandonment of the 'Hawaiian custom'. A group of brothers would now marry someone else's set of sisters. Marriage would remain a combination of polyandry and polygamy. But the practice of exogamy would result in the separation of the children of brothers and the children of sisters into distinct categories. A man's brothers' children would still count as his children; and a woman's sisters' children as her children. But:

All the children of my several sisters, myself a male, are my nephews and nieces. Reason: Since under the tribal organization my sisters ceased to be my wives, their children can no longer be my children, but must stand to me in a different and more remote relationship. Whence the relations of nephew and niece.[43]

In the jargon of a later generation, cross-cousins were distinguished from parallel cousins, and parallel cousins were identified with siblings. Other classifications were similarly explained with reference to group marriage arrangements. Problematic features were said to represent survivals of an earlier state of affairs.

The other stages in the development of the family were sketched in the most casual fashion. In conclusion, Morgan presented a fifteen-stage evolution (see Table 3.1)[44] rather like a magician drawing rabbits out of a hat, remarking:

It may be confidently affirmed that this great sequence of customs and institutions, although for the present hypothetical, will organize and explain the body of ascertained facts, with respect to the primitive history of mankind, in a manner so singularly and surprisingly adequate as to invest it with a strong probability of truth.[45]

The one principle which apparently operated throughout human history was a tendency to moral progress. For example:

the Hawaiian custom still embodies the evidence of an organic movement of society to extricate itself from a worse condition than the one it produced. For it may be affirmed, as a general proposition, that the

---

43 Ibid.
44 This table occurs in Morgan's (1868b) 'A conjectural solution. . . .', p. 463 and his (1871) *Systems in Consanguinity and Affinity*, p. 480.
45 Morgan (1868b), 'A conjectural solution of the origin of the classificatory system of relationship', pp. 463–4.

Table 3.1 THE DEVELOPMENT OF FAMILY TYPES

I	Promiscuous intercourse
II	The intermarriage or cohabitation of brothers and sisters
III	The communal family (first stage of the family)
IV	The Hawaiian custom, giving
V	The Malayan form of the classificatory system of relationship
VI	The tribal organization, giving
VII	The Turanian and Ganowanian system of relationship
VIII	Marriage between single pairs, giving
IX	The barbarian family (second stage of the family)
X	Polygamy, giving
XI	The patriarchal family (third stage of the family)
XII	Polyandria
XIII	The rise of property with the settlement of lineal succession to estates, giving
XIV	The civilized family (fourth and ultimate state of the family), producing
XV	The overthrow of the classificatory system of relationship, and the substitution of the descriptive

principal customs and institutions of mankind have originated in great reformatory movements.[46]

Similarly, the tribal organization 'was designed to work out a reformation with respect to the intermarriage of brothers and sisters', and 'it seems extremely probable that it can only be explained as a reformatory movement'.[47]

More specific mechanisms, however, might explain the change from one stage to another – the need for mutual defence leading to tribal organization, genetic advantages favouring exogamy, and so forth. The only mechanism which Morgan handled in any detail was the development of private estates, which explained the emergence of the 'civilized family' and the final 'Overthrow of the classificatory system of relationship, and the substitution of the descriptive'. Morgan ascribed this very last stage of man's social development to the influence of property relationships. Indeed, the emergence of property relationships was the mark of civilization.

---

46 Morgan (1871), *Systems of Consanguinity and Affinity*, p. 481.
47 *Op. cit.*, p. 490.

With the rise of property, considered as an institution, with the settlement
of its rights, and above all, with the established certainty of its
transmission to lineal descendants, came the first possibility among
mankind of the true family in its modern acceptation ... It is impossible
to separate property, considered in the concrete, from civilization, or for
civilization to exist without its presence, protection, and regulated
inheritance. Of property in this sense, all barbarous nations are necessarily
ignorant.[48]

This view was commonplace in the Scottish tradition,[49] and was
essentially identical to that of McLennan and of Maine.

Encountering the British anthropologists

Morgan visited Europe in 1871, taking delivery of his first copies
of *Systems* in London. He visited Maine, McLennan, Lubbock
(whom he found playing cricket), and even Darwin and Huxley;
and found himself welcomed as a colleague into the inner circle of
the new anthropology.

And 1871 was the year in which Darwin published his *Descent
of Man*. This book was, of course, of capital importance to all
anthropologists. Darwin paid attention to McLennan's theory of
matriarchy, and he raised the question of intellectual development,
which was to become the central issue in anthropology in the
following decades. Also in 1870–1 Tylor and Lubbock each published his most important book – Tylor his *Primitive Culture*,
and Lubbock his *Origin of Civilization*. Both profoundly affected
Morgan's thinking.

Lubbock had been responsible for popularizing the new prehistory.[50] He had translated the crucial Scandinavian texts, which
introduced a three-stage model of development through stone,
copper (or bronze) and iron 'ages'. Following Nilsson, he had
identified these archaeological phases with the classical Scottish
'stages of progress' – through savagery (hunting and gathering),
barbarism (nomadism and pastoralism, and then agriculture) and
finally industrial civilization. On the basis of this proven technological advance he and Tylor rejected the hypothesis that men
had degenerated from a higher state. The fossils and survivals of
human industry demonstrated, on the contrary, a regular progress.

48 *Op. cit.*, p. 492.
49 See Meek (1975), *Social Science and the Ignoble Savage*.
50 See Daniel (1950), *A Hundred Years of Archaeology*.

Lubbock and Tylor also argued that this unmistakable technological progress was matched by a 'mental' progress – physically,
in that man's cranial capacity actually expanded, and also in the
sense that there was improvement in the beliefs and institutions
which man developed. Tylor was particularly interested in the
development of religious ideas, but Lubbock recognized the potential interest of the conjectural histories of marriage and the family
proposed by McLennan and Morgan. He discussed them at length,
and in a friendly, though not uncritical, fashion. Morgan, in turn,
took the Lubbock-Tylor model back to America, and applied it to
his own ends. He now became a universal historian.

Ironically, however, just as Morgan embraced the British school,
it was preparing a rejection of his major theses. In 1876, McLennan
published an attack on Morgan entitled 'The classificatory system
of relationships'.[51] He poured scorn on Morgan's notion that even
early man might have been ignorant of his mother (and he pointed
out that Darwin had expressed puzzlement on this score in the
second edition of *The Descent of Man*). On the contrary, recognition
of the tie to the mother was very primitive, and formed the basis
of the original condition of matriarchy. Further, Morgan's reliance
on the evidence of kinship terminologies was methodologically
unsound. The classificatory system 'is a system of mutual salutations merely'.[52] These lines of criticism persuaded most of the
leading British scholars, at least for a while, but they did not reach
Morgan in time to influence the writing of *Ancient Society*.

'Ancient Society'

Ancient Society, Morgan's most famous book, appeared in 1877. It
begins with a resounding affirmation of the antiquity of human
history and the uniformity of man's progress through the ages that
could well have come from either Tylor or Lubbock. 'It can now
be asserted upon convincing evidence that savagery preceded barbarism in all the tribes of mankind as barbarism is known to have
preceded civilization. The history of the human race is one in
source, one in experience, and in progress.'[53]

---

51 This paper appeared in McLennan's new volume (1876), *Studies in Ancient
   History*, which included a reprint of *Primitive Marriage*.
52 McLennan (1876), *Studies in Ancient History*, p. 366.
53 Morgan (1877), *Ancient Society*, p. 6.

Progress had been made on two levels, one technical, the other social. In each field it exhibited different characteristics. Broadly speaking, technical development resulted from invention and diffusion and exhibited sharp discontinuities. Social development, on the other hand, was the product of steady growth.

Part I of *Ancient Society*, entitled 'Growth of intelligence through inventions and discoveries', was taken over directly from Lubbock and Tylor. The development of subsistence techniques provided the basis for the classification of cultures into seven distinct 'ethnical periods' (see Table 3.2). These ethnical periods had

Table 3.2   MORGAN'S 'ETHNICAL PERIODS'[54]

I	Lower status of savagery	From the infancy of the human race to the commencement of the next period
II	Middle status of savagery	From the acquisition of a fish subsistence and a knowledge of the use of fire, to etc.
III	Upper status of savagery	From the invention of the bow and arrow, to etc.
IV	Lower status of barbarism	From the invention of the art of pottery, to etc.
V	Middle status of barbarism	From the domestication of animals on the eastern hemisphere, and in the western from the cultivation of maize and plants by irrigation, with the use of adobe-brick and stone, to etc.
VI	Upper status of barbarism	From the invention of the process of smelting iron from ore, with the use of iron tools, to etc.
VII	Status of civilization	

a direct relationship to stages of social progress, for 'the great epochs of human progress have been identified, more or less directly, with the enlargement of the sources of subsistence'.[55]

54 *Op. cit.*, p. 12.
55 *Op. cit.*, p. 19.

Technical and social progress were in turn matched by a correlative growth in the human brain, 'particularly of the cerebral portion'.[56]

The different human groups progressed at different speeds, the Aryans taking the lead. 'The Aryan family represents the central stream of human progress, because it produced the highest type of mankind, and because it had proved its intrinsic superiority by gradually assuming the control of the earth.'[57] But inventions are commonly borrowed, and so the Aryans – and Semites – drew others in their wake as they advanced.

The bulk of the book was devoted to the growth of 'ideas' of civil institutions – the 'growth of the idea of government' (Part II), of the family (Part III) and of property (Part IV). While movement from one phase to another might be triggered by a technical advance, the lines of social development are predetermined and inevitable. Here Morgan adopted the idiom of Agassiz – evolutionary development expressed God's thoughts. The content of these divine ideas was, however, already familiar enough.

The 'growth of the idea of government' recapitulated the phases defined by Maine and by Grote; the movement from a kinship-based polity to a territorial state which ordered property relations.

It may be here premised that all forms of government are reducible to two general plans, using the word plan in its scientific sense. In these bases the two are fundamentally distinct. The first, in the order of time, is founded upon persons, and upon relations purely personal, and may be distinguished as a society (*societas*). The gens is the unit of this organization; giving as the successive stages of integration, in the archaic period, the gens, the phratry, the tribe, and the confederacy of tribes, which constituted a people or nation (*populus*). At a later period a coalescence of tribes in the same area into a nation took the place of a confederacy of tribes occupying independent areas. Such, through prolonged ages, after the gens appeared, was the substantially universal organization of ancient society: and it remained among the Greeks and Romans after civilization supervened. The second is founded upon territory and upon property, and may be distinguished as a state (*civitas*).[58]

56 *Op. cit.*, p.57.
57 *Op. cit.*, p. 553.
58 *Op. cit.*, pp. 6–7.

The gens formed the basis of social organization even as late as the final stages of barbarism, since successively more complex kin-based units developed in its image – 'the gens, the phratry, the tribe, and the confederacy of tribes'. This model is once again traceable to Grote, and Morgan cited Grote's description of the Greek gens at length. Another source was obviously McLennan, as both Tylor and Lubbock commented in their reviews.[59]

Since the gentile system survived for most of human history, Morgan devoted over half his book to detailing its development. The stages of its progress were illustrated by five crucial case-studies, dealing respectively with the Australians, the Iroquois, the Aztec, the Greeks and the Romans. Each of these cases had a special relevance for Morgan.

The Australian case represented the most primitive extant system, only a step away from the initial condition in which brothers married their sisters in an incestuous form of group marriage. The Australians had introduced the improvement which in *Systems* (Morgan, 1871) had been termed the 'Hawaiian custom' and now appeared as 'the Punaluan custom', whereby a group of brothers had wives in common, a group of sisters husbands in common, but brothers could not marry sisters. This division of the sibling group by sex into marriage classes provided the potential for the development of the gens, since it allowed the unilineal reckoning of descent. Initially the maternal line was used for counting descent and so matrilineal gentes were generated. Once the rule of exogamy was introduced into the gens, the way was prepared for the gentile system itself.

This model was a slight variant of that presented in *Systems*, but the new version was greatly enriched by new Australian materials, provided by the Rev. Lorimer Fison, one of the first converts to Morgan's thesis as presented in *Systems*. Fison was a missionary who had been inspired to conduct anthropological research as a consequence of filling in Morgan's questionnaire for *Systems*. His fieldwork in Australia was conducted with Morgan's detailed guidance, and although he later mildly criticized aspects of Morgan's rendition of the Australian case, he was on the whole fiercely loyal, and was vituperative about McLennan's critique of Morgan.[60]

59 Stern (1931), *Lewis Henry Morgan*, p. 141.
60 Chapter 5 of this book takes up Fison's story.

Morgan's own Iroquois material was used to illustrate the next stage of evolution, in which the democratic gentes were associated in larger federations.

The following level of development was represented by the Aztecs. Morgan's reanalysis of the Aztec case was extremely influential. Indeed, one of his biographers has suggested that 'Morgan's recognition in America by his contemporaries came primarily through his work on a critical reconstruction of the culture of Mexico and Central America'.[61] His particular concern was to discredit the Spanish chroniclers, who had 'adopted the erroneous theory that the Aztec government was a monarchy, analogous in essential respects to existing monarchies in Europe'.[62] He rejected this judgment on *a priori* grounds. The Aztecs were clearly only at the level of 'the middle status of barbarism'. If they were indeed monarchical, then monarchy was an early and basic form of political organization. But if monarchies were primitive human institutions, then they should perhaps continue to exist in a modified form (on the Lamarckian theory that primitive stages of evolution were overlaid rather than displaced). Such a line of argument might even justify the survival of European monarchies themselves. But such a conclusion was abhorrent to Morgan. His recent European journey had confirmed him in his detestation of monarchical and aristocratic institutions.[63]

Morgan's solution was to reinterpret the Aztec materials. His criterion for using or rejecting his Spanish sources is very telling:

The histories of Spanish America may be trusted in whatever relates to the acts of the Spaniards, and to the acts and personal characteristics of the Indians; in whatever relates to their weapons, implements and utensils, fabrics, food and raiment, and things of a similar character. But in whatever relates to Indian society and government, their social relations, and plan of life, they are nearly worthless, because they learned nothing and know nothing of either. We are at full liberty to reject them

---

61 Stern (1931), *Lewis Henry Morgan*, p. 109.
62 Morgan (1877), *Ancient Society*, p. 186.
63 See his repeated diatribes in White (1937), *Extracts from the European Travel Journal of Lewis Henry Morgan*. Stern (1931), commented: 'Throughout Morgan's writings, from the first in 1843 to the last in 1880, ran the theme of contrast of American republican institutions with those of the aristocratic institutions of Europe' (*Lewis Henry Morgan*, p. 35).

in these respects and commence anew; using any facts they may contain which harmonize with what is known of Indian society.[64]

Using this convenient formula, he was able to recast the Aztec state as a more advanced version of the Iroquois federation. Once again he inspired an ethnographer, in this case Adolphe Bandelier, who produced data which apparently supported his argument.

Turning to the Greeks, Morgan based his case on Grote's description of the gens, which he quoted at length, commenting that 'The similarities between the Grecian and Iroquois gens will at once be recognized'.[65] This was not surprising, since Grote's model of the Greek gens had from the first provided Morgan with his model of the Iroquois system. Indeed, all the characteristics of the gentile system had been defined by Grote.[66] But Morgan now differed from Grote on two counts. First of all, Grote had erred in placing the family early on in Greek development – even making it anterior to the gens. Morgan had no doubt that he was mistaken, and did not hesitate to pit his theories against the conclusions of one of the leading classical scholars of the day.

Secondly, Morgan disputed Grote's view that the Greek state had begun as a monarchy. Once more he resorted to *a priori* argument, phrased in a particularly enlightening form:

The true statement, as it seems to an American, is precisely the reverse of Mr. Grote's; namely, that the primitive Grecian government was essentially democratical, reposing on gentes, phratries and tribes, organized as self-governing bodies, and on the principles of liberty, equality and fraternity. This is borne out by all we know of the gentile organization, which has been shown to rest on principles essentially democratical.[67]

Finally, Morgan discussed the Romans. He had to admit that their political development had ended in a form of undemocratic government, though he refused to accept that such a development was either desirable or inevitable. The Roman Empire 'was artificial, illogical, approaching a monstrosity; but capable of won-

64 Morgan (1877), *Ancient Society*, pp. 186–7, fn.
65 *Op. cit.*, p. 222.
66 *Op. cit.*, pp. 221–2.
67 *Op. cit.*, p. 247.

derful achievements ... The patchwork in its composition was the product of the superior craft of the wealthy classes.'[68]

In general, however, the development of political institutions demonstrated that a democratic order which builds upon the gentile tradition is natural to humanity.

As a plan of government, the gentile organization was unequal to the wants of civilized man: but it is something to be said in its remembrance that it developed from the germ the principal governmental institutions of modern civilized states ... out of the ancient council of chiefs came the modern senate; out of the ancient assembly of the people came the modern representative assembly ... out of the ancient general military commander came the modern chief magistrate, whether a feudal or constitutional king, an emperor or a president, the latter being the natural and logical results.[69]

The constitution of the United States is therefore the logical and natural flower of the ancient order of the gens.

Part III of *Ancient Society* described the development of the 'idea of the family', providing, in half the space given over to the gens, a summary of the argument of *Systems of Consanguinity* (1871). A brief chapter offered a revised sequence of family development, linked to the development of modes of subsistence and of gentile organization.

Only the final twenty-nine pages of this 560-page opus were devoted to the growth of the idea of property. Technical development increased the amount of property and its variety. The growth of property was a sign of progress, rather than a cause; but it stimulated the change from matrilineal to patrilineal gentile organization, and the development of the monogamous family. These institutions arose in order to deal with fixed property. They allowed a man to settle his possessions on his sons. Morgan regarded this as natural and proper, but he did not countenance the concentration of inherited wealth and privilege which characterized aristocratic societies. There was nothing natural or inevitable about institutionalized inequality.[70]

---

68 *Op. cit.*, p. 340.
69 *Op. cit.*, p. 341.
70 Although several thousand years have passed away without the overthrow of privileged classes, excepting in the United States, their burdensome character upon society has been demonstrated. Democracy in government, brotherhood in society, equality in rights and privileges, and universal education foreshadow the next higher plane of society to which

But his was by no means a materialist theory of history. Political and social progress was ultimately a sign of God's purpose. The heroic achievements of our primitive ancestors 'were part of the plan of the Supreme Intelligence to develop a barbarian out of a savage, and a civilized man out of this barbarian'.[71]

Marx, Engels and the legacy of Morgan

In later chapters I shall be returning to Morgan's theory, since his work dominated the field of kinship studies for many years, and had direct repercussions for the ethnographic study of North America and Oceania. But another tradition also stems from Morgan's writing, for he was adopted into the Marxist canon by Marx and Engels themselves. Reinterpreted by Engels, Morgan became the most important ancestral figure for Soviet ethnology, and he is a revered – though perhaps seldom read – authority in the broader tradition of Marxist theory.

Marx himelf published little on either non-European or 'pre-feudal' societies. His best-known contribution on these subjects was his model of an 'Asiatic mode of production'. This was a type of society in which a state organization existed in a primitive form. It was concerned only with war, taxation and public works, and was superimposed upon a series of otherwise independent village communities. These village communities held land in common and redistributed their agricultural surplus internally, except for a proportion which was appropriated by the state. This model posed serious theoretical problems for later Marxists, in part because it was not evident whether Marx thought of such systems as a geographically-specific Asian development, and in part because it was not clear in what direction societies of this type might subsequently evolve.[72]

Towards the end of his life, Marx took an interest in the new anthropology. He wrote extensive notes on the work of Morgan, Maine and Lubbock, evidently with a view to using them later in

---

experience, intelligence and knowledge are steadily tending. It will be a revival, in a higher form, of the liberty, equality and fraternity of the ancient gentes. (Morgan, 1877, *Ancient Society*, p. 522)

71 *Op. cit.*, p. 554.

72 There is a large literature on the 'Asiatic mode of production'. See Bailey and Llobera (1981), *The Asiatic Mode of Production* for a useful review. Cf. Krader (1975), *The Asiatic Mode of Production*.

a book.[73] After Marx's death, Engels used these notes as a starting-point for his own book (1884), *The Origin of the Family, Private Property and State*, which is essentially a popularization and development of Morgan's theories. It was first published in German in 1884. For present purposes it is unnecessary to enquire to what extent Engels exaggerated Marx's faith in Morgan, or to guess at the manner in which Marx himself would have reconciled Morgan's developmental sequence with the existence of an 'Asiatic mode of production'. In the event it was the Morgan as defined by Engels who became crucial for the Marxist tradition.

The element of Morgan's theory on which Engels seized was his 'rediscovery of the primitive matriarchal gens as the earlier stage of the patriarchal gens of civilized peoples'; a discovery which (so Engels claimed in his preface to the first edition) 'has the same importance for anthropology as Darwin's theory of evolution has for biology and Marx's theory of surplus value for political economy'. The evolutionary importance of this discovery was that it opened the way to a history of the development of the family, regarded not as a natural institution but as the product of historical processes. In its modern form, the family was just a way of organizing private property – it 'was the first form of the family to be based not on natural but on economic conditions – on the victory of private property over primitive, natural communal property'.[74]

No more was there anything natural or morally superior about monogamy. The civilized monogamous family was not (as Morgan in fact firmly believed) the ultimate realization of man's best instincts. It was a form of exploitation, comparable to the exploitation of one class by another. 'Within the family [the husband] is the bourgeois, and the wife represents the proletariat.' The family 'is based on the supremacy of the man, the express purpose being to produce children of undisputed paternity; such paternity is demanded because these children are later to come into their father's property as his natural heirs'.[75]

The state itself was as temporary and artificial as the family. Morgan had revealed that before the state existed, political systems had been based upon kinship. The state had emerged only as a

---

73 These have been transcribed and edited. See Krader (1974), *The Ethnological Notebooks of Karl Marx.*
74 Engels (1972), *The Origin of the Family, Private Property and the State*, p. 128.
75 *Op. cit.*, pp. 137, 125.

consequence of the growth of property and the evolution of class conflict; and it would break up when production was ordered on the basis of a free and equal association of the producers.

These ideas all have a recognizable point of origin in Morgan's work, but Engels himself conceded that he had 'moved a considerable distance' from Morgan on some matters.[76] Morgan would certainly have repudiated Engels' analysis of monogamy, and he would probably have had great difficulty with other aspects of his theory. This is not in itself a criticism of Engels, but it does mean that the Morgan who took his place in the Marxist tradition was already at several removes from the historical Morgan.

In the American anthropological tradition Morgan figures especially in debates about kinship systems. The tradition of analysis which Engels inaugurated was concerned rather with stages of social evolution and with the 'origin of the state'. More recently some feminist anthropologists have found inspiration in Engels' discussion of the monogamous family, so providing yet another context in which the implications of these ideas may be worked out, but one in which the contribution of Morgan himself can hardly be discerned any longer.

Morgan's transformations

It can be argued that Morgan's greatest influence was in the accumulation of data. He himself collected a great deal of ethnographic material by fieldwork and through questionnaires. He even invented a whole new category of data, kinship terminologies, and persuaded generations of anthropologists that they were the key to defining systems of kinship and marriage. And he inspired others to do fieldwork on his behalf, notably Bandelier and Fison. In the next generation the Bureau of American Ethnology was set up in the Smithsonian Institution essentially to carry out Morgan's programme of ethnological research.

Nevertheless, it must be admitted that Morgan's reputation has depended largely on his theory; and on the face of it this is strange, since his organizing ideas were derivative. His theoretical progress is replete with transformations in Cohen's sense. Again and again he borrowed an established framework and adapted it to his needs. Müller's philology, the 'gens' of Grote, McLennan's exogamy and

76 *Op. cit.*, pp. 145–6.

his matriarchy, Lubbock and Tylor's intellectual and technological evolutionism; all were grist to his mill. It is almost as though he believed the person he had last read.

Reviewing his career one cannot fail to be impressed by the contingent nature of his various syntheses. The history of his 1871 *Systems*, in particular, is an extraordinary chapter of accidents. Perhaps this element of chance is intrinsic to this sort of transformation, since its author depends, like a magpie, on what others have left lying about. To borrow one of Lévi-Strauss's images, this is the science of the *bricoleur*. And yet this account seems ultimately unpersuasive; there is clearly an underlying direction behind Morgan's work, at some level at least.

His political inspiration is very evident at several points, perhaps most particularly in his insistence on monogenesis and in his revulsion from monarchies. Nevertheless it would not be easy to account for his model in terms of his politics. After all, it could be used by Engels as an argument for communism, and by Morgan himself in defence of American capitalism and democracy.

I think that the fundamental consistency of Morgan's thinking has to do with religious rather than political beliefs. His ultimate aim was to demonstrate that human history made moral sense, that it was a history of progress, and that it united all branches of the species. If he could borrow ideas so promiscuously from Müller and McLennan and Tylor, it was because they all shared this faith.

CHAPTER 4

The question of totemism

The reception of *Ancient Society* was generally friendly, an indication that a new consensus had established itself on the question of primitive social structure. The degree of consensus might be obscured by the continuing controversies, which had begun with polemical exchanges between Maine, McLennan and Morgan, yet the disputes were increasingly technical and limited in scope. They tended to concern such recondite matters as the meaning of kinship terms. Agreement on fundamentals became more general. Most authors now converged on a single model of primitive society. The conflict between the advocates of primitive 'matriarchy' and 'patriarchy' was resolved. 'Matriarchy' was generally held to characterize the most primitive societies; 'patriarchy' typified a higher level of social development. Both forms of organization were based upon group exogamy. Primitive societies had all been organized on these principles of descent and exogamy for many millennia, until at last the revolutionary transition occurred from the original kinship-based polity, in which property was held in common, to a territorially-based state and a system of private property.

The agreement on substantive issues was matched by a convergence on questions of method. Maine's approach – loosely inspired by the example of Indo-European philology – had restricted comparison to societies within a single cultural tradition, which might be identified with a particular 'race'. In the 1860s this version of the comparative method lost ground in Britain and America, at least among those writers who were interested in 'primitive societies'. The more universal, not to say promiscuous, scope of Enlightenment historiography made a comeback. McLennan, Morgan and above all Tylor assumed that successive types of society all over the world had developed out of one primitive ancestral form, according to a fixed programme.[1] In other words, a unilinear evolutionism was an unquestioned component of the new consensus.

But just when a consensus was established on the nature of 'primitive society', the focus of anthropological interest shifted. The first wave of anthropological studies had responded to a variety of political concerns. Its authors belonged to a generation coming to terms with the Reform Bill, the crisis in India, and the Civil War in America. The main theme of their anthropology was the development of political institutions. But, increasingly, political issues began to seem less important than questions of belief and rationality.

The publication in 1871 of Darwin's *The Descent of Man* served to concentrate the minds of many intellectuals. Its effect was twofold. First of all, anthropologists were bound to ask what the connection was between man's biological evolution and his intellectual development. In *The Descent of Man* Darwin emphasized the evolutionary significance of language and other cultural techniques, which depended on man's powers of observation, memory, curiosity, imagination and reason.[2] He suggested that the growth of language might even have stimulated the development of the brain. The attention of anthropologists, accordingly, was now firmly directed on the evolution of language and cultural techniques, and on man's intellectual development.

Secondly, *The Descent of Man* reinforced the scientific challenge to the traditional religious view of creation. Many intellectuals now believed that science was actually taking over the explanatory role of religion. Perhaps the intellectual development of mankind was tending to a stage at which faith in magic and religion would be abandoned and man would turn to rationality and science.

The anthropology which emerged to deal with this new agenda was personified above all by an English scholar, E. B. Tylor. Tylor had been born in 1832 and, as his friend Marett remarked, he grew up just when the political preoccupations of the old generation gave way to the religious obsessions of the new.

1 This shift was by no means total. Much German and French writing continued to use the culture-area framework. In France, the rise of Durkheimian sociology brought with it an acceptance of Anglo-American evolutionism, but the German geographical school persisted in their preference for culture-area approaches.
2 This is a central theme of Part 1 of *The Descent of Man*. Another is the question whether – and to what degree – animals share these capacities.

Fortunate in the time of his birth – the hour of the Reform Bill – Tylor had reached his prime just when in England intellectual, following on the heels of political, liberation was calling for recruits in the inevitable struggle with the die-hards of the old order.[3]

From the first he took little interest in political or social questions: his anthropology dealt with man's intellectual development.

The rise of E. B. Tylor[4]

Born into a well-to-do Quaker industrial family, Tylor did not attend a university. On a youthful tour abroad a chance meeting on a Havana omnibus with a fellow-Quaker, Henry Christie, led him to accompany Christie to Mexico, where he was engaged in archaeological research. Christie had been an early convert to Darwinism, and his interest in archaeology had been quickened by Boucher de Perthes's discoveries in the Somme valley which established the antiquity of man.

In Mexico Christie and Tylor became fascinated by the complex pre-Conquest Mexican civilization. How had it arisen? Was it the result of diffusion from the Old World, or the fruit of independent development? Did it provide evidence for human progress, or, on the contrary, for degeneration?

The leading theorist in Britain concerned with these questions was Tylor's contemporary, Sir John Lubbock (Lord Avebury).[5] Lubbock was even more of a Darwinian than Christie – almost a birth-right Darwinian in fact, as a country neighbour of the Darwins and a lifelong friend. When the storm broke over him with the publication of *The Origin of Species*, Darwin had written to Lubbock (then only twenty-six years old), 'I settled some time ago that I should think more of Huxley's and your opinion – than of that of any other man in England'.[6]

Lubbock's *Prehistoric Times*, published in 1865, established a

---

3 Marett (1936), *Tylor*, pp. 212–13.

4 An account of Tylor's thought is to be found in J. Leopold (1980), *Culture in Comparative and Evolutionary Perspective*. Burrow (1966), in *Evolution and Society*, pp. 234–59, is particularly good on Tylor's 'ulterior motives' which he sees as broadly theological. Marett's *Tylor* (1936) is still worth reading, as the appreciation of a friend.

5 See Daniel (1950), *A Hundred Years of Archaeology*. Cf. Burrow (1966), *Evolution and Society*, pp. 228–9.

6 Quoted by Burrow (1966), *Evolution and Society*, pp. 228–9.

quasi-evolutionary theory for archaeology. The remains of ancient cultures exhibit a serial progression, like the fossil varieties of contemporary animal species. Strata of social evolution could be uncovered and related in sequences. Technology demonstrated unmistakably that progress had occurred. Later techniques were obviously advances on earlier techniques. This proved that man himself had progressed in his capacities, and put paid to any talk of degeneration from a higher condition. In the late 1860s Tylor formed a close alliance with Lubbock and with the other Darwinians, Huxley and Wallace, and technological progress became one of his major themes.

A second issue which concerned Tylor from the period of his Mexican fieldwork was the development of language. This was an interest of Darwin, but perhaps the key influence on Tylor was Max Müller. Müller had brought from Germany both the narrower philological tradition and also a more speculative interest in the notion of linguistic development. Tylor was especially interested in the evolutionary view of language, and his second major theme was the development of forms of language, including the language of children, gesture language, picture writing, etc. The assumption was that advances in language reflected intellectual progress. The activity which most clearly exhibited these relationships was mythology, to which Tylor, like his German models, devoted considerable attention. In his *Researches into the Early History of Mankind and the Development of Civilization* (1865), Tylor brought together the themes of linguistic, mythological and technical development to buttress a general argument about the intellectual progress of mankind.

But Tylor skirted the problem of religion in his *Researches*, rather as Darwin had postponed a detailed consideration of the evolution of the human species itself in *Origins*. Yet in both cases the next question on the agenda was obvious. In 1866 Tylor published an essay entitled 'The religion of savages', which appeared in *The Fortnightly Review*. The argument was expanded and developed in his *Primitive Culture*, published in 1871. The first volume of that book was essentially a revamp of his earlier *Researches*, but the second volume was devoted to the development of religion.

It must be remembered that 1871 was also the year that Darwin's *Descent of Man* was published, applying the theory of evolution to explain the emergence of the human species. Tylor's book added what was potentially an equally devastating challenge to orthodox

Christians. He argued that even the earliest men had some form of religious belief. Religions could be ranged in a series according to intellectual sophistication, but later religions all derived from a primitive system of theology, and retained traces of their origins. The clear implication was that classical Christianity might have been outgrown by modern man. Increasingly, religious belief would yield place to scientific theory.

The earliest religion was based upon a series of intellectual (and partly linguistic) confusions between the self and the other. In dreams people saw themelves roaming about in strange places, where they met other people, some of them long dead. This experience led to the belief that every man had a double existence, corporeal and spiritual. And if people had spirits, why not animals, or even inanimate natural objects? The earliest coherent form of religion was based on 'the theory which endows the phenomena of nature with personal life'. Tylor called it 'animism'.[7]

This primitive animism was not merely of antiquarian interest. Even the most civilized societies suffered something of a hangover from the animism of their forefathers. Vestiges of outworn primitive cults could be traced in the ceremonies of the most advanced religions. These were 'survivals', the fossils of cultural institutions. Quite often an ancient rite was still celebrated, even though it might be given a fresh rationale. Tylor's main example of such a rite was sacrifice, and this was a most significant choice. The question of sacrifice was central to the exegesis of Biblical Judaism. In the context of communion, it was also a major point of contention between Catholics and Protestants, and indeed between more ritualistic Protestants and the anti-ritualists, prominent among whom were, of course, the Quakers.

Tylor argued that rituals of sacrifice preserved very primitive religious notions. Sacrifice was so ancient, indeed, that even the explanations given in the Old Testament were anachronistic. To understand the primordial purpose of sacrifice, it was necessary to place it in its original context, animism. In animistic religions, offerings were made to the spirits of the dead after they had appeared in dreams. Later, sacrifices were made to 'other spiritual beings, genii, fairies, gods'. The rationale was quite evident: 'the

7 Tylor (1866), 'The religion of savages', p. 84.

object of sacrificing to the gods is that they are to consume or enjoy the souls of the things sacrificed'.[8]

Tylor's ideas had a remarkable success. In 1871, the year of *Primitive Culture*, not yet forty years old, he was elected a Fellow of the Royal Society. In 1875 Oxford awarded him an honorary degree. In 1881 he published the first general textbook in English on the subject, his *Anthropology*, which held the field for a generation. In 1884 Oxford created a Readership in Anthropology for him, and in 1896 he was made a Professor by personal title. By now the likes of Max Müller were talking of anthropology as 'Mr Tylor's science'.

Yet however timely, his work was clearly not original. His theory of technological progress was drawn from Lubbock, his notions about the development of language and mythology (despite some differences of opinion) from Müller. His theory of religious development owed a great deal to Comte, and his 'animism' is hardly to be distinguished from Comte's 'fetichism'. Even his ideas about sacrifice owed much to the German biblical scholar Wellhausen.

To a later generation Tylor's most memorable contribution was his idea that technology, language, myth and belief formed a single entity, which, following an already well-established German tradition, he termed 'culture or civilization'. This he defined as 'that complex whole which includes knowledge, belief, art, morals, law, custom and any other capabilities and habits acquired by man as a member of society'.[9] Tylor emphasized man's intellectual development, and he increasingly distinguished the history of culture from the history of race (in his practice if not in principle). Yet the introduction of the German idea of culture history did not seem a great novelty to contemporaries. British scholars would certainly have noticed an obvious kinship with Spencer's idea of the 'super-organic'.

Andrew Lang, reviewing his friend's career in his introduction to Tylor's *Festschrift*, conceded Tylor's lack of originality but suggested that 'his merit lay in his patient, sagacious, well "documented", and, at last, convincing method of exposition'.[10] In other words, Tylor was a synthesizer. The reception of his synthesis

8 *Op. cit.*, p. 77.
9 This famous definition is given in the opening sentence of *Primitive Culture* (Tylor, 1871).
10 In Balfour *et al.* (1907), *Anthropological Essays Presented to E. B. Tylor*.

reflected his identification with the Darwinians and also the swing of interest away from political issues and towards religious questions.

Yet despite the new prominence of religious questions in anthropology, the consensus about the form of primitive society was not abandoned. Rather, it now became desirable to relate it to Tylor's ideas about the origin of religion. What was the link between animism and exogamy? The theory which made the strongest bid to resolve this question was put forward by McLennan, who called it 'totemism'.

McLennan and the invention of totemism

Frazer's biographer pointed out that totemism, 'like radar, whiskey and marmalade, was a Scottish discovery or invention, for it was first defined by the Edinburgh lawyer John Ferguson McLennan, and Frazer, Robertson Smith and Andrew Lang were among the first to discuss it'.[11] Of these McLennan was the least scholarly but perhaps the most original. At any rate, it fell to him for the second time to launch a theory, one which was to have an even greater long-term impact than his theory of primitive marriage. The new theory was set out in a two-part essay entitled 'The worship of animals and plants', and was published in *The Fortnightly Review* in 1869–70.[12] Tylor's essay, 'The religion of savages', had appeared in the same journal three years earlier.

McLennan took for granted Tylor's thesis that primitive peoples worshipped fetishes, which they believed to be animated by anthropomorphic spirits. Man was conscious of his own spiritual force, and ascribed a similar power to natural objects. These animistic beliefs, however, gave rise to a new religion that McLennan called 'totemism'. 'Fetishism resembles Totemism', he wrote with splendid effrontery, and indeed it turned out that totemism 'is Fetishism *plus* certain peculiarities. These peculiarities are, (1) the appropriation of a special Fetich to the tribe, (2) its hereditary transmission through mothers, and (3) its connection with the *jus connubii*.'[13] In other words, totemism was fetishism but given a sociological anchor in McLennan's primordial society.

---

11 Downie (1970), *Frazer and the Golden Bough*, p. 76.
12 But cf. his entry, 'Totemism', in *Chambers' Encyclopaedia* (1868).
13 McLennan (1869–70), 'The worship of animals and plants', part 1, p. 422.

According to McLennan, some primitive peoples believed that they were of the same species as their totem. They were descended (in the female line, of course) from the original totemic animal. Some had even developed theories about such transformations from animals to men. Totemism might therefore almost be regarded as a first, faint hint of Darwinian evolution. The most primitive religion sowed the seeds not only of later religions, but also of science.

Most of McLennan's paper was given over to illustrations of 'totemism'. The key areas were aboriginal America and Australia. Basing himself on Sir George Grey, and allowing himself remarkable interpretative licence, McLennan deduced the existence in Australia of exogamous matrilineal groups, gentes, whose members share a common totem. Despite the absence of further evidence, he expressed his confident belief that a similar system prevails, or prevailed, throughout Oceania. For America, he relied especially on Gallatin, concluding that here too totems were associated with matriarchal, exogamous groups. A rapid review of world ethnography revealed elements of a totemic system among the tribes of Siberia, Peru, Fiji, and even in classical India. Classical Europe itself exhibited traces of totemism, as did ancient Israel – what else was the serpent story in Genesis? The use of animal terms for constellations of stars was equally a totemic derivation.

Robertson Smith *and* 'The Religion of the Semites'

In 1866 a group of intellectuals had formed the Edinburgh Evening Club. McLennan was a founder member. Another was the theologian W. Robertson Smith, who became his friend.[14] In 1870 Smith was appointed to the chair of Hebrew and Old Testament at the Free Church College at Aberdeen. Here he began to propagate the new critical approach to the Bible which he had learned in Germany from Julius Wellhausen, and which was to lead him to heresy – and also to the adoption of his friend's theory of totemism.

Another Scottish intellectual institution was implicated in Robertson Smith's first crisis. This was the *Encyclopaedia Britan-*

14 See John Black and George Chrystal (1912), *The Life of William Robertson Smith*. Another useful source is Beidelman (1974), *W. Robertson Smith and the Sociological Study of Religion*.

nica, which published the first volume of a new edition in 1876, carrying articles by Smith on 'Angel' and 'Bible'. These expressed his view (derived from Wellhausen) that the Bible was a compilation of sources of various dates, and including mythological as well as historical elements. In 1878 he answered charges of heresy before the Church Assembly, and eventually, in May 1880, he was cautioned. In April, however, he had visited McLennan in Italy, and in June he published an essay entitled 'Animal tribes in the Old Testament', which applied McLennan's theory of totemism to the Bible. A decade after the publication of McLennan's original article, his theory was to receive extraordinary publicity as the central issue in a theological *cause célèbre*.

In his new essay, Robertson Smith argued that his own researches in the Semitic field confirmed McLennan's theory of totemism. Arabic pre-Islamic sources indicated that tribal groupings were often named after animals, and sometimes after the moon and sun. Since sun and moon were evidently worshipped as gods, animals presumably once had a similar status. Furthermore, tribes worshipping the moon were believed to be descended from their god. The same might well have been true of tribes named after animals.

This demonstration seems peculiarly thin, and Robertson Smith himself admitted 'that we have very little direct information connecting these facts with animal worship'. But there was a reason for the absence of direct evidence. Greek sources are unreliable on these topics, and Islamic authors censored heathen ideas – 'we must remember the nature of the records'.[15]

McLennan's theory also required that the original totemic tribes should be matriarchal and exogamous. Robertson Smith claimed that this was indicated by some sub-tribe names, which might 'denote the offspring of one mother'.[16] Furthermore, some sources seemed favourably disposed to female infanticide, which again supported McLennan's theory. Strabo also reported traces of polyandry. The marriage rites of some Arab peoples apparently contained survivals of exogamy and marriage by capture. The Queen of Sheba's existence pointed to a pre-patriarchal form of organization. Taken together, 'These facts appear sufficient to prove that Arabia

15 Robertson Smith (1889), *Religion of the Semites*, p. 84.
16 *Op. cit.*, p. 86.

did pass through a stage in which family relations and the marriage law satisfied the conditions of the totem system'.[17] There was evidence of the same sort which suggested that totemic elements had survived in ancient Israel, if in an attenuated form. Robertson Smith suggested that the heathen practices against which the prophets inveighed were totemic in origin, and that the second commandment itself was directed against nature worship.

Coming from a man who had just been warned to mind his step by the Church Assembly, this was a provocative argument. The General Assembly did not mince words in its reaction to the paper.

First, concerning marriage and the marriage laws in Israel, the views expressed are so gross and so fitted to pollute the moral sentiments of the community that they cannot be considered except within the closed doors of any court of this Church. Secondly, concerning animal worship in Israel, the views expressed by the Professor are not only contrary to the facts recorded and the statements made in Holy Scripture, but they are gross and sensual – fitted to pollute and debase public sentiment.[18]

Smith was removed from his professorship in May 1881, but he was not cast into the outer darkness. He became co-editor of the famous ninth edition of the *Encyclopaedia Britannica* (and was reputed to have read every entry). In 1883 he was appointed Reader in Arabic at Cambridge and in 1889 he became Professor. When he died in 1894, at the age of forty-eight, he was already widely regarded as a great scholar.

In Cambridge Smith acquired his most important apostle, another fellow of Trinity, and another Scot, James George Frazer, whom he at once commissioned to write an entry on 'Totemism' for the *Encyclopaedia*. He also developed his own ideas on early Semitic religion and social organization, notably in his entry on 'Sacrifice' in the *Encyclopaedia*, in his book *Kinship and Marriage in Early Arabia* (1885), and finally in his masterpiece, *Lectures on the Religion of the Semites* (1889).

Kinship and Marriage in Early Arabia is far more fully argued and documented than the original 1880 essay on 'Animal worship', but the ideas on primitive Semitic society are essentially the same. The main thrust of the book is that, despite obvious indications to the contrary, the strongly 'patriarchal' societies of ancient Arabia

17 *Op. cit.*, p. 88.
18 Cited in Beidelman (1974), *W. Robertson Smith*, p. 21.

were preceded by 'matriarchal' communities. The evidence was (necessarily) indirect and slight. The conclusions which were drawn could be sustained only if McLennan's theory of a universal totemic stage was correct. Smith wrote:

In enquiring whether the Arabs were once divided into totem-stocks, we cannot expect to meet with any evidence more direct than the occurrence of such relics of the system as are found in other races which have passed through but ultimately emerged from the totem stage.[19]

The stagnation of Robertson Smith's thinking on primitive social structure contrasts strikingly with the vitality of his later work on totemic religion, which was concerned especially with the problem of sacrifice. The traditional theological view derived from the priestly code, according to which sacrifices were essentially acts of atonement. Smith's mentor Wellhausen had rejected this interpretation as anachronistic. Textual criticism revealed that the priestly code was a post-Exilic document. It superimposed a late-priestly theology on earlier ritual practices. Originally sacrifices were not even performed in the Temple. They were associated with what Wellhausen called a natural religion, which was situated within the life of the family. Smith developed this conception and linked it with totemism.

The argument was most fully developed in *Lectures on the Religion of the Semites* (1889), Smith's last book and by a considerable margin his best. He emphasized particularly two themes. The first was methodological. Rites were the most authentic pointers to earlier religious ideas. The myth or dogma with which a rite is associated may be a later accretion. As Smith put it, the 'ritual was fixed and the myth was variable, the ritual was obligatory and faith in the myth was at the discretion of the worshipper'.[20] A later generation read this as a proto-functionalist statement. It was, rather, a methodological principle, derived from Tylor, for the identification of survivals.

Secondly, Roberton Smith developed a sociological argument: 'the fundamental conception of ancient religion is the solidarity of the gods and their worshippers as part of one organic society'. And again: 'gods and men, or rather the god and his proper worshippers, make up a single community, and ... the place of the god in the

---

19 Robertson Smith (1885), *Kinship and Marriage in Early Arabia*, pp. 187–8.
20 Robertson Smith (1889), *Religion of the Semites*, p. 18.

community is interpreted on the analogy of human relationships'.[21] There was in fact a religion especially appropriate to a clan-based society, and another more appropriate for a state. 'We now see that the clan and the state are both represented in religion: as father the god belongs to the family or clan, as king he belongs to the state.'[22]

In ancient Israel this relationship of divine fatherhood was conceived of in spiritual terms. In more primitive societies, people believed that they were physically descended from the founding god. This was the original religious conception. It was equally the origin of morality, for 'the indissoluble bond that united men to their god is the same bond of blood-fellowship which in early society is the one binding link between man and man, and the one sacred principle of moral obligation'.[23]

Totemism represented perhaps the earliest stages of this conception. In a totemic religion, the gods were natural species, generally animals. These gods were associated with natural sanctuaries, which followers had to visit. Even early religions had holy places, shrines. But at certain times a yet more intimate contact with the gods was required. This was achieved through sacrifice, 'the typical form of all complete acts of worship in the antique religions'.[24]

Sacrifices could take one of two main forms. A vegetable sacrifice was thought of as a tribute or gift (which was Tylor's conception). Alternatively, one could sacrifice an animal, but animal sacrifices were a different matter entirely. They 'are essentially acts of communion between the god and his worshippers'. 'The god and his worshippers are wont to eat and drink together, and by this token their fellowship is declared and sealed.'[25] Since pastoralism preceded agriculture, animal sacrifices were anterior to vegetable sacrifices.

But what animals were sacrificed and eaten at these feasts? Originally, one of the sacred animals themselves. A totem animal could not normally be killed or eaten, but this very taboo made the sacrifice sacred. 'The evidence ... is unambiguous. When an unclean animal is sacrificed it is also a sacred animal.'[26] Among the

21 *Op. cit.*, pp. 32 and 85.
22 *Op. cit.*, p. 40.
23 *Op. cit.*, p. 53.
24 *Op. cit.*, p. 214.
25 *Op. cit.*, p. 243 and p. 271.
26 *Op. cit.*, p. 294.

Semites, then, 'the fundamental idea of sacrifices is not that of a sacred tribute, but of communion between the god and his worshippers by joint participation in the living flesh and blood of a sacred victim'.[27] Ideas of atonement through sacrifice were a later, more sophisticated gloss on a primitive totemic rite.

The argument was clearly leading up to a climax in which something would have to be said about the sacrifices of gods themselves in Semitic religions, perhaps during communal meals. Smith took the step in this passage:

That the God-man dies for His people and that his Death is their life, is an idea which was in some degree foreshadowed by the oldest mystical sacrifices. It was foreshadowed, indeed, in a very crude and materialistic form, and without any of those ethical ideas which the Christian doctrine of the Atonement derives from a profound sense of sin and divine justice. And yet the voluntary death of the divine victim, which we have seen to be a conception not foreign to ancient ritual, contained the germ of the deepest thought in the Christian doctrine: the thought that the Redeemer gives Himself for his people.

Frazer cited this passage in his obituary essay on Smith and remarked that it was dropped in a later, revised edition of the *Lectures*.[28] Yet even if it was left implicit, the theological implications of this view of sacrifice would have been evident to any contemporary scholar. They were certainly clear enough to Robertson Smith. The theological reverberations are enough to account for Smith's obsession with McLennan's theory of totemism; and they account also for the extraordinary fame later enjoyed by Frazer, who developed and popularized Robertson Smith's theories.

Frazer and 'The Golden Bough'

Frazer was a shy young classicist, upon whom the charismatic Robertson Smith initially exercised a most powerful intellectual influence. Robertson Smith commissioned from him entries on 'Taboo' and 'Totemism' for the *Encyclopaedia Britannica*, and Frazer fulfilled this commission with the thoroughness which became his hallmark. Characteristically, the resulting entry on

---

27 *Op. cit.*, p. 345.
28 Frazer's 1894 obituary of Robertson Smith.

totemism was far too long.[29] In the event, an abridged version appeared in the *Encyclopaedia*, but the complete essay was published by Black in book form in 1887. It was to be the authoritative source on the topic for the next decade. Baldwin Spencer himself recorded that when he went into the field, 'my anthropological reading was practically confined to two works, Sir Edward Tylor's "Primitive Culture" and Sir James Frazer's little red book on "Totemism".'[30]

McLennan had been working on a refinement of his theory of totemism, but he died before it could be completed. His brother, Donald McLennan, issued some of his unpublished work in a book entitled *The Patriarchal Theory*, which appeared in 1885, and in his introduction he remarked that his brother had hoped to relate totemism to exogamy. He had come to believe that totemism preceded exogamy. It had existed in all 'rude societies', though its origin remained mysterious.

Frazer's contribution was less imaginative, but more methodical. He distinguished different categories of totem. There were clan totems, sex totems and individual totems. Clan totems were by far the most important, and clan totemism was at once a religious system and a social system. Its social form was a system of exogamous clans in which descent was traced in the female line. The religious aspect 'consists of the relations of mutual respect and protection between a man and his totem'.[31] Normally there was a prohibition on killing and eating the totem. These religious and social aspects had drifted apart in the course of time, but originally they were inseparable – 'the further we go back, the more we should find that the clansman regards himself and his totem as beings of the same species'.[32] The most primitive form of the belief was that the totem was the ancestor of the clan.

29 Robertson Smith wrote to the publishers:

I hope that Messrs. Black clearly understand that Totemism is a subject of growing importance, daily mentioned in magazines and papers, but of which there is no good account anywhere – precisely one of those cases where we have an opportunity of being ahead of everyone and getting some reputation. There is no article in the volume for which I am more solicitous. I have taken much personal pains with it, guiding Frazer carefully in his treatment; and he has put about seven months' hard work on it to make it the standard article on the subject. We must make room for it, whatever else goes. (Cited by Beidelman (1974), *W. Robertson Smith*, p. 24)

30 Spencer (1928), *Wanderings in Wild Australia*, vol. 1, p. 184.
31 Frazer (1887), *Totemism* (first edition), p. 3.
32 *Ibid.*

Frazer reviewed the ethnography far more systematically than McLennan or Robertson Smith had done, providing a genuinely encyclopaedic review of the available literature. He suggested that totemism existed in many culture areas, although without making definite claims for its original universality. But he did not commit himself to a theory of totemism. 'No satisfactory explanation of the origin of totemism has yet been given.'[33]

In his most famous book, *The Golden Bough*, first published in 1890, Frazer took up Robertson Smith's central preoccupation, the sacrifice of the god.[34] He constructed an ethnological detective story which began with the ritual killing of the priest of Aricia, 'the King of the Wood'. This sacred king was the embodiment of a tree-spirit, and it turned out that he was not simply murdered, but rather sacrificed to ensure the fertility of nature. The clues were drawn from a vast range of ethnographic sources, all tending to show that primitive people identified their well-being with the fate of animistic spirits, whose priests were sacrificed in fertility rituals. The precise motive, however, remained a little mysterious. Perhaps it all had something to do with ancient beliefs about the trans-migration of human souls into natural objects.[35]

The Golden Bough was enormously successful. For many educated readers it offered an irresistible combination of classical scholarship, exoticism and daring rationalism. It was far more appealing than his study of totemism, and Frazer soon began to distance himself from totemism and also from Robertson Smith. In the preface to the second edition of *The Golden Bough*, which appeared in 1900, he strengthened his own claims to originality with the statement that 'the worship of trees and cereals ... is neither identical with nor derived from a system of totemism'. And he positively disavowed the theories of Robertson Smith. 'I never assented to my friend's theory, and, so far as I can remember, he never gave me a hint that he assented to mine.'[36]

33 *Op. cit.*, p. 95.
34 He also drew heavily on the work of the German folklorist, Mannhardt, who had tried to construct an 'Aryan' mythology from peasant folktales. Mannhardt's theory drew upon ideas about animism, and he explained peasant rites in Germany as 'survivals' of ancient fertility rituals. See, e.g., his *Der Baumkultus der Germanen und ihrer Nachbarstämme* (1875).
35 Frazer borrowed this idea from a Dutch scholar, Wilken, who reported a belief along these lines in Malaya.
36 Frazer (1890 (1900)), *The Golden Bough*, 2nd edition, p. 3. Cf. R. Ackermann (1975), 'Frazer on myth and ritual'.

One reason for this shift was presumably simple vanity. However, Frazer preferred to attribute any changes in his thinking to the impression of new ethnographic materials, and he set great store by his accumulation of data.[37] He quite compulsively expanded his store of ethnographic analogies, and stimulated ethnographers in the field with his letters and questions. In time he built up what amounted to an international intelligence service, sending out questionnaires on topics which interested him, urging on his protegés, passing on and publishing their letters.

Frazer's network eventually extended into Africa and Asia, but he believed, with other experts, that ethnographic materials from Australia were going to prove of decisive importance. By the turn of the century, totemism had come to be equated with Australian totemism. The speculations of McLennan and Robertson Smith were being put to the test in the central and northern territories of the vast island continent.

37 'Hypotheses are necessary but often temporary bridges built to connect isolated facts,' he remarked in the Preface to the second edition of *The Golden Bough* (1900). 'If my light bridges should sooner or later break down ... I hope that my book may still have its utility and its interest as a repertory of facts.'

CHAPTER 5

Australian totemism

It is difficult to exaggerate the impact of the Australian ethnographers on the idea of primitive society, especially after the publication of Fison and Howitt's *Kamilaroi and Kurnai* in 1880; but it is essential to be clear about the nature of that impact. Even before there were any detailed ethnographic descriptions, Australia had already been identified as the crucial anthropological laboratory. The reasons were obvious enough. The Australian aborigines were naked, black hunters and gatherers. Compared with the American Indians, they had limited contact with Europeans. In other words, they were as close as could be to the Victorian image of primitive man. There was also the seductive analogy of Darwin's explorations, which had shown that isolated island populations were particularly instructive, sometimes nourishing primitive biological forms which had died out elsewhere. The pioneer ethnographer Lorimer Fison wrote in a letter to Lewis Henry Morgan in 1879: 'To use your own words, in the Australian field we are "working at the very foundations of that great Science of Anthropology which is sure to come"'.[1] The same belief inspired the next generation. Twenty years later, Frazer wrote to Spencer: 'The anthropological work still to be done in Australia is ... of more importance for the early history of man than anything that can now be done in the world.'[2] If something like the earliest form of society was to be found, if a primeval religious ceremony was still being celebrated, this could only be in Australia. That was the place to hunt cultural dinosaurs.

---

1 Stern (1930), 'Selections from the letters of Lorimer Fison and A. W. Howitt to Lewis Henry Morgan', p. 271.
2 Marett and Penniman (1932), *Spencer's Scientific Correspondence with Sir J. G. Frazer*, p. 22.

Yet the information available on the Australian aborigines was very slight.[3] There soon built up a considerable demand for information on Australia. Coupled with the lack of an indigenous tradition of ethnography, this gave rise to a remarkable situation. The first serious students of Australian aboriginal society were in thrall to opinionated outsiders, who inspired, and often even arranged the finance for, their expeditions.

Fison and Howitt

The subservience of the Australian ethnographers to anthropological theorists was facilitated by a curious accident. The two great Australian studies of the late nineteenth century were made by partnerships in which a foreign intellectual, without previous firsthand experience of Australia, but directly inspired by metropolitan theorists, joined up with a local expert who had a rich store of information. The first partnership, between Fison and Howitt, was inspired by Morgan. It investigated the established theories of descent and exogamy, what Frazer would later call 'totemism as a social system'. In the next generation Spencer and Gillen, directed by Frazer himself, studied Australian totemism as a religious system.

Fison had been recruited by Morgan to fill in his kinship questionnaire while working as a missionary in Fiji. In 1871 he went to Australia, and advertised in the newspapers for help in the study of Australian kinship. A response came from Alfred William Howitt, an experienced bushranger who had led the expedition which attempted to rescue Burke and Wills. Howitt was now a magistrate in the interior, and a well-known amateur geologist. In the 1860s he had begun to read the new literature on evolution, and he was ripe for Fison's invitation.

---

3 McLennan, for example, had given Australia a privileged place in his theory of totemism, but could only cite Sir George Grey's remarkably concise description. Grey had specified the basic laws of aboriginal social organization in these terms: '1st. That children of either sex, always take the family name of their mother. 2nd. That a man cannot marry a woman of his own family name.' He had then added that each 'family' had an animal or vegetable crest, a *kobong*, and commented: 'A certain mysterious connection exists between a family and its *kobong*, so that a member of the family will never kill an animal of the species to which the *kobong* belongs'. (George Grey (1841) *Journals of Two Expeditions of Discovery in North-Western Australia*, vol. 2, pp. 226–8)

The two men were also in constant correspondence with Morgan,[4] and exchanged letters with Tylor and other authorities. In 1880, after a decade of this three-cornered collaboration, they published a monograph, *Kamilaroi and Kurnai*. This slim book effectively established the tradition of Australian ethnography but, despite the ostentatiously ethnographic title, neither author was content with mere description. Fison especially was determined to address the theoretical issues of the day. Specifically, their work was designed to advance the cause of Morgan as against McLennan.

McLennan and Morgan had both argued for 'matriarchy' in the face of Maine's patriarchal theory, but they disagreed about how this matriarchy was organized. Morgan believed that whole descent groups were linked in marriage. The clan was exogamous, and a set of brothers from one clan communally married a set of sisters from another. Traces of this ancient system could be found in kinship terminologies, which still grouped relatives into the old categories, separating the marriageable from the unmarriageable. McLennan denied that the kin terms had any sociological significance. Moreover, exogamy was an act of war. Individual women were captured from foreign communities. The original form of marriage was polyandry. Brothers might share a single wife, but there was no ordered system of marriage exchange.

On all these points, Fison was determined to support Morgan against McLennan. He subtitled *Kamilaroi and Kurnai* 'Group-marriage and relationship, and marriage by elopement', and wrote:

> The chief object of this memoir is to trace the formation of the exogamous intermarrying divisions which have been found among so many savage and barbaric tribes of the present day, and to show that what the Hon. Lewis H. Morgan calls the Punaluan family, with the Turanian system of kinship, logically results from them. The Australian classes are especially valuable for this purpose, because they give us what seem to be the earliest stages of development.[5]

'Class' was the term upon which Fison had settled for the basic unit of the system,[6] and he identified the class with 'the exogamous

---

4 See Stern (1930), 'Selections from the letters of Lorimer Fison and A. W. Howitt to Lewis Henry Morgan'.

5 Fison and Howitt, (1880), *Kamilaroi and Kurnai*, p. 23.

6 I have used the word 'class' in preference to tribe, sept, or clan, because each of these words is apt to have a sort of confused meaning to the reader which might tend to produce a wrong impression. The Greek 'phratria' would be the most correct term: but, for several reasons,

intermarrying tribal divisions which have been observed in so many other parts of the world'.[7] But he did not go so far as to claim that the Australians still actually practised group marriage. Undeniably

certain modifications as to the extent of the matrimonial privilege have been introduced. Here, as elsewhere, present usage is in advance of the ancient rules. But those rules underlie it, and are felt through it, and the underlying strata crop up in many places'.[8]

Fison believed that the Australians had begun with two classes. Subsequently these had subdivided, producing a four-class system. In a four-class system the range of permitted spouses was further narrowed, but the basic structure persisted: 'marriage must still be without the class, and descent is still reckoned in the female line'.[9]

In a fascinating appendix, Fison developed an abstract model of cross-kin marriage between two classes, in which 'John Smith and John Brown, two first cousins, marry one another's sisters. Each has a son John and a daughter Jane. These first cousins marry, and have issue, a son and a daughter to each marriage. The same Christian names are continued.'[10] ('The surnames represent the two intermarrying phratriae, or gentes' – see Figure 5.1.) The importance of this model was that it drew out the implications of running such a marriage system over several generations. (Tylor was soon to generalize the model.)

As this instance clearly suggests, Fison's thinking was notably abstract and deductive. In a letter to Morgan he even suggested that the laws of the Turanian system could be demonstrated from the Australian materials by steps 'as conclusive as any one of Euclid's demonstrations, if we can only establish three preliminary propositions'; namely that marriages united groups, that the kinship terminology identified these groups, and that each group was exogamous.[11]

This elegant model was complicated by the presence of two extraneous features. First, there were cross-cutting groups which had animal totems. These groups were probably exogamous too,

'class' seemed to be the more convenient for the special purpose of this memoir, to designate the primary divisions of a community, and their first subdivisions. (*Op. cit.*, p. 24)

7 *Op. cit.*, p. 32.
8 *Op. cit.*, p. 29.
9 *Op. cit.*, p. 40.
10 *Op. cit.*, p. 95. The diagram is on p. 96.
11 Stern (1930), 'Selections from the letters of Lorimer Fison and A. W. Howitt to Lewis Henry Morgan', p. 268.

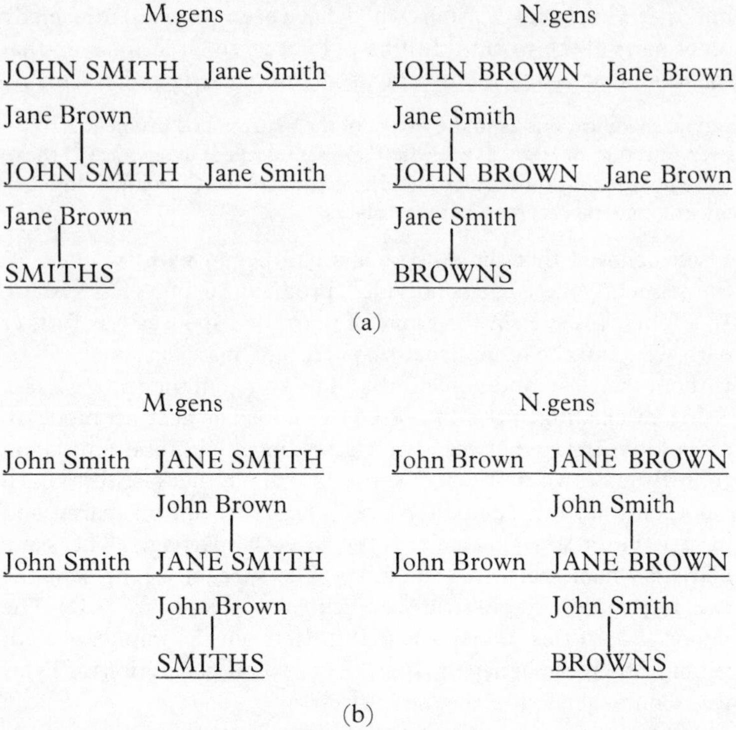

```
           M.gens                          N.gens

JOHN SMITH    Jane Smith      JOHN BROWN    Jane Brown

Jane Brown                    Jane Smith
      |                             |
JOHN SMITH    Jane Smith      JOHN BROWN    Jane Brown

Jane Brown                    Jane Smith
      |                             |
SMITHS                        BROWNS
```

(a)

```
           M.gens                          N.gens

John Smith    JANE SMITH      John Brown    JANE BROWN

     John Brown                    John Smith
          |                             |
John Smith    JANE SMITH      John Brown    JANE BROWN

     John Brown                    John Smith
          |                             |
     SMITHS                        BROWNS
```

(b)

Figure 5.1 Fison's model of the Australian 'class' system. (a) Descent through males (Turanian system). (b) Descent through females (Gonowanian system). From *Kamilaroi and Kurnai*, p. 96.

though Fison had to admit that 'our information is not sufficiently complete to enable us to assert that this is always the case'.[12]

Secondly, there were distinct local communities which did not coincide with marriage classes or with totemic categories of people. This difficulty was dealt with in later publications, where, after first suggesting the term 'local clan' for these communities, Howitt and Fison settled on the term 'horde'. They could not properly be called clans, because descent was not in the female line. On the contrary, a child belongs to the horde in which it was born, normally his father's. These hordes were particularly important since they signalled the future development of a patriarchal society and the state.[13]

12 *Ibid.*
13 See particularly Howitt and Fison (1885), 'On the deme and the horde'.

All these complications were secondary, however. Whatever the rôle of the totemic groups and hordes might be, the classes were the key to Australian social structure.[14] They constituted the original basis of Australian society. The evidence for their priority was provided above all by the kinship terminologies.

In the end, therefore, their thesis, like Morgan's, depended on the evidence of the kinship terminology. This was one of the main issues on which McLennan had attacked Morgan, claiming that kin terms were mere salutations of no great historical interest. Determined to prove Morgan right, Fison tried to show that among the Australian aborigines the division of relatives into marriage classes was mirrored in the terminology (though he also claimed to detect traces of an even more ancient 'Malayan' system). This demonstration was no easy task. An Australian aborigine,

when asked to define the relationship in which he stands to other persons, frequently takes into consideration matters other than relationship, and so gives words which are not specific terms of kinship. After years of inquiry into this matter, the humiliating confession must be made that I am hopelessly puzzled.

Yet Fison claimed that, notwithstanding such difficulties,

enough can be made out from the terms of kinship in present use to show that relationship is based upon the same ideas with those which form the foundation of the system called by Mr Morgan the Turanian. Most certainly ... the terms of that system are the logical outcome of the Australian classes.[15]

Fison contributed the theoretical and synthesizing element in the book, while Howitt's ethnography of the Kurnai formed the descriptive core. Remarkably enough, this ethnography diverged from Fison's model on many points. Most significantly, Howitt made it clear that Kurnai marriage was an individual matter, and that the social groups were all organized on a basis of locality rather than kinship. He suggested that this was because the Kurnai were excep-

---

14 'Australian exogamy ... is the plain outcome of the class divisions' (Fison and Howitt (1880), *Kamilaroi and Kurnai*, pp. 67–8). Matrilineal descent was 'the necessary consequence of the matrimonial regulations of the class divisions' (*op. cit.*, p. 73).

15 *Op. cit.*, pp. 58 and 60.

tionally advanced, though Fison preferred to believe that they simply had a very odd history.[16]

Fison's model rather than Howitt's ethnography was to be the leading influence on the next generation of Australian studies. Readers seemed to have more faith in its clear lines than in the messier account which Howitt provided, and in any case both Howitt and Fison were quite definite that the Kurnai diverged from the Australian pattern. Fison's model accordingly provided the paradigmatic account of how the most primitive of social systems operated.

Tylor on exogamy

The most important step in the generalization of the new Australian model occurred back in the metropolis, where Frazer and Tylor were beginning to collate the results of the first generation of ethnographers, of whom Fison and Howitt were the most notable. In 1889 Tylor read a paper to a meeting of the Anthropological Institute. It is remembered above all for its methodological contribution; indeed it was entitled 'On a method of investigating the development of institutions; applied to laws of marriage and descent'. And the methodological innovations were certainly remarkable, for where even Frazer relied on the accumulation of apt illustrations, Tylor prepared a sample of exotic cultures and tried to measure associations between cultural traits. He was directly influenced by Darwin's cousin Francis Galton, the pioneer statistician. Galton – a president of the Anthropological Institute – was in fact in the chair when Tylor delivered the paper (and he rather unkindly pointed out one of its weaknesses, the fact that Tylor had not controlled for historical relationships between the cases in his sample). Yet whatever the importance of this methodological innovation, it was not imitated for many years, and Tylor seemed not to have pressed on with it. The substantive argument of the paper was, however, immediately interesting and influential.

Up to this point, Tylor had paid little attention to theories of

16 Fison attributed the unexpected features of Kurnai custom to historical accidents:

> The Kurnai are the descendents of an isolated division of a tribe which formerly consisted of two exogamous intermarrying divisions ... and their regulations as to marriage and descent are such as would arise from an endeavour to follow the regulations of such divisions under circumstances of peculiar difficulty. (*Op. cit.*, p. 297, italicized in the original)

primitive social structure. Now he attempted to weigh the evidence, and to decide the main issues in contention between McLennan and Morgan. He began by listing indirect pieces of evidence which combined to suggest that societies had indeed passed 'from the maternal to the paternal systems', as had been suggested by Bachofen, McLennan, *et al.*[17] Tylor even detected traces of McLennan's marriage by capture, though he argued that it would not make much sense to capture wives in a matriarchal system, and that the custom would rather signal the passage to a patriarchal society.

On the question of exogamy, however, Tylor supported Morgan's position rather than McLennan's. It was now evident 'that exogamy was hardly to do with the capture of wives in war between alien nations, but rather with the regulation of marriages within groups or clans or tribes who have connubium'. Exogamy was a process within a political society. 'It is now also understood that a people may at once practice endogamy or 'marrying-in' within its borders, and exogamy or 'marrying-out' of its clans with one another.'[18] He further accepted that the classificatory terminology mirrored this system. Fison and Howitt had demonstrated that clan exogamy and classificatory kinship terminologies were 'in fact two sides of one institution'.[19]

One of Tylor's findings was that twenty-one societies practised a peculiar and striking form of exogamy, in which 'the children of two brothers may not marry, nor the children of two sisters, but the child of the brother may marry the child of the sister.' He called this 'cross-cousin marriage', and argued that it was 'the direct result of the simplest form of exogamy, where a population is divided into two classes or sections, with the law that a man who belongs to Class A can only take a wife of class B'.[20] He pointed out that this arrangement broke down if there were more than two clans involved, and concluded 'that the dual form of exogamy may be considered the original form'.[21] Fison had already made

17 Tylor (1889), 'On a method of investigating the development of institutions; applied to laws of marriage and descent', p. 256.
18 *Op. cit.*, p. 261.
19 *Op. cit.*, p. 262.
20 *Op. cit.*, p. 263.
21 *Op. cit.*, p. 264.

precisely the same point, but Tylor claimed to have reinvented it himself, only later recalling having seen it in Fison's writings.[22]

Up to this point Tylor had refined Morgan and Fison's conclusions, and subjected them to a crude statistical test. He now added a novel and powerful sociological hypothesis to explain the development of endogamy and exogamy, which he termed 'a political question of the first importance'. The formulation was clearly influenced by Malthus and Darwin.

when tribes begin to adjoin and press on one another and quarrel, then the difference between marrying-in and marrying-out becomes patent. Endogamy is a policy of isolation, cutting off a horde or village, even from the parent-stock whence it separated ... Among tribes of low culture there is but one means known of keeping up permanent alliance, and that means is intermarriage. Exogamy enabling a growing tribe to keep itself compact by constant unions between its spreading clans, enables it to overmatch any number of small intermarrying groups, isolated and helpless. Again and again in the world's history, savage tribes must have had plainly before their minds the simple practical alternative between marrying-out and being killed out.[23]

Tylor therefore returned to McLennan's starting point, the struggle for survival, but went off in a diametrically different direction. McLennan had imagined a war of all against all, complete with ghastly atrocities, notably infanticide and rapine. Tylor was a Quaker, and perhaps for this reason he preferred to imagine a struggle for survival which produced a system of alliances.

Tylor did not refer to totemism as a religious system, but he had always doubted whether McLennan's theory had added anything of value to his own description of animism. Clearly the theory of McLennan and Robertson Smith had now to be subjected in its turn to the test of Australian ethnography. Precisely at this juncture an associate of Tylor travelled to Australia and prepared to make investigations among the aborigines.

---

22 Having come to this point, it seemed to me that I had seen something like it elsewhere, and on looking back to 'Kamilaroi and Kurnai' I found that Fison had thus worked out the origin of the Turanian classificatory system. (*Op. cit.*, p. 263)

23 *Op. cit.*, p. 267. This hypothesis applied regardless of the mode of descent, 'it making no difference politically whether kinship follows the female or male line, if only marrying-out causes the requisite intermixture of the clans' (*op cit.*, p. 268). Exogamy could even be based on locality as well as upon kinship.

Totemism as a religious system: Spencer and Gillen

Baldwin Spencer was a naturalist. In 1887, at the age of twenty-seven, he went out to Australia to take the chair of biology in Melbourne University. He had collaborated with Tylor on the removal of the Pitt Rivers collection to Oxford, and he carried with him a letter in which Tylor suggested that 'I might be able to do some work of value if ever I chanced to come into contact with savage peoples'.[24] But first – in July 1894 – he made what Elliot Smith later called his most important discovery, namely Frank Gillen, the postmaster of Alice Springs. Gillen had already been collecting materials on the Aranda tribe, 'with whom he was on the most friendly terms and by whom he was completely trusted'.[25] Together they organized special fieldwork expeditions to the centre and north of the country, and eventually published two classic Australian ethnographies, *The Native Tribes of Central Australia* (1899) and *The Native Tribes of the Northern Territory* (1914).

The partnership between Spencer and Gillen was structurally rather similar to that between Fison and Howitt. Again there was a metropolitan intellectual paired with a man who had outstanding local knowledge. But in the case of Spencer and Gillen, the difference between the two was more marked. Spencer was a trained scholar and experienced naturalist, while Fison was rather a self-trained intellectual; and Gillen was a man of very little education, whereas Howitt – for all his familiarity with the bush – was a professional man. In consequence, Gillen's ethnography was completely subordinated to Spencer's ideas. 'Do please let me have a list of questions by each mail', he would write to Spencer. 'I must have the guidance of your scientifically trained mind to work or I shall accomplish very little.'[26] Spencer confirmed this mode of operation in a letter to Frazer. 'I send him up endless questions and things to find out, and by mutual agreement he reads no one else's work so as to keep him quite unprejudiced in the way of theories.'[27]

---

24 Spencer (1928), *Wanderings in Wild Australia*, vol. 1, p. 185.
25 *Ibid.* However, Spencer's biographers conclude that Gillen was not fluent in Aranda and that he and Spencer used pidgin English for most of their work, and depended upon interpreters (Mulvaney and Calaby (1984), *So Much That is New*, p. 174).
26 Mulvaney and Calaby (1984), *So Much That is New*, p. 169.
27 *Op. cit.*, p. 172.

But just as Fison and Howitt took their broader theoretical directions from Morgan, so Spencer (and in his turn Gillen) were under the ultimate command of Frazer. Spencer was quite clear that a fieldworker required detailed guidance.[28] Without such direction, he could simply miss what was of importance. That was how Spencer explained Howitt's failure to report on the religious aspects of totemism, writing to Frazer that

in those days with no work such as yours and Tylor's to guide him there was little to show him what to look for in this line, and therefore there will be little reference in his book to customs associated with totemism other than in regard to its relationship to marriage.[29]

He depended on Frazer, just as Gillen depended upon him, for ideas and for encouragement. 'The knowledge that there is some one like you', he wrote to Frazer, 'who can piece together the odd fragments of information which isolated workers can acquire is a great stimulant.'[30]

Frazer accepted that he should give the lead, but he repeatedly told Spencer that the ethnographer's data had a more permanent value than any metropolitan theorizing.[31] And certainly Spencer was by no means constrained to endorse the ruling theories. He accepted Frazer's rule that 'Descriptive and comparative ethnology should be kept most rigidly apart; to try to combine both is to spoil both.'[32] There was almost a contract between them. The metropolis put the questions, but the fieldworker was in the business of checking, documenting and, if necessary, refuting the speculations of the metropolis. The fieldworkers also relied on Frazer to bolster the authority of their reports. Spencer reminded him more than once that 'Australian anthropology is badly in want of a committee of expurgation'.[33] And Frazer recorded that Howitt's very last message to the metropolis, dictated from his death-bed, was addressed to those who made use of ethnographic information,

28 See Marett and Penniman (1932), *Spencer's Scientific Correspondence*, pp. 47, 58.

29 *Op. cit.*, p. 79. Fison had, however, speculated about 'totemism' with reference to McLennan's theory and garnered some information from informants. See Fison and Howitt (1880), *Kamilaroi and Kurnai*, pp. 165–71.

30 Marett and Penniman (1932), *Spencer's Scientific Correspondence*, p. 58.

31 E.g. *op cit.*, p. 22.

32 *Op. cit.*, p. 23.

33 *Op. cit.*, p. 22.

'impressing on them the importance of caution in accepting information drawn from the Australian tribes in their present state of decay'.[34]

There was, then, something of a chain of command which ran from Frazer through Spencer to Gillen, but the fieldworkers retained their special integrity and influence. Though this hierarchical, *dirigiste* approach to fieldwork did not determine what he and Gillen actually found out, it set the questions which Spencer chose to investigate. It is indeed quite extraordinary how Spencer disciplined his curiosity, how narrowly his attention and Gillen's were directed to the study of totemic beliefs and practices. They accepted Fison and Howitt's group-marriage thesis almost without enquiry, and added little to their description of the aboriginal social system. On the other hand, anything relevant to totemism as a religious system was investigated in unprecedented detail, and given great prominence in their reports.

This sharply-focused research yielded authoritative answers to some of the central questions of contemporary anthropology. Spencer and Gillen's findings were picked over time and again in the next decade. They demonstrated that totems were distributed by locality and not according to descent-group membership. There was no relationship between the marriage classes and the totemic groups. At least in Central Australia, there were no restrictions on eating the totem. On the contrary, members of the totem group took a leading part in killing and eating the totemic animals in the 'intichiuma' ceremony, which they took to be the archetypal totemic rite. Nor was there a belief that totems had souls or should be worshipped.

Only one element of the original theory found support in Spencer and Gillen's field researches. Robertson Smith had claimed that the sacrifice of the totem was the central rite in the original totemic religion. Among the Aranda, Spencer and Gillen discovered a fertility rite in which totemic animals or plants were killed to increase the number of the species. This Aranda 'intichiuma' seemed to correspond to Robertson Smith's expectations, and its description was given pride of place in their vivid and detailed monograph on the tribe – though they did not suggest that it was of central significance for the Aranda themselves.

---

34 Frazer (1909), 'Howitt and Fison', p. 171.

Frazer's faith in his own mentor was briefly rekindled. He wrote that he welcomed the description of the Aranda 'intichiuma' as

a very striking proof of the sagacity of my brilliant friend, whose rapid genius had outstripped our slower methods and anticipated what it was reserved for subsequent research positively to ascertain. Thus from being little more than an ingenious hypothesis the totem sacrament has become, at least in my opinion, a well-authenticated fact.[35]

But soon his enthusiasm cooled. Spencer did not agree that the totem was being worshipped, and he even rejected Frazer's suggestion that there was at least an element of 'conciliation' of the totem.[36] Frazer began to question whether totemic rituals were religious. Perhaps they did not imply a belief in the divinity of the totem, were no more than crude magical exercises. If that was the case then they need have little bearing on the history of religion.

Tylor had already expressed his own scepticism. In an essay published in 1899 (the year in which Spencer and Gillen's monograph appeared), he reiterated his faith in animism. Totemism 'has been exaggerated out of proportion to its real theological magnitude. The importance belonging to totem-animals as friends or enemies of man is insignificant in comparison with that of ghosts or demons, to say nothing of higher deities.' The relationship of totemic beliefs to clan organization and exogamy was also put in question. Spencer had begun to express his doubts in letters to Frazer, and now Tylor concluded bluntly that 'Exogamy can and does exist without totemism, and for all we know was originally independent of it'.[37]

---

35 Frazer (1890 (1900)), Preface to the second edition of *The Golden Bough*, p. xix.
36 Marett and Penniman (1932), *Spencer's Scientific Correspondence*, pp. 45–54.
37 Tylor (1899), 'Remarks on totemism', pp. 144 and 148.

CHAPTER 6

Totem and taboo

Tylor's authority was still unchallenged and his judgments carried great weight. In 1889, reflecting on Fison and Howitt's monograph, he had reviewed the state of thinking on exogamy and endorsed the theory of Morgan as modified by Fison. Ten years later, with the publication of Spencer and Gillen's book, he dismissed the theory of totemic religion, and denied its connection with exogamy. A decade later, in 1910, Frazer published a typically exhaustive review of the field. Where Tylor had dealt with exogamy and totemism in two lectures, Frazer's *Totemism and Exogamy: A Treatise on Certain Early Forms of Superstition and Society* filled four large volumes. He painstakingly reviewed the theories and materials which had been produced, but his conclusions in the fourth volume by and large echoed Tylor's.

In totemism a man 'identified himself and his fellow-clansmen with his totem'. This does not, however, amount to a religion – 'it is a serious, though apparently a common, mistake to speak of a totem as a god, and to say that it is worshipped by the clan'. A man may be prevented from eating and killing the totem, but not invariably. Nor had totemism ever been universal. He specifically rejected Robertson Smith's thesis that there were traces of totemism in pre-Islamic Semitic religions. It was rather a peculiar mutation of the black races.[1]

---

1 Thus if civilisation varies on the whole ... directly with complexion, increasing or diminishing with the blanching or darkening of the skin, we may lay it down as a general proposition that totemism is an institution peculiar to the dark-complexioned and least civilised races of mankind. (Frazer (1910), *Totemism and Exogamy*, vol. 4, p. 14)

This forthright racism was of course in direct contradiction to Frazer's evolutionism, which took for granted that every human society had passed through the same stages of development.

Quite commonly members of a totemic clan were prohibited from marrying one another, but this generalization was also subject to numerous exceptions. Moreover, there were people in Melanesia and Australia who practised both exogamy and totemism without connecting the two institutions; and in some areas one of the customs might be found without the other. There was, then, a 'radical distinction of totemism and exogamy'.[2]

When it came to explaining totemic beliefs, Frazer was equally negative, dismissing all current ideas, including his own of the day before yesterday, that totemism was to be understood as an organized system of cooperative magic. This was to overrate the philosophical subtlety of totemic man. It now appeared to him that totemism was simply the effect of the primitive theory of conception. Ignorant of the biology of conception, savages assumed that local natural objects somehow quickened the child, and this led to ideas of individual totemism.

Frazer therefore shared Tylor's scepticism about totemic religions. With Tylor again, he pretty much endorsed the now established theory of primitive social organization. Drawing especially on Fison he argued that an original two-class system had developed into a four- and then an eight-class system. Such systems might be associated with the tracing of descent in either the female or the male line. The classes probably arose by way of segmentation. The purpose of these systems – and they were certainly deliberately designed – was progressively to rule out more and more relatives as marriage partners. This was due to a fundamental dread of incest.

The class system also imposed a classification of kin. Father's brothers' children and mother's sisters' children were members of a man's own exogamous class, and were called brother and sister. His mother's brothers' children and father's sisters' children were members of the other class, and intermarriage with them was possible. This classificatory system of kinship terminology 'simply defines the relations of all the men and women of the community to each other according to the generation and the exogamous class to which they belong'.[3]

Also in 1910 an American student of Boas, Alexander Golden-

---

2 *Op. cit.*, vol. 4, p. 10.
3 *Op. cit.*, p. 124.

weiser, published a yet more negative summary of the situation, in which he dismantled even more conclusively the elaborate structure which had dominated anthropological theory for a generation. With his more incisive style – and unburdened by hostages to fortune – his critique was more swiftly and completely accomplished.[4]

Up to this point, the story of totemism may appear to conform to the orthodox notion of scientific progress. McLennan put up a new theory – or rather, he yoked together two established theories, one about the primeval society, another about the original religion. Robertson Smith elaborated the idea. Frazer systematized it. Then came ethnographic tests by the Australian specialists. These failed to confirm Robertson Smith's ideas. Tylor expressed scepticism. Finally, Frazer and Goldenweiser independently reviewed the accumulated evidence, and concluded that totemism as a religion was a dubious construct, and certainly never universal; and that it had no necessary connection with exogamy.

But the story could equally be rewritten to emphasize the political reasons for the theoretical shift. Tylor was the dominant figure in British anthropology in the last decade of the nineteenth century, and he saw no reason to concede that totemism should share the limelight with animism. Frazer himself was engaged in developing his own reputation, which involved distancing himself from his mentor Robertson Smith. That was enough to put paid to the theory of McLennan and Robertson Smith, both of whom had long passed from the scene.

On the other hand, neither Tylor nor Frazer had a special investment in the theory of exogamy, and they were content to exalt the claims of their Australian clients. Power within the intellectual establishment was certainly at the least a crucial part of the story, for when an outsider formulated a devastating critique of the established theory of the evolution of the family he was largely ignored.

Westermarck and the family

Edward Westermarck, a Finn, was drawn into anthropology as a result of reading Darwin's *Descent of Man*.[5] His starting-point was an interest in the origins of sexual shame and morality. Reading Darwin he found that, according to some scholars, primitive man

4 Goldenweiser (1910), 'Totemism, an analytical study'.
5 Westermarck (1927), *Memories of My Life*.

was sexually promiscuous. He learnt to read English and began to follow up Darwin's sources – Morgan, McLennan and Lubbock. Initially he was inclined to credit the theory of primitive promiscuity, despite Darwin's own reservations; but quite soon he began to doubt that customs could be interpreted as survivals of early forms of organization. Gradually he became more and more sceptical of the orthodox reconstructions of primeval marriage and began to collect fresh information. He pursued his researches in the British Museum and sent out questionnaires to missionaries and others. When he finally published his findings in 1891, at the age of thirty, he was a master of the field.

The theoretical inspiration of Westermarck's encyclopaedic *History of Human Marriage* (1891) was strictly Darwinian, free of any Lamarckian vestiges. Perhaps the first orthodox application of modern evolutionary theory in anthropology, it was enthusiastically endorsed by Alfred Wallace (who shares the credit with Darwin for the formulation of modern evolutionary theory).[6]

Following Darwin, Westermarck included the primates in his argument. The higher mammals care for their own young. This is especially true of the higher apes and, above all, of 'the man-like apes'. The gorilla and chimpanzee 'lives in families, the male parent being in the habit of building the nest and protecting the family . . . Passing from the highest monkeys to the savage and barbarous races of man, we meet the same phenomenon.' Everywhere 'it is to the mother that the immediate care of the children chiefly belongs, while the father is the protector and guardian of the family . . . the simplest paternal duties are . . . universally recognized'.[7]

The universal existence of the family is to be explained by natural selection. The protection of the husband/father offers mother and children an advantage, given the small number of progeny among humans, the extended period of gestation, and the length of time during which the child is unable to fend for itself. The male protector need not always be the biological father, but each female requires a male partner who will also protect her offspring. Where this protection is provided, more children will survive.

Writing to Westermarck, Tylor admitted that he was largely

6 See Wikman (1940), 'Letters from Edward B. Tylor and Alfred Russel Wallace to Edward Westermarck'.

7 Westermarck (1891), *History of Human Marriage*, pp. 14 and 15.

persuaded by his arguments,[8] but he was now entering the long twilight of his dotage, and he published nothing further on the matter. In the next generation Westermarck was ignored by Rivers, the central figure in the study of social organization in Britain.[9] The one leading scholar of the next generation who did pick up his argument was another exotic immigrant, the Pole Bronislaw Malinowski.

Malinowski on the family in Australia

Like many of his generation of anthropologists, Malinowski began as a natural scientist. After taking a first degree in physics in Cracow he studied in Germany under Wundt, a pioneer in the field of experimental psychology and a polymath with an interest in ethnology. In 1910, at the age of twenty-six, he moved to the London School of Economics to work with Westermarck. Here he completed a study, begun in Germany, on the problem of the family among the Australian aborigines.

Malinowski felt a special intellectual kinship with Westermarck, to whom, he once wrote, he owed more than to any other scientific influence. For his part, Westermarck welcomed Malinowski's study of the Australian family as a model of its kind.[10] Nevertheless, Malinowski's study of the Australian family (*The Family among the Australian Aborigines*, published in 1913) was far more than a straightforward reprise of Westermarck's masterpiece. Central to the argument were two novel assumptions – novel, at least, in the mainstream anthropology of the time. First of all, context was crucial. The operation of any institution is modified by other institutions with which it is associated. Consequently the family will have specific and perhaps unique features in any particular society. Secondly, an institution is also informed by the perceptions,

---

8　See his letters in Wikman (1940), 'Letters from Edward B. Tylor and Alfred Russel Wallace to Edward Westermarck'.

9　In 1913 Rivers delivered a course of lectures at the London School of Economics which were published in the following year under the title *Kinship and Social Organization*. In the preface he notes that 'A few small additions and modifications have been made since the lectures were given, some of these being due to suggestions made by Professor Westermarck and Dr Malinowski in the discussions which followed the lectures'. It would be fascinating to know more about these suggestions.

10　See Firth (1957), 'Malinowski as scientist and as man', pp. 5–6.

emotions and ideas of the people who use it. In short, the 'family' must be studied in operation. As Westermarck indeed had insisted, it was not the ideal of family life which counted, not the rules and pious formulae, but the practice.

It had been widely reported that the Australian aborigines were ignorant of physiological paternity. If one concentrated on practice rather than ideology it was apparent that the mother's husband had special responsibility for her children, and that the unit of mother, children and mother's husband was a recognizable and important isolate. It followed that 'individual' relationships of kinship, traced through the father in a matrilineal society, were signiifcant. They coexisted with 'group' kinship relationships. Relationships of descent were evidently secondary, and emphasis on one line of descent did not exclude the use of the other.

Freud's 'Totem and Taboo'

If the foreign prophets in England were ignored, it is equally the case that the leading Anglo-American anthropologists could not impose their views on foreign scholars. To some of the enquiring minds on the continent, Frazer's new compendium was a challenge rather than a warning. At the same time as Malinowski's funda-mental critique of kinship theory appeared, Durkheim in France and Freud in Austria harked back to the assumptions of the pre-vious century, and produced the most brilliant and influential formulations of classic totemism.

In 1912 Durkheim published his *Les Formes élémentaires de la vie religieuse: le système totémique en Australie* (English translation, 1915). The following year Freud's *Totem und Tabu* appeared. The fame and influence of these books were to rival, perhaps surpass, Frazer's *The Golden Bough* itself. And both authors set out to explain the connection between the taboo on the totem and the rule of exogamy within the clan. Freud and Durkheim – especially Durkheim – were familiar with Frazer's work and with other recent sources; but all doubts were brushed aside in the pursuit of a grand foundation myth for Western civilization. They were closer in their inspiration to Robertson Smith and to the Frazer of *The Golden Bough* than to Tylor or the later Frazer.

Freud's thesis was certainly the most imaginative version of totemism. It had little impact within anthropology, but it was also perhaps the most influential in the intellectual world at large in the long run. His starting-point was Darwin, or at least a book by Andrew Lang and an obscure English author (Lang's cousin), J. Atkinson. Atkinson's *Primal Law* (1903) was one of the flood of idiosyncratic fantasies on human social origins which had been launched with the work of Maine and McLennan, but it is notable since it is among the very few which began from Darwin's reconstruction of the early human band.

In *The Descent of Man* (1871) Darwin had reviewed the evidence for the social organization of various primate species. He emphasized the importance of sexual jealousy and rivalry, and concluded that early man probably 'lived in small communities, each with a single wife, or if powerful with several, whom he jealously guarded against all other men'. Alternatively, a powerful male might have lived alone with several mates and their offspring, like the gorilla. When a young male matured he would be engaged in a contest by the dominant male. Either the older male would be killed or the young would be expelled. 'The young males, being thus expelled and wandering about, would, when at last successful in finding a partner, prevent too close interbreeding within the limits of the same family.'[11]

Atkinson speculated that mothers would in time rebel against the expulsion of their sons. First the youngest son would be allowed to stay, then others. The prohibition on incest would have been introduced to guarantee the old male's sexual monopoly of his spouses. Freud's fantasy was more violent. There would have been an uprising of the young males against the patriarch, motivated by the desire to share his women. This act of parricide was the more heinous since the patriarch was also revered as a god. A guilty memory of the terrible crime would haunt mankind. Totemic taboos and sacrifices were acts of appeasement, the totem standing for the murdered god. Rules against incest were also instituted in reaction to this awful deed.

Freud believed in the inheritance of acquired traits. That was why the descendants of the original parricides – all mankind – still dealt with their ancestral guilt by making the totem taboo and banning incest. But he also believed that as the individual grew up he relived the experience of the race. Ontogeny recapitulated phylogeny. Therefore every boy had to deal with a guilty desire to

11 Darwin (1874), *Descent of Man* (second edition), p. 901.

murder his father and marry his mother. This was the 'Oedipus complex'. Neurotics (who were very like both primitives and children) failed to resolve their ambivalent feelings for their parents. They protected themselves from their conflicting urges by obsessional practices which were private versions of incest taboos.

Freud's own totemic myth did not impinge upon the major traditions of anthropology until the 1930s, and then only marginally. By that stage totemism was so discredited that Freud's influence imposed itself despite *Totem and Taboo* rather than because of it. The Durkheimian version, in contrast, was seen as a challenge from the very first, not least because it was based upon a detailed reading of the Australian sources.

Durkheim and the anthropologists

As the founding father of modern French social science, Émile Durkheim's writings have been the subject of an immense body of exegesis.[12] Virtually all accounts of his sociology are dominated by his theory of religion. This seems reasonable, on the face of it. After the early works – notably *The Division of Labour in Society* (1893; English translation, 1915), *The Rules of Sociological Method* (1895) and *Suicide* (1897) – Durkheim devoted himself to problems of religious sociology, and his next (and last) major study, *The Elementary Forms of the Religious Life*, published in 1912 (English translation, 1915), fifteen years after *Suicide*, is generally regarded as his masterpiece.

Nevertheless, Durkheim himself did not expect this study of religion to represent the crowning achievement of his career. His nephew, Marcel Mauss, reported that on his death-bed Durkheim had made a supreme effort to begin writing his planned book on morality, which he had looked forward to as the 'but de son éxist-

---

12 The study of Durkheim was transformed by Stephen Lukes' excellent *Emile Durkheim: His Life and Work* (1973). A good sampling of current French research on Durkheim is to be found in P. Besnard (1983), *The Sociological Domain: The Durkheimians and the Founding of French Sociology*. On Durkheim's use of ethnology see especially V. Karady (1981), 'French ethnology and the Durkheimian breakthrough' and (1983), 'The Durkheimians in academe. A reconsideration'. See also W. P. Vogt (1976), 'The use of studying primitives: a note on the Durkheimians'. For Durkheim's theory of totemism, see Robert Jones (1977), 'On understanding a sociological classic'; (1981) 'Robertson Smith, Durkheim, and sacrifice'; and (1986) 'Durkheim, Frazer and Smith'. On his theory of kinship see my essay (1985), 'Durkheim's theory of primitive kinship'.

ence, fond de son ésprit'.[13] Moreover he also set great store by his uncompleted work on the family. He had written only part of it (in Bordeaux between 1890 and 1892), but these pages were so precious to Durkheim that he would not be separated from them, even when he travelled. Durkheim had 'wished to devote the rest of his life to this comparative natural history of the family and marriage up to the present'.[14] He had taken personal responsibility for the sections on the family and marriage in the *Année Sociologique* when it began to appear under his editorship, in 1898. Towards the end of his life he had even considered cutting the planned book on morality, and making it into an introduction to the book on the family.

In fact these three projects – the studies of religion, morality and the family – were closely united in Durkheim's mind. Durkheim's fundamental concern had always been to provide a scientific basis for morality. He viewed this as a matter of urgent political necessity. He was a secular republican, wary of the political power of the Catholic Church. He was also a Jew – and a Jew from Alsace, at that – a member of a newly-enfranchised minority, but one very much under threat. It was in 1894 that Dreyfus was prosecuted for treason, and his trial unleashed a frightening alliance of militarists, Catholic reactionaries and anti-Semites.

A secular morality required a theory of religion and a theory of the family. Conservative writers believed that church and family were the sources which fed morality. If a new moral order was to be established, appropriate to the social forms which were emerging, then alternative sources of morality had to be constituted. This was not a promising venture unless it could be shown that religion and the family system had not been constant, but had changed as fundamental social forms had altered. Ethnology offered precisely this assurance. The new consensus asserted that the family was a recent innovation, and that religious beliefs had evolved through various stages and were in imminent danger of being displaced by science.

Like Engels then, Durkheim was clearly attracted by the relativizing potential of ethnology. If things were very different in the past, they may be very different again in the future. The present institutional arrangements are not facts of nature, they are human

---

13 Karady (1969), *Marcel Mauss, Oeuvres*, vol. 3, p. 475.
14 *Op. cit.*, p. 480–1.

constructs. There were other reasons too for Durkheim's interest in ethnology.[15] The Durkheimians were seeking an academic niche, and it made tactical sense to lay claim to an unclaimed field of scholarship. Finally, the appeal to ethnology also made sense in terms of Durkheim's evolutionism. This owed much to Spencer and nothing to Darwin, who in any case had little influence in France at the time, even among natural scientists.[16]

Spencer believed that all societies shared a common point of origin. Moreover, the original institutional forms were never lost, but were simply recombined in various, more complex, new forms. (This was a form of social Lamarckism. Spencer was himself a believer in the inheritance of acquired characteristics, and Durkheim shared the Lamarckian assumptions, which were common currency in France at the time.) Durkheim further concluded from these premises that institutions could be most easily understood in their simplest, original form, and that if they were studied in a primitive state their relations with other institutions would be most readily apparent. All these considerations reinforced the appeal of ethnology.

Durkheim on the family

In his early lectures on the family and in *The Division of Labour*, which appeared in 1893 (1915 in English translation), Durkheim accepted the orthodox Anglo-American account of the evolution of the family from an original horde by way of matriarchy and patriarchy; but he situated this conventional model in a new, more sociological context. Spencer had speculated that the original society must have been unicellular, as it were, and internally undifferentiated. By segmentation it gave rise to more complex social forms. The original horde split into two, yielding a society made up of two clans (or moieties). Durkheim identified this type of system with the Australian society described by Fison and Howitt. Morgan had described the Iroquois as having eight clan units, and so clearly they were a yet more advanced system, having segmented not once but three times. The terminology for these segments was

15 See Karady (1981), 'French ethnology and the Durkheimian breakthrough'.
16 See Corning (1982), 'Durkheim and Spencer'. The best account of Spencer is Peel's *Herbert Spencer: The Evolution of a Sociologist* (1971). He has also edited a valuable reader (1972), *Herbert Spencer on Social Evolution*. Medawar has a marvellous essay on Spencer in his *Pluto's Republic* (1982).

borrowed from the anthropologists, but the terminology for the structure which they formed was Spencer's. 'The horde which had ceased to be independent, and become an element in a more extended group, we call the clan. Peoples formed by an association of clans we call segmentary clan-based societies [sociétés segmentaires à base de clans].'[17]

The repetitive, internally undifferentiated units of the segmentary, clan-based social system were bound together by what Durkheim called 'mechanical solidarity'. This society of clones was very different from the modern social structure, which was based on the division of labour. The specialized elements of a modern society were intricately related to each other in a web of interdependencies. People in such a society had a very different sense of how they fitted into the broader society. Instead of mechanical solidarity, such societies created 'organic solidarity'.

Family units were the typical elements of the ancient social system, though a clan system might just as well be based upon local groups. In modern societies, however, the family had lost its pivotal social role. Other, more specialized, institutions had taken over many of its erstwhile functions. Accordingly the family became smaller, feebler, and more internally differentiated. The old ties of descent, which had regulated communal property relationships, were now less important, while the individualized conjugal bond had become relatively more significant.

True to his Spencerian views, Durkheim believed that the earlier family forms survived on the margins of the more evolved institutions. The kindred, for example, surrounds the modern nuclear family, recalling the extended patriarchal family of an earlier period. 'The modern family contains within it, as if in miniature, the whole historical development of the family.'[18]

Durkheim's main point was that the form of the family was a function of the social structure. In the old segmental type of society, the units all had to be alike, though they might be organized on the basis of consanguinity or of locality. That was a secondary issue. 'The organization with a clan-base is really only a species of a larger genus, the segmental organization. The distribution of

---

17 Durkheim (1893), p. 150.
18 Karady (1975), *Emile Durkheim, Textes*, vol. 3, p. 73.

society into similar compartments corresponds to persisting necessities.'[19]

If family organization was structured by other, more significant, overarching forms of social organization, then clearly it made little sense to talk about the abstract advantages of one or other kind of family institution. Nostalgia for 'traditional' family forms was irrational. 'The family of today is not more or less perfect than that of old: it is different, because the circumstances are different. It is more complex, because the environment in which it exists is more complex: that is all.'[20]

In *The Division of Labour* Durkheim argued that the family was withering away, and that its moral, disciplinary and organizational functions would be taken over by corporations which were economically specialized, that is, by professional associations. The new organic societies and their institutions were no less moral or natural than the old clan-based systems, although they were inevitably more evolved, more complex, more differentiated. Criticizing Tönnies, Durkheim wrote in 1889: 'I believe that the life of the great social agglomerations is just as natural as that of the small communities. It is neither less organic nor less internalized [interne].'[21]

But was there not something *natural* about family organization? Le Play, for example, had argued that the family was in some sense prior to, and independent of, society, and that it was a primordial source of moral values. The French ethnologist Letourneau had insisted that the primitive family forms were more natural than, and morally preferable to, our own. Westermarck, in his *History of Human Marriage* (1891), had argued that the basic family institutions were derived from our primate ancestors. If arguments of this type were correct, then the value of the family was not contextual at all, but independent of other social institutions. The family would be a natural and permanent institution.

The issue was vital to Durkheim's whole attempt to formulate a scientifically-based morality. If certain institutions, notably the family, were 'natural' to man then, although they might 'evolve', they could not be jettisoned without serious risk. But if they

---

19 Durkheim (1915b), *The Division of Labour in Society*.
20 Karady (1975), *Emile Durkheim, Textes*, vol. 3, p. 25.
21 *Op. cit.*, p. 390.

were social artifacts then they might well be replaced by more sophisticated institutions.

In 1895 Durkheim realized that Robertson Smith's theory of totemism offered a powerful, fresh perspective on these questions.[22] Above all, the theory of totemism promised to relativize both the family and religion at a single stroke. He began to work out the implications of this theory in a long essay, 'La prohibition de l'inceste et ses origines'. It was given pride of place in the first issue of the *Année sociologique*, which appeared in 1898.

The origin of the incest taboo

Durkheim began by restating the old idea of totemism. Totemic clans were exogamous and matrilineal. Clan members believed themselves to share a common substance of some kind with each other and with their clan totem. Exogamous (localized) patrilineal clans developed later, but they adopted the exogamous rules of the uterine clans by way of analogy. He added that the Australian 'marriage-classes' resulted from the combination of exogamous uterine clans and exogamous patrilineal local units. In time, more complex family forms developed, and the rules of exogamy were adapted accordingly.

Yet while Durkheim's description was orthodox, he rejected the explanations of exogamy which were available to him. The leading anthropologists had explained exogamy in terms of the clan structure. (He cited Lubbock, Spencer, Morgan and McLennan.) These writers assumed mistakenly that exogamy was in essence a general prohibition of marriage with consanguines. Durkheim countered that the exogamy rules might also prohibit marriage with non-relatives, and that certain very close blood relatives might be marriageable, including, for example, mother's brother's children in a

---

22 In 1907, in a letter to the editor of a scholarly journal, he wrote:

it was only in 1895 that I clearly recognized the crucial role played by religion in social life … for the first time I found the means to tackle the study of religion sociologically. It was a revelation to me. The course of 1895 marks a line of demarcation in the development of my thought, to the point that all my previous researches had to be started afresh in order to harmonize them with these new opinions. This was due entirely to the studies of the history of religion which I had recently undertaken, and notably to reading the works of Robertson Smith and his school. (Durkheim (1907), *Revue néo-scolastique*, pp. 606–7, 612–14)

The meaning of this statement has been endlessly debated (for example, Jones (1985), 'Durkheim, totemism, and the *Intichiuma*').

uterine system. He rejected the view that there was a universal horror of sexual contact with consanguines.

Durkheim looked for the causes of exogamy not directly in the clan system, but rather in totemism itself. This was to make exogamy the consequence of religious beliefs, or, more precisely, a special instance of a general religious institution, fundamental to all primitive religions, namely taboo.

He argued that women are typically subject to ritual segregation at puberty, menstruation and childbirth. This was because their blood was regarded as especially dangerous. These taboos on women were connected with the taboo on shedding the blood of a clansman and with the taboos on killing or eating the totem. The key to the whole intellectual complex was the belief that the clansmen shared a common substance with the totem. 'Thus the totemic being is immanent in the clan; it is incarnated in each individual, and it resides in the blood. It is itself the blood.'[23] The notional consanguinity of clansmen has nothing directly to do with kinship. Rather it is a religious belief, a statement of the solidarity of the congregation and its god.

Sociological determinism

It is possible to read Durkheim's argument as a kind of ideological determinism. A religious belief – totemism – generated an idea of consanguinity and a rule of exogamy. This seems to echo Fustel de Coulanges' argument in *La Cité Antique* (1864), in which he argued that a succession of forms of family organization followed from changes in religious belief. Fustel had been a teacher of Durkheim's, and although Durkheim initially criticized this ideological determinism, his later position may appear to be fairly similar. I believe, however, that this is an oversimplification.[24] Durkheim's fundamental premise was that the structural type of a society determined the nature and function of the social units. Institutions, rituals and beliefs were determined by the same structural matrix.

The argument was elaborated in *The Elementary Forms of the Religious Life* (1915a). The basic thesis was that the family was not

23 Durkheim (1898), 'La prohibition de l'inceste', p. 39.
24 For the contrary view see Lukes (1973), *Emile Durkheim*, pp. 58–63.

really 'about' consanguinity, nor was religion really 'about' gods.[25] The simplest societies were composed of undifferentiated and repetitive clans. But each clan was nevertheless particular, and so it needed a badge of identity, an emblem. The emblem was the origin of the totem. The religious features of totemism – the rituals, the prohibitions, the beliefs – followed from the identification of the social unit, the clan, with an emblem, the totem. When the group came together at certain seasons it did so under the common banner of its emblem, the totem. The sentiments aroused by collective action were then projected on to the emblem itself. The emblem became a sacred object, and so the focus of ritual. The effect was

to raise man above himself and to make him lead a life superior to that which he would lead, if he followed only his own individual whims: beliefs express this life in representations; rites organize it and regulate its working.[26]

And the subordination of individual 'whims' to the interests of the group was what Durkheim meant by morality.[27]

The line of causality in Durkheim's argument is therefore strictly sociological. The structure of the total society – its form – generates particular types of segment. These develop a symbolic expression in the course of their social activity. This symbolic identity produces ritualized behaviour, which sustains the individual's sentiment of solidarity with his group. These beliefs and rituals, finally, maintain

25 In the first chapter of *Elementary Forms* Durkheim wrote:

Primitive civilizations offer privileged cases ... because they are simple cases. That is why, in all fields of human activity, the observations of ethnologists have frequently been veritable revelations, which have renewed the study of human institutions. For example, before the middle of the nineteenth century, everybody was convinced that the father was the essential element of the family; no one dreamed that there could be a family organization of which the paternal authority was not the keystone. But the discovery of Bachofen came and upset this old conception. Up to very recent times it was regarded as evident that the moral and legal relations of kindred were only another aspect of the psychological relations which result from a common descent; Bachofen and his successors, McLennan, Morgan and many others still laboured under this misunderstanding. But since we have become acquainted with the nature of the primitive clan, we know that, on the contrary, relationships cannot be explained by consanguinity, To return to religions, the study of only the most familiar ones has led men to believe for a long time that the idea of god was characteristic of everything that is religious. Now the religion which we are going to study presently is, in a large part, foreign to all idea of divinity. (Durkheim (1915a), pp. 6–7)

26 Durkheim (1915a), *The Elementary Forms of the Religious Life*, p. 414.

27 For an excellent discussion of Durkheim's theory of morality see Lukes (1973), *Emile Durkheim*, Chapter 21.

the moral basis of the society – the subordination of individual wishes to group requirements. Religion and the family are commonly the immediate sources of morality, as the conservatives had always argued, but they are themselves the product of a broader structure; and either – or both – could be replaced by alternative institutional forms. These sociological truths are exemplified in the primitive totemic stage of social organization.

Durkheim's was a Cartesian argument. Like Descartes he was looking for the first step in the dialectic,[28] and he assumed that this could be found at the beginning of human evolution. This first step – Durkheim's *cogito* – was not an institution but a structure. An abstract form of organization – segmental or differentiated – determined the type of family structure or religion.

The fate of totemism

The theory of totemism may be traced to McLennan's essay of 1869, although it was only when Robertson Smith linked totemism to the religion of the ancient Semites, a decade later, that the theory attracted broad attention. The debate on totemism then occupied an entire generation, but it was clearly fizzling out by the time that the journal *Anthropos* published a disillusioned symposium on the subject in the early years of the First World War.

This debate was initiated by Goldenweiser, who in 1912 wrote to the editor of *Anthropos*:

The appearance of Durkheim's brilliant but unconvincing treatise on religion brings home the fact that one of the phases of socio-religious thought, namely the problem of totemism, remains as replete with vagueness and mutual misunderstanding as ever.'[29]

Despite the war, *Anthropos* published a symposium on the subject, in which specialists from a number of countries expressed their measured disillusionment with the old models.[30]

Many of the leading scholars of the new generation contributed – Thurnwald, Graebner and Schmidt in Central Europe; Rivers and

---

28 See Durkheim (1915a), *The Elementary Forms*, pp. 3–6.

29 *Anthropos*, 1915, vol. 9, p. 288.

30 The symposium was published in the following numbers of *Anthropos*: 1914, vol. 9, pp. 287–325, 622–52; 1915–16, vols 10–11, pp. 234–65, 586–610, 948–70; 1917–18, vols 12–13, pp. 338–50, 1,094–113; and 1919–20, vols 14–15, pp. 496–545. Further contributions were published occasionally thereafter.

Radcliffe-Brown in Britain; and Boas, Goldenweiser and Swanton in the United States. Virtually all insisted on separating the social and religious models of totemism, though there was less agreement as to which model then offered the better prospects for research. Rivers, for example, wished to restrict attention to totemism as a form of social structure, while his student Radcliffe-Brown suggested that the term should be used to connote only a magico-religious system. This general scepticism was fed by a more general disenchantment with broad evolutionist models. Of the major contributors to the *Anthropos* symposium, only Radcliffe-Brown would probably have called himself an evolutionist, and he certainly had no sympathy with the unilinear models of the classic British anthropology. If Durkheim's formulation remained influential for rather longer in France, it was badly dented by Van Gennep's powerful polemic, *L'Etat actuel du problème totémique*, which appeared in 1920.

But although totemism was abandoned by the anthropologists between 1910 and 1920, it is arguably the most pervasive and enduring anthropological contribution to the European conception of primitive society. Because of its significance for Durkheimian sociology it remains a disturbing presence in the literature of mainstream sociological thinking about religion. It became a central myth of Freud's psychoanalysis. *The Golden Bough* generated a whole theory of drama and ritual, permeating the study of the classics to this day, and inspiring T. S. Eliot's *The Waste Land*.

The reason is evident. With totemism, anthropology achieved for the first and only time an agreed myth of the origin of human society, which accounted for the family and for religion, and represented both as contingent, irrational, but temporary constraints on the potentialities of civilized man. Totemism therefore served as a foundation myth of rationalism; yet at the same time it offered a symbolic idiom in which a poet could celebrate a more natural time, when man's spirit was at one with plants and birds and beasts, and mythical, poetic thought was commonplace, and sexual instincts uninhibited. It was the anthropologists' Garden of Eden. In contrast, the modern age was a waste land indeed.

The anthropologists nevertheless abandoned totemism. Soon even the established model of primitive society came under fire. There were some political considerations behind these shifts, which will be touched upon, but the most obvious structural correlate was institutional. The next generation of anthropologists became academics. Less ambitious than their predecessors to change the world, they were less affected by it. In academe they turned inwards, upon themselves, and, of course, upon one another.

PART II

Academic anthropologists and primitive society

CHAPTER 7

The Boasians and the critique of evolutionism

At the turn of the century, the increasingly dominant Anglo-American anthropology was challenged by a distinctive German ethnological tradition. The central issue was the validity of evolutionism. This engagement was fought out not in Europe but in the United States, where Boas and his students were ranged against the disciples of Lewis Henry Morgan. The United States was then on the periphery of the scientific world, and these transatlantic polemics were largely neglected in Europe. Yet the Boasian critique of evolutionism was enormously significant; and as American anthropology grew, so the Boasian critique became increasingly influential.

The impact of the Boasians within the United States was never doubted, but later American students did not always appreciate how deep were the German roots of Boas's anthropology. This was partly because Boas's career was such a very long one. Some of his best-known students – including Ruth Benedict and Margaret Mead – were part of a second generation, who came to him only after World War One, when he was already over sixty. By then the old battles had been won, and Boas's preoccupations had altered. I am concerned here with the earlier period and with Boas's most creative years, from the mid-1880s to the 1920s.

The German tradition

Franz Boas was born in Minden, Westphalia, in 1858.[1] (Durkheim

---

1 One of his students, Melville Herskovits (1953), published a rather conventional account of the man and his ideas, *Franz Boas: The Science of Man in the Making*. Modern biographies of Boas have been promised, but none has yet appeared.

was an exact contemporary, Freud two years older.) His family was fairly typical of the assimilated German Jewish middle-class of the time – prosperous, liberal and well educated. Boas himself later wrote[2]:

The background of my early thinking was a German home in which the ideals of the revolution of 1848 were a living force. My father, liberal, but not active in public affairs; my mother, idealistic, with a lively interest in public matters, the founder about 1854 of the kindergarten of my home town, devoted to science. My parents had broken through the shackles of dogma. My father had retained an emotional affection for the ceremonial of his parental home, without allowing it to influence his intellectual freedom.

As he grew up, Boas was torn between his respect for the natural sciences and the appeal of a more humanistic and 'emotional' study, his personal conflict mirroring the more general intellectual division in Germany between the positivists and subjectivists, the proponents of the natural sciences and the defenders of the humanities. In the end, 'My university studies were a compromise. On account of my intense emotional interest in the phenomena of the world, I studied geography; on account of my intellectual interest, I studied mathematics and physics'. But even his physics tended towards 'psychophysics'. His apprentice research involved the measurement of light intensities, which led him to consider the subjective elements in the measurement of sensations. Eventually he formulated the broad parameters of his personal project, which synthesized his major concerns. His aim was now 'to understand the relation betweeen the objective and the subjective worlds'.

After graduation and a period of military service, Boas spent the winter of 1882–3 in Berlin. Here he came under the influence of Adolf Bastian, the ethnologist, and the anatomist Rudolf Virchow, and he decided that the relationship between 'the objective and the subjective worlds' could be studied in some exotic field just as well – if not better – than in a psychological laboratory. Accordingly, 'by

---

There are, however, numerous articles and reminiscences, and Boas himself published a brief autobiographical sketch, reprinted in Stocking (1974), *A Franz Boas Reader*, under the title 'The background of my early thinking'. See also, Goldschmidt (1959), *The Anthropology of Franz Boas*, and some of the essays in Stocking (1968), *Race, Culture and Evolution*.

2 The quotations in this and the following paragraph come from Boas's autobiographical sketch, 'The background of my early thinking' in Stocking (1974).

a peculiar compromise presumably largely dictated by the desire to see the world, I decided to make a journey to the Arctic for the purpose of adding to our knowledge of unknown regions and of helping me to understand the reaction of the human mind to natural environment'. The expedition which he proposed was to go to Baffin Island to investigate the physical determinants of Eskimo migrations.

This plan was very much in the mode of the rather deterministic geography then current in Germany, and which continued a tradition going back to Humboldt.[3] The central issue was the relationship between natural environment and human mentality. Boas's immediate link with this tradition was through Bastian, with whom he was working in Berlin, and Bastian represented a reaction to the orthodox environmental determinism.[4] In an earlier generation the pioneer ethnologist Waitz had argued that man's intellectual capacity was uniform in all human populations, although secondary variations had developed as a consequence of historical accidents. Bastian pressed this notion further, writing of the 'psychic unity of mankind'. Not only were all human beings similarly endowed, all cultures could ultimately be reduced to the same basic mental principles, the *Elementargedanken*.[5] Local circumstances produced modifications in custom and organization, but the common principles of human mental operation could be identified everywhere.

Other geographers tended to give much more weight to environmental factors in intellectual and cultural development. There were, however, more and less radical environmentalists. Some

---

3 Boas's relationship to the tradition of German geography is helpfully discussed by Kluckhohn and Prufer in their essay (1959) 'Influences during the formative years' and by Speth in his (1978) 'The anthropogeographic theory of Franz Boas'. A good introduction to German geography can be found in Dickenson (1969), *The Makers of Modern Geography*.

4 On Bastian see Koepping (1983), *Adolf Bastian and the Psychic Unity of Mankind*.

5 Koepping asks whether Bastian actually identified any of these *Elementargedanken* operationally and the only instance he finds is a very vague notion of 'differentiation' based upon sexual complementarity, on age succession, and on the likelihood that neurotics will become prophets (*op cit.*, p. 37). Later he remarks:

It is true that we never find the 'core' or elementary ideas summarized in Bastian's works, but some good examples for the reconstruction of the elementary idea from diverse folk ideas are taken from material objects ... Bastian considers all tools and weapons of propulsion as an example of the underlying elementary idea of extending one's body and limbs externally, and this can lead to such diverse folk ideas – according to environmental conditions – as the bola, the lasso or spear-thrower. (*Op. cit.*, pp. 57–8)

favoured a form of environmental determinism. Others, like Ratzel, paid special attention to the history of contact and the diffusion of ideas, techniques and institutions. 'The fundamental theory of world-history,' as Ratzel once put it, 'is the history of migration'. Change and variation were to be explained with reference to migration.[6]

Except in their most extreme forms, these positions were not necessarily mutually exclusive, and even such leading protagonists as Bastian and Ratzel might sometimes adopt compromise formulations. Ratzel's textbook, *Völkerkunde*, published between 1885 and 1890, supported a rather strong environmentalist position. Bastian was himself willing to recognize the modifying influence of environment and diffusion, and indeed he developed the notion of the 'geographical province', a region defined both by environment and history, which should serve as a focus of ethnological research.

The central issue in all these theoretical tendencies was the role of the environment. Was man's culture and intellect shaped by his material environment? Alternatively, was the human environment decisive, migration the key to culture change? A similar question arose in the field of human biology in Germany, and there were virtually the same tensions between a purely physical, mechanistic form of explanation and a historical, particularist approach. It was assumed that the human body was liable to radical alterations as a result of environmental influences. Were these physical alone, or also cultural? Waitz had suggested that cultural variations were accidental and secondary, but he had nevertheless believed that once these variations were established they could feed back and influence fundamental mental capacities, eventually precipitating changes in head shape (for head shape was, he assumed, related to mental capacities). Virchow also argued that skull proportions were plastic traits, which could be influenced directly by environment, or indirectly by mental development.

Boas was sufficiently interested in this debate to follow it up in an early piece of research. When he settled in the USA he studied the head shapes of immigrants, coming to the conclusion that the head forms of American-born individuals changed 'almost immediately after the arrival of their parents in America'. The

6 Cited in *op cit.*, p. 62.

younger the age at which a child arrived in America the narrower his face was relative to that of his parents and older siblings. This was, Boas believed, a reflection of what was going on inside that narrower head. Changes in the mental constitution of the child skewed its skull-shape towards the white American mean. In more general terms, 'the mental make-up of a certain type of man may be considerably influenced by his social and geographical environment'.[7]

These questions had a special resonance because they were relevant to the debate on evolution. One of Virchow's students, Haeckel, had become Germany's leading advocate of Darwin, but Darwinian thought had never found general favour in German scientific circles. Moreover, the last decade of the nineteenth century witnessed a marked decline in support for Darwinian thinking. The temporary 'eclipse of Darwinism' (as Julian Huxley later called it) was accompanied by a revival of Lamarckism, which in turn favoured environmental determinism. Even moderate Lamarckians believed that environmental forces could precipitate rapid and enduring change in the organism, for which no basis existed in the germ plasm.[8] In consequence, there was an affinity between the Lamarckians and the geographical determinists.

Virchow[9] repudiated the ideas of Haeckel and made scathing attacks on the Darwinians, insisting on the range of historical variation in the development of biological forms. He rejected all forms of evolutionary determinism. His reiterated assaults upon

---

7 Boas's paper on this subject, 'Changes in bodily form of descendants of immigrants' (1912) – from which the quotations are taken – was his most substantial contribution to physical anthropology. The paper was reprinted in his collected essays (1940), *Race, Language and Culture*. See T. M. Tanner (1959), 'Boas's contributions to knowledge of human growth and form' for a discussion of his work in this field.

8 See Peter J. Bowler (1983), *The Eclipse of Darwinism*.

9 See Ackerknecht (1953), *Rudolf Virchow: Doctor, Statesman, Anthropologist*. Boas was as impressed by Virchow's liberal politics as by his science. He wrote a fulsome tribute to Virchow (reprinted in his *Race, Language and Culture* (1940)) and, as has been remarked by several commentators, his description of Virchow might have been applied to himself. He particularly emphasized Virchow's critical contributions. 'His critical judgment was so strong that, in an address delivered in the summer of 1900, he was even led to doubt the desirability of the strong preponderance of his influence upon current opinion' (Stocking (1974), *A Franz Boas Reader*, p. 41).

Haeckel's Darwinism was to provide the dialectical basis for Boas's later critique of evolutionism in anthropology.

Boas in America

Boas spent a year in Baffin Island engaged in perhaps the most intensive anthropological fieldwork which he was ever to undertake.[10] After his Alaskan expedition he returned to Germany via the United States. He was engaged to Marie Krackowizer, a woman of Austrian origin who had settled in New York. He also had an uncle in the city, Abraham Jacobi, an established figure in the intellectual life of New York. At this point he seriously considered making New York his home, largely because he was conscious of anti-Semitic forces in German academic life; but he responded to the urgings of his parents and rejoined Bastian at the ethnographic museum in Berlin. Here he prepared a report on his Baffin Island journey for his *habilitation* (the German university teacher's qualification). His thesis criticized the environmental determinist position.

In 1886 he returned to North America, and spent three months on the Northwest coast of Canada, where he began his life's main work, the ethnography of the Kwakiutl Indians and their neighbours. He then went back to New York, where he married his fiancée and found a job as geographical editor of *Science* magazine. Now began the protracted, lonely and often painful process of establishing a position for himself in American anthropology.

In the closing years of the nineteenth century the one significant concentration of anthropologists in the USA was at the Smithsonian Institution in Washington, which housed the Bureau of American Ethnology (BAE). Under the leadership of John Wesley Powell, the BAE organized the only substantial American research programme in anthropology.[11] A geologist by training, Powell was a strong advocate of Morgan's theories, and believed that the BAE's mission was to extend and complete Morgan's American researches. Powell recruited a number of enthnographers, and supervised the ethnographic exploration of large tracts of aboriginal North America. He was supported by the first curator of ethnology

---

10 See Boas's Baffin Island letter-diary, edited and translated by Cole (1983).
11 See Hinsley (1981), *Savages and Scientists: The Smithsonian Institution and the Development of American Anthropology, 1846–1910.*

at the Smithsonian museum, Otis T. Mason, who held office from 1884 to 1908. Mason shared Powell's theoretical orientation, and his museum exhibits were arranged to illustrate technological evolution and to bring out the underlying unity of man's development.

The Darwinian anthropology which reigned at the Smithsonian was, of course, unacceptable to Boas, the student of Virchow and Bastian. In 1887, the year after he had settled in the USA, he published an attack on the principles behind an exhibition of Eskimo artifacts which Mason had mounted. Mason, he complained, had arranged ethnographic objects as though they were specimens in a natural history collection, which could be sorted into genera and species. Objects from remote places were grouped together on purely typological grounds. The classification was then made to yield a theoretical conclusion: 'like causes produce like effects. Under the same stress and resources the same inventions will arise.' Man was everywhere essentially the same, and men everywhere would react in the same fashion, given the same external stimuli.

As against Mason, Boas insisted on the necessity of adopting a regional, cultural focus.

We have to study each ethnological specimen individually in its history and in its medium, and this is the important meaning of the 'geographical province' which is so frequently emphasized by A. Bastian ... we want a collection arranged according to tribes, in order to teach the peculiar style of each group.

More generally, he argued that 'classification is not explanation', and that, even if resemblances were found between institutions, this did not necessarily mean that similar causes were at work; sometimes 'unlike causes produce like effects'.

Powell and Mason both responded, Powell arguing that Boas's alternative was itself not viable. Tribal groups had undergone so many changes that a settled classification on ethnic grounds was impossible. He concluded that 'there is no science of ethnology, for the attempt to classify mankind in groups has failed on every hand ... The unity of mankind is the greatest induction of anthropology.'[12]

12 Boas's critique was published in *Science* in 1887 and is reprinted in Stocking (1974), *A Franz Boas Reader*, pp. 61–7. A good account of the debate can be found in Hinsley (1981), *Savages and Scientists*, pp. 98–100.

There were very few positions in anthropology outside the Smithsonian, but in 1889 Boas was given a post at the newly-founded Clark University. He stayed long enough to produce the first American PhD in anthropology, but he quarrelled with the University's founder and by 1892 he was unemployed once more. His prospects were bleak, but while Boas's theoretical ideas set him against the Smithsonian people, they won him an influential sympathizer at Harvard, in F. W. Putnam.[13]

A student of Agassiz, Putnam was also anti-Darwinian and inclined towards Lamarckism, and sceptical of the developmental schemes of the Smithsonian anthropologists. Just when Boas was looking for a new position, Putnam was made responsible for the anthropological section of the Chicago World Fair, and he appointed Boas his assistant. Both men expected this appointment to lead to a permanent position at the Field Museum which grew out of the Exposition, but the Smithsonian group secured the appointment of their protegé, Holmes.[14]

At the end of 1895 Putnam appointed Boas assistant curator at the American Museum of Natural History. Boas also began to teach at Columbia University, where he became a full professor in 1899. In 1905 he resigned his position at the Museum, and it was Columbia which at last provided the institutional base he had wanted, allowing him to begin training a new generation of American anthropologists. In 1899, when his position at Columbia was stabilized, he was already over forty.

Fieldwork

Boas's year in Baffin Island – and his subsequent period in Berlin – had seen him abandon environmental determinism and the study of Eskimo seasonal migration routes.[15] He was now interested in historical questions, one of them the relationship between the Eskimo and the North American Indians. This was not simply a

13 On Putnam see Joan Mark (1980), *Four Anthropologists*.
14 There is a good account of Holmes in Mark's *Four Anthropologists* (1980).
15 Stocking writes that

> The change [from environmental determinism] was not abrupt. It apparently took place only over the course of the two years after his return from Baffin-land as he worked through his materials for publication and as he attempted to establish himself professionally.

> He particularly stresses the influence of Bastian as Boas's supervisor (Stocking (1968), *Race, Culture and Evolution*, pp. 151–2).

change in subject-matter. He had come to believe that history was of primary importance in shaping the psychology of a people – history in Ratzel's sense, essentially the history of migration and contact. As he explained in 1887 to the Director of the Bureau of Ethnology,

the phenomena such as customs, traditions and migrations are far too complex in their origin, as to enable us to study their psychological causes without a thorough knowledge of their history. I concluded it necessary to see a people, among which historical facts are of greater influence than the surroundings and selected for this purpose Northwest America.[16]

After his first visit to the Northwest coast in 1886, Boas made five visits, each lasting several months, between 1888 and 1894.[17] He worked first under the direction of a British Association for the Advancement of Science Committee for the Study of the Northwest Tribes of Canada, under the remote but benevolent chairmanship of E. B. Tylor, and later with the support of the Bureau of American Ethnology. In 1897 Boas and Putnam persuaded Morris Jesup (the president of the Board of Trustees of the American Museum of Natural History) to support a large expedition to the North Pacific Coast which would determine whether the New World had been colonized by the movement of Siberian peoples across the Bering Strait. The 'Jesup Expedition' continued for five years, and involved the cooperation of American and Russian anthropologists. Boas directed the research, although he made only two field trips himself in this period. Even after World War One, Boas regularly visited the Northwest coast for fieldwork, and his publications on Kwakiutl ethnography eventually ran to over 5,000 printed pages.

Boas's fieldwork has been contrasted, to his detriment, with the participant observation of Malinowski. He did sometimes live on fairly intimate terms with the Kwakiutl, and he regularly attended ceremonies and public events, but his work lacked the directness, the personal involvement, which was later to become a distinguishing feature of anthropological fieldwork. Boas was perhaps not altogether satisfied with the nature of his own materials, and Lowie remarked that

16 In Stocking (1974), *A Franz Boas Reader*, p. 60.
17 *The Ethnography of Franz Boas* (1969), compiled and edited by Ronald Rohner, is an essential guide to Boas's field expeditions.

he was especially appreciative of men who had achieved what he never attempted – an intimate, yet authentic, picture of aboriginal life. I have hardly ever heard him speak with such veritable enthusiasm as when lauding Bogora's account of the Chukchi, Rasmussen's of the Eskimo, Turi's of the Lapps.[18]

Nevertheless, there were several good reasons for Boas's procedures.

In Boas's day the Northwest coast Indians were already by no means 'traditional' peoples. Involved in the wide-open frontier economy and society, and under constant political pressure, they were ambivalent about their cultural heritage, and deeply suspicious of white people. Certain ceremonies continued to be held – though in a radically different setting – but several, including the potlatch, were under threat from the authorities.

These factors may have helped to shape the course taken by Boas's fieldwork, but the guiding principles were also, at least in part, theoretical. Boas was especially concerned to capture the Kwakiutl view of the world and he considered it best to let the people speak for themselves, as directly as possible. In the German tradition, he believed that folktales offered a privileged point of access to the folk mentality, and that they even preserved layers of historical experience.

Boas's ethnographic procedures were very similar to those of other German ethnologists (though his ethnography was eventually far more extensive than that of any contemporary). They operated in the European tradition of Oriental studies or classical studies, the central aim being the compilation, annotation and translation of texts. His own ethnography consisted very largely of texts dictated to him in Kwakiutl or written out for him, often by his main informant George Hunt. These texts were generally published with an absolute minimum of scholarly apparatus, or even organization. Irving Goldman, who has reanalysed the Kwakiutl ethnography, commented that:

the Kwakiutl texts were not organized by Boas in conformity with traditional anthropological schedules ... each of the published volumes of text materials seems to have been assembled at random. For the most

18 Lowie (1947), 'Franz Boas', p. 311.

part, each text around a subject stands within the corpus of the entire work unconnected, unannotated, and uninterpreted for the reader.[19]

The austere research strategy was meant to expose the authentic mental processes of the Kwakiutl. It was also intended to provide materials for historical reconstructions. Boas believed that such specific local histories would demonstrate the crudity of evolutionist generalizations. Culture history was to provide the critical materials with which to puncture the pretensions of the evolutionist writers. Using Kwakiutl data he attacked the Morgan dogma that all societies progressed from a matrilineal to a patrilineal form of organization, and criticized the orthodox theory of totemism.

Totems and descent

In some of his early essays Boas endorsed the orthodox Anglo-American ideas about the evolution of marriage, descent and totemism.[20] In his first report to the British Association on his Northwest coast research he dealt with the classic issues, remarking that Frazerian animal totems were found among the Tlingit, Tsimshian and Heiltsuk (see Figure 7.1), but not among the Kwakiutl, although they were of the same linguistic stock as the Heiltsuk. The Kwakiutl had 'crests', however, and these were perhaps attenuated versions of totems. All these peoples – including the Kwakiutl – had legends which apparently accounted for the adoption of these totems by their ancestors. The totemic groups were matrilineal gentes, which were ordered into phratries (also named for animals).

To the south of this cluster, however, things were very different. There

the patriarchate prevails. The social organization of these tribes differs fundamentally from that of the northern group. We do not find a single clan that has, properly speaking, an animal for its totem; neither do the clans take their names from their crest, nor are there phratries. It seems as though the members of each gens were really kindred.[21]

---

19 Goldman (1980), 'Boas on the Kwakiutl', pp. 335–6.
20 See, for example, 'The aims of ethnology', a lecture given by Boas in 1888. He reprinted it in his *Race, Language and Culture* (1940), because he said that 'it illustrates my early views regarding ethnological problems' (p. 626, note).
21 Boas (1889), 'First general report on the Indians of British Columbia', p. 825.

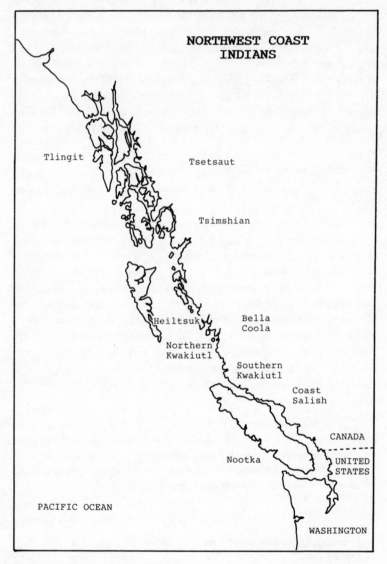

Figure 7.1 Northwest coast Indians.

Boas had worked especially among the Kwakiutl, who lived between these two clusters; and he suggested that they might represent an intermediate condition. Their marriage customs 'seem to show that originally matriarchate prevailed among them'. Before his marriage a man assumed his wife's father's name and crest, 'and thus becomes a member of his wife's clan'. His children take the same name and crest, but his sons lose them on marriage. 'Thus the descent of the crest is practically in the female line, every unmarried man having his mother's crest.'[22]

These general conclusions were repeated in his 1890 report: 'the tribes speaking the Heiltsuk and Gyimano-itq dialects are in the maternal stage, and are divided into gentes having animal totems; while the southern group are in the paternal stage, and are divided into gentes which have no animal crest'. In terms of this contrast, the Kwakiutl remained anomalous – or, at least, very puzzling. 'The social organisation of the Kwakiutl is very difficult to understand. It appears that, in consequence of wars and other events, the number and arrangement of tribes and gentes have undergone considerable changes.' The determination of group affiliation seemed particularly complex.

The child does not belong by birth to the gens of his father or mother, but may be made a member of any gens to which his father, mother, grandparents, or great-grandparents belonged. Generally, each child is a member of another gens.[23]

Although Boas did not draw that conclusion, it seems obvious that these new findings weakened his former claim that the Kwakiutl showed traces of 'matriarchy'. Were the Kwakiutl indeed really so fascinatingly transitional? In a report published in 1897, Boas reaffirmed the transitional status of the Kwakiutl, but he reversed their postulated historical transformation. The Kwakiutl were not in the process of moving from matriarchy to patriarchy, in the orthodox Morgan fashion. Rather, they were moving in the direction of matriarchy, from an original paternal form of organization. 'Matriarchy' was not a past but a future condition. Formerly the Kwakiutl had been organized in 'a series of village communities'.

22 *Op. cit.*, p. 829.
23 Boas (1890), 'Second general report on the Indians of British Columbia', pp. 604 and 609. Compare his subsequent report (1897), 'The social organization and the secret societies of the Kwakiutl Indians', especially pp. 332–3.

Descent had been traced in the paternal line, the members of each village being considered the descendants of a single ancestor. Later these communities had amalgamated to form tribes and lost their local identity, becoming dispersed and increasingly 'maternal' clans within the tribe.

The movement from patriliny to matriliny had two basic causes; the exigencies of the new tribal organization (though these were not specified), and diffusion from the northern, matrilineal tribes. One mechanism was the adoption of the northern, matriarchal legends legitimating the transmission of rank and privileges. The Kwakiutl arrangements were so complicated because they represented 'an adaptation of maternal laws by a tribe which was on a paternal stage'.[24]

The traces of this transition remained somewhat exiguous, though Boas identified one relic of the ancient system, the rule by which certain privileges, notably names and crests, were transmitted in the paternal line. However, he laid much store by the evidence of the legends, even if this was largely negative in character. The Kwakiutl must have been patriarchal originally, for otherwise in their legends 'the tribes would have been designated as the descendants of the ancestor's sisters, as is always the case in the legends of the northern tribes'.[25]

This was a noteworthy transformation (in Lévi-Strauss's sense). Boas had argued in 1890 that their legends and their system of transmitting crests showed the Kwakiutl to have been originally matriarchal and totemic, though they were so no longer. In 1897 he was using essentially the same evidence to argue that they had on the contrary been originally patriarchal, and were now in the process of becoming matriarchal.

To judge by Boas's own later writings, this new formulation was itself extremely dubious. In a paper published in the *American Anthropologist* in 1920[26] he abandoned all talk of totems, crests, gentes or clans as misleading, and provided instead an exegesis of the Kwakiutl concept *numaym*, a term which evidently referred less to any group than to a bundle of 'privileges' perpetuated by an intricate series of alternative rules of inter-generational trans-

---

24 Boas (1897), 'The social organization and secret societies of the Kwakiutl Indians', pp. 334–5.
25 *Op. cit.*, p. 335.
26 Boas (1920), 'The social organization of the Kwakiutl'.

mission and, at the higher levels of society, by endogamous marriage. In order to secure a privilege, a man had to have a claim to it through a parent or wife, but within these limits an office-holder could assign his privileges to one of a variety of possible candidates of different kinds. If a son-in-law succeeded, then the privilege was regarded as a return for the bridewealth which the son-in-law had paid. There was no evidence that the privilege was passed down a line of sons-in-law. Finally, the *numaym* did not have any communal property, and the crests had none of the attributes of totems.

One would have thought that this mature revision would have brought in its train a reconsideration of the historical trans-formation. Yet Boas reaffirmed his view that the complex system of transmitting privileges had been superimposed upon a simpler, paternal, village-based social system. However, he did qualify the claim that a paternal system had given way to a maternal system. His earlier formulation, he conceded, had been open to mis-interpretation. In a 'maternal' system, rights were transmitted from a mother's brother to a sister's son. Obviously, the Kwakiutl mode of transmission, from a father-in-law to a son-in-law, was very different.

The transformation in Boas's views owed little to new eth-nographic discoveries. At first he endorsed the orthodox expec-tation that societies moved from a matriarchal to a patriarchal form of organization. Later he claimed that the people of the Northwest coast – or at least the Kwakiutl – were moving in the opposite direction. But the evidence for both transformations was essentially the same – namely the curious system of succession, together with some deductions from the corpus of legends.

Since there was no new empirical evidence which supported the new hypothesis rather than the old, Boas's change of opinion may be attributed to other causes. One candidate is what might be termed tactical advantage. In his early and more orthodox days in America, Boas's research was financed by a British anthropological committee under the chairmanship of Tylor. It was for this body that his first reports were prepared. When he was appointed to Columbia he began to establish his own American base and became more boldly heterodox. He now turned again on the Establishment of American anthropology, the Bureau of Ethnology at the Smith-sonian Institution, and began a frontal attack on their ruling doctrine, which was Morgan's evolutionism.[27] His initial resources were his ethnographic materials from the Northwest coast and the arguments which Virchow had directed against the Darwinians. Soon he would add the support of his own cadre of students.

Columbia

Boas introduced the German intellectual tradition into American anthropology at Columbia University. The students who were first attracted to this exotic discipline in the United States at the beginning of the twentieth century were overwhelmingly of German extraction. Most of them had come to America as children, but their homes and schools in New York city were culturally German. Radin wrote of Lowie, for example, that:

The atmosphere in which he was raised in New York was a completely German one. All his parents' friends were Austrians, mainly Viennese, and Viennese German was the only language spoken in the home. To all intents and purposes, the United States was a foreign and somewhat shadowy land, with which one came into contact when leaving the house and with which one lost contact on reentering.

And he added that 'much of his inner life was concerned with German culture and cultural ideals', a fact which manifested itself 'in the direction of much of his scientific work – in the influence that Haeckel, Ostwald, and Wundt once had on him, and the influence which Boas and Mach had to the end of his life'.[28]

Almost the same has been said of Kroeber. His widow reported that 'German was Alfred's first language ... The elder Kroebers, like their relatives and friends, wanted their children to be bilingual. They particularly wanted them to know their Goethe, Heine and Schiller and to read Shakespeare first in German translation'.[29] Other members of Boas's entourage at Columbia were from a similar cultural background, notably Goldenweiser, Sapir, and Radin himself.

It made little difference that Kroeber came of a German and non-Jewish family, while most of the others were Jewish. Kroeber himself remarked that the Jewish and Gentile German families

27 See Hinsley (1981), *Savages and Scientists: The Smithsonian Institution and the Development of American Anthropology, 1846–1910*.

28 Radin (1958), 'Robert H. Lowie', p. 359.

29 Theodora Kroeber (1970), *Alfred Kroeber*, p. 12.

alike 'took it for granted that one did not believe in religion'.[30] The Ethical Culture movement provided for the spiritual needs of many German-speaking upper-middle-class families, Gentile and Jewish, in New York. Their schools also brought together Gentile and Jewish German-Americans. Kroeber was sent to Dr Sachs's Collegiate Institute, which was modelled on a European gymnasium. Four-fifths of the pupils were Jewish.[31] This was a transplanted version of the world in which Boas himself had grown up.

But while the German-speaking intellectuals of New York might be internally tolerant of religious and national differences, there was a definite element of ethnic confrontation in the relations between the Boasians and the WASP establishment at the Smithsonian. To this was added a political strain between the liberalism of the New Yorkers and the more conservative and nationalist attitudes which dominated the nation's capital. Boas claimed that the Spanish-American war of 1898 was his 'rude awakening' to the real nature of American politics, obliging him to recognize that his adopted country was 'dominated by the same desire of aggrandise-ment that sways the narrowly confined European states'.[32] His Establishment colleagues in Washington had no such reservations.

This is not to say that a break was inevitable between the Boasians and the Smithsonian people, on either intellectual or political grounds. Indeed relations remained correct enough for some years. In 1901 the BAE appointed Boas honorary philologist. Powell and Mason also accommodated ideas taken from regional, geographic German thinking. Powell's map of American Indian language groups (which provided the centre-piece of Mason's exhibit at the Chicago World Fair) would have been perfectly acceptable to any student of Bastian.

It is difficult to avoid the conclusion that Boas had decided that it was politically necessary to challenge the hegemony of the Smithsonian people. In 1904 an international conference was held at St Louis, and Boas was invited to deliver an address on the history of anthropology.[33] In his talk he represented the modern development of the discipline in terms of a struggle between two

30 *Op. cit.*, p. 26.
31 *Op. cit.*, p. 21.
32 Hinsley (1981), *Savages and Scientists*, p. 283.
33 This address is reprinted in Stocking (1974), *A Franz Boas Reader*, pp. 23ff.

opposed positions. On the one side were the universalists, who believed that cultural traits exhibited a remarkable uniformity all over the world. Two types of explanation were advanced to account for this phenomenon, one associated with Tylor (culture evolved along the same tracks in every part of the globe), the other with Bastian (there are certain universal 'elementary ideas' which recur in every culture). The alternative view was that cultural similarities were the consquence of borrowing. Historical research was required to resolve the issues, and Boas instanced studies in train of European folklore.

The striking feature of the lecture, in context, was not so much what was said as what was omitted. Boas's talk was studded with examples of research and with the names of distinguished anthropologists, but the audience was not informed that anything in American anthropology was worth the slightest consideration. As a modern commentator has remarked, Boas:

mentioned only one American anthropologist, Daniel G. Brinton, whom he called an 'extremist' in his support of independent invention of myths ... This paper ... dropped a whole generation of American anthropologists from the historical record. There was no mention of Lewis Henry Morgan, no mention of John Wesley Powell, William Henry Holmes, Frank Hamilton Cushing, Alice C. Fletcher, and others whose work at the Bureau of American Ethnology and elsewhere was arousing the admiration of European scholars, and no mention of the man to whom Boas owed so much, F. W. Putnam.[34]

Established now at Columbia with his own Europe-oriented students, Boas was effectively denying the significance of the American tradition of anthropology.

The critique of evolutionism

Boas's Columbia students were presented with two tasks. One was ethnographic and documentary. There were vast gaps in the knowledge of the North American Indians, and these had to be filled. The students were expected to combine research in linguistics, folklore, material culture and social organization. The final goal was to establish the local historical relations between aboriginal cultures. The second task was theoretical, or, rather, critical. The facts had to be allowed to speak for themselves, and to this end

34 Mark (1980), *Four Anthropologists*, p. 48.

cant had to be cleared away. In particular, the Boasians were determined to root out evolutionist schemas and crude natural-science classifications.

This critical empiricism fitted in with the general spirit of Columbia at the turn of the century. By 1900 the Darwinian tide had receded at Columbia, as it had somewhat earlier in the German universities. Lowie described the shock of this reorientation on the basis of his personal experience:

A Columbia student who from a boy had accepted Darwinism as a dogma, who had steeped himself as an undergraduate in Herbert Spencer's *First Principles* and hailed Ernst Haeckel's *Die Welträtsel* as a definitive solution of all cosmic enigmas, was profoundly disturbed when browsing in the departmental libraries of Schermerhorn Hall or talking to age-mates who majored in zoology. Bewildering judgments turned up in the new books and journals. For William James, Herbert Spencer was a 'vague writer', and in Pearson's opinion the British philosopher cut a sorry figure when using the terms of physics. Darwin himself, esteemed for his monographs, was not always taken seriously as a theorist. In the building where our student spent most of his time Thomas Hunt Morgan, a prophet of the new dispensation, held forth on the weaknesses of the Darwinian philosophy.[35]

But there was something bracing about this new scepticism.

The transports of delirious rapture were succeeded by the mood of the *Katzenjammer*. What had figured as the quintessence of scientific insight suddenly shrank into a farrago of dubious hypotheses. In short, sobriety reigned once more in professional circles.[36]

Boas's critique matched that of Lowie's other heroes, Mach, the empiricist philosopher, and the psychiatrist Adolf Meyer.

They were severely scrutinizing such blanket terms as 'schizophrenia', 'totemism', 'matter' and trying to discover their factual basis. When later I grappled with Schurtz's notion of 'age-society' and with L. H. Morgan's of 'classificatory terms of relationship', I more or less consciously applied the principles of these scientific thinkers. We had learned to view catchwords with suspicion.[37]

---

35 Lowie (1956), 'Reminiscences of anthropological currents in America half a century ago', p. 1005.
36 *Op. cit.*, pp. 1005–6.
37 *Op. cit.*, p. 1013.

From the point of view of the Boasians, Lewis Henry Morgan was the main source of error in American anthropology. Their critique of Morgan's theories was launched by one of Boas's first followers, John Reed Swanton. A rare WASP in this circle, Swanton came to work with Boas in 1900. He had studied with Putnam in Harvard, where he eventually submitted his doctoral thesis, but it was under Boas's direction that he undertook ethnographic work on the Northwest coast between 1900 and 1904. He then published three major critical reviews of Morgan's theories which appeared between 1904 and 1906.[38] These set out the views which Boas's students were to develop for the next twenty years. Swanton never again published any original theoretical work, and it seems plausible enough that although the hands were the hands of Esau, the voice was the voice of Jacob. Certainly Swanton later merged happily into the Smithsonian establishment. He was perhaps a *Parade-Goy*, a respectable American front for the subversive views of the immigrant Boasians. In any case, Swanton was effectively no more than a spokesman for a Columbia consensus, which derived from Boas.

Swanton's first paper simply extended the argument sketched by Boas in 1895. The Kwakiutl, originally patrilineal, were acculturating to the mainstream, matrilineal and totemic cultures of the Northwest coast, represented especially by the Tlingit, Haida and Tsimshian. He added little even at the level of ethnography to Boas's arguments, apart from some new material on Haida oral traditions. In a second paper he suggested that 'the curious phenomenon here presents itself of a loosely organized tribe changing to a gentile and afterwards to a clan system'.[39] This was in direct contradiction to the line of development postulated by Morgan. It illustrated rather the significance of diffusion in cultural convergence.

The evidence for classical totemism was also fragmentary and dubious. On the Northwest coast the crests were personal badges, not an essential feature of the clan structure. Even the kinship terminology could not be made to fit a Morgan model. If two female relatives were classified together, this need not be evidence

---

38 Swanton (1904), 'The development of the clan system and of secret societies'; (1905), 'The social organization of American tribes'; and (1906), 'A reconstruction of the theory of social organization'.
39 Swanton (1905), 'The social organization of American tribes', p. 671.

of some former system of marriage claims. Such a usage might equally well signal the possibility of future marriages. For instance, a man may call his wife's sister 'wife' because she can be claimed in marriage if her sister dies.

Swanton also attacked the 'catchwords' of the evolutionists (to borrow Lowie's term of denigration). Exogamous, totemic clans were not like natural species; they were merely shaky hypothetical constructs.

Thus we can conceive of descent as reckoned through the mother without the existence of clans, of a clan system in which the clans are without totems, and of one in which, while totems exist, there are no special tabus, names, or ties accompanying them.[40]

Moreover, unilineal descent was not exclusive: 'the authority of the clan has been greatly exaggerated and the power and importance of the father's clan placed at a too low value'.[41]

Finally, Swanton argued that patrilineal societies rarely showed traces of previous matrilineal institutions. Moreover, they often seemed to be at a lower general level of development than matrilineal peoples.[42]

These arguments were elaborated by other students of Boas. Kroeber (Boas's first Columbia PhD) began with the issue of the classificatory kinship terminology, the foundation of Morgan's edifice. He argued that Morgan's opposition between classificatory and descriptive types of kinship system was crude. One should penetrate beyond the terms and the relationships they designed to the 'principles or categories of relationship which underlie these'. There were eight such priniciples – *Elementargedanken* he might have said – such as generation, lineality and collaterality, age, sex and so forth.[43] The differences between kinship terminologies arose

---

40 *Op. cit.*, p. 664.
41 *Op. cit.*, p. 667.
42 *Op. cit.*, passim.
43 Kroeber's eight categories were:

1 The difference between persons of the same and of separate generations ...
2 The difference between lineal and collateral relationship ...
3 Difference of age within one generation ...
4 The sex of the relative ...
5 The sex of the speaker ...
6 The sex of the person through whom relationship exists ...
7 The distinction of blood relatives from connections by marriage ...
8 The condition of life of the person through whom the relationship exists (... the person

because some did not use all the eight principles, and because in different systems various of the principles were weighted differently.

The crucial argument, however, was that there seemed to be no sociological basis for these variations.

The causes which determine the formation, choice, and similarities of terms of relationship are primarily linguistic. Whenever it is desired to regard terms of relationship as due to sociological causes and as indicative of social conditions, the burden of proof must be entirely with the propounder of such views.[44]

Morgan was not the only enemy. The theory of totemism was also ripe for deconstruction. In a lecture delivered at Clark University in 1909 (to an audience which included Sigmund Freud), Boas argued that totemism was 'not a single psychological problem, but embraces the most diverse psychological elements'. Moreover, 'the anthropological phenomena, which are in outward appearances alike, are, psychologically speaking, entirely distinct, and . . . consequently psychological laws covering all of them can not be deduced from them'.[45] Goldenweiser took this up as his major theme, elaborating a critique of totemism which followed the familiar Boasian lines – it was not a unified institution, but a construct, whose elements might, and indeed often did, occur independently of each other.[46]

New field studies fed the critique. Frank Speck published studies of Algonkian social organization which showed that these simple hunter-gatherers were ordered into a series of nuclear families, and that family groups controlled specific territories.[47] This was, of course, in direct contradiction to the Morgan dogma that the most primitive peoples – by definition hunters and gatherers – were organized into matrilineal hordes without property rights.

Kroeber's monograph 'Zuni kin and clan', which appeared in 1919, was an exceptionally powerful ethnographic critique of the orthodox model of primitive social structure. His target was Cush-

---

serving as the bond of relationship may be alive or dead, married or no longer married). (Kroeber (1909), 'Classificatory systems of relationship', pp. 78–9)

44 *Op. cit.*, pp. 78 and 83.
45 Stocking (1974), *A Franz Boas Reader*, p. 246.
46 Goldenweiser (1910), 'Totemism, an analytical study'.
47 Speck published two essays on the family hunting band among the Algonkian in 1915.

ing's description of Zuni as a classic matrilineal society. Kroeber insisted that the individual Zuni was attached to his father's and his mother's people in much the same way. The matrilineal clans had ritual functions, but they hardly affected the individual in his or her daily affairs. They were 'only an ornamental excrescence upon Zuni society, whose warp is the family of actual blood relations and whose woof is the house'.[48] The clans were not localized. Indeed, the only social basis for matrilineal institutions was the fact that the house was transmitted from mother to daughter.

Had the Zuni perhaps once been more matrilineal? Were some of their institutions the relics of a more thoroughgoing ancient matriarchate? This sort of speculation was completely unacceptable.

It is clear that once this method of interpretation is adopted, it can be eternally applied without let or hindrance. Every irregularity, every subsidiary feature even, can be construed as a survival, and every survival as evidence of a former different plan.[49]

The clan model simply did not apply to the Zuni, and probably never had. The reality had been distorted as a consequence of theoretical bias:

it grew the fashion often to look only for clans, and to overlook actual family life, among nations whose society after all conforms in many respects to ours. I venture to believe that in many another totemic and clan-divided tribe the family of true blood-relatives is fundamental.[50]

By the outbreak of World War One the critique of evolutionist anthropology had essentially been accomplished. Lowie's books summed up the results for the general public. He proved to have a useful gift for readable synthesis, and he developed the Boasian critique with a wealth of illustration, dealing in particular with the evolution of the sib, the gens and the state.[51] New schools of anthropology were established in other universities, and were

---

48 Kroeber (1919), 'Zuni kin and clan', p. 49.
49 *Op. cit.*, p. 187.
50 *Op. cit.*, p. 49.
51 See especially Lowie's 'Social organization' (1914); 'Exogamy and the classificatory systems of relationship' (1915); *Primitive Society* (1920); and *The Origin of the State* (1927).

staffed by Boasians – Kroeber and Lowie going to Berkeley, and Speck to Philadelphia. The gospel spread quickly.

Yet the very triumph of the Boasian critique left it vulnerable to the charge that it was merely destructive and that it offered no positive new theory to replace the old orthodoxy. Reviewing Lowie's *Primitive Society*, Kroeber tempered his praise with the observation that 'As long as we continue offering the world only reconstructions of specific detail, and consistently show a negativistic attitude towards broader conclusions, the world will find very little of profit in ethnology. People do want to know why'.[52] But this negativism was inherent in the Boasian project. Critical arguments and empirical findings were marshalled in the first instance to attack false science. As Roman Jakobson was to remark, with affectionate irony, had it fallen to Boas to announce the discovery of America he would have begun by saying that the hypothesis that there was an alternative route to India had been disproved. Then he would incidentally report what was known about the new part of the world.[53]

Patriots and immigrants

The intellectual triumph of the Boasians was marred by a final, embittered political conflict with the Smithsonian anthropologists. During World War One Boas and his circle were pro-German or neutral. The director of the BAE, Holmes, a long-standing rival of Boas, led a nationalistic group of scientists in Washington, who were strongly committed to the Allied cause. In 1917 Holmes became chairman of the anthropology committee in the National Research Council, a grouping of scientists founded the previous year to advise the government on its war effort. It transpired that some of his associates were even more actively engaged with the American armed forces. Sylvanus G. Morley, a protegé of Holmes, spent part of the war gathering information for Naval Intelligence under cover of doing archaeological work in Central America. This incident provided the occasion for the final confrontation between Boas and Holmes, whose enmity dated back at least to the time of

---

52 Kroeber (1920), review of Lowie's *Primitive Society*, p. 380.
53 Jakobson (1944), 'Franz Boas's approach to language', p. 194.

the Chicago Fair, when Holmes had been given the position at the Field Museum on which Boas had been counting.[54]

In 1919 Boas wrote a letter to *The Nation* denouncing men who 'have prostituted science by using it as a cover for their activities as spies'.[55] Holmes reacted vituperatively, writing to an associate about 'the traiterous article by Boas', anathemizing 'Prussian control of Anthropology in this country' and demanding an end to 'the Hun regime'.[56] Boas was censured at the next meeting of the American Anthropological Association and, although a former president of the Association, he narrowly escaped expulsion. But Boas's students had by now established themselves in a number of university departments, and were quickly able to reimpose Boasian control of the institutions of American anthropology. In 1920 Holmes became first Director of the National Gallery of Art and moved out of anthropology. Hostility towards the foreign-born and largely Jewish anthropologists continued to fester for many years, however, and can be clearly discerned in the polemics of Leslie White, who tried much later to mount a Morgan revival.[57]

Boas the theorist

I have not discussed the linguistic researches of Boas, Sapir and Kroeber, and have totally neglected Boas's work on mythology, art and religion. My treatment of Boas and the Boasians has necessarily been shaped by the theme of this book; but the whole body of Boas's work was informed by philosophical themes and methodological concerns which derived largely from his German education, and which gives his anthropology a certain unity despite the diversity of his preoccupations.

Boasian anthropology was clearly an expression of the German ethnological tradition. It had a close affinity with the contemporary work of Bastian's German students. Frobenius might have been too much a romantic, his sweep too ambitious for the austere Boasians, but they were forced to recognize how much they shared with other German ethnographers. In 1905 they were startled to read papers published in Berlin by two young scholars at the

---

54 Stocking provides a detailed account of this crisis. See his *Race, Culture and Evolution* (1968), Chapter 11.
55 Stocking (1974), *A Franz Boas Reader*, p. 336.
56 Mark (1980), *Four Anthropologists*, pp. 161–2.
57 White (1966), *The Social Organization of Ethnological Theory.*

ethnological museum, Graebner and Ankermann, which could have come from within their own circle.[58]

And yet, as Boas would immediately have granted, migration had also left its mark. In America he was confronted with the Morgan tradition, finding in it a distinctive focus for the anti-evolutionist arguments he derived from Virchow. His polemics with the Smithsonian anthropologists were also to be sharpened by iedological differences, and by rivalry for jobs and influence.

I have represented Boas as above all a theorist. Admittedly his rhetoric was fiercely empiricist. (He once told a graduate student that 'there are two kinds of people: those who have to have general conceptions into which to fit the facts; those who find the facts sufficient. I belong to the latter category'.[59]) None the less it was his theory – in the guise of a critique of theory – rather than his ethnography which provided the basis for his influence. He gave priority to ethnographic data in the rawest form, and his critique of established theory was generally illustrated by ethnographic examples, often taken from the Kwakiutl. Yet the theoretical impulse behind the critique was obviously more powerful than the empirical support which he might be able to conjure up for it. Even within his own universe of discourse, the empirical evidence could be made to support contradictory conclusions, as can be seen in his shifts on the question of Kwakiutl social evolution, or the presence or absence of totems.

The scepticism which Boas conveyed to his students, together with his demand for empirical research, did provide a remarkably powerful impetus. The best work of the Boasians combined ethnographic sensitivity and theoretical relevance, although, as Kroeber for one admitted, the final product might be unnervingly negative in tone.

But, as Kroeber also remarked, people did still want to know why, and the demolition of the Anglo-American orthodoxies left many dissatisfied. In the 1920s and 1930s a new generation of Boasians developed a theory of cultural determinism, partly to fill the void left by the destruction of the old theories, partly in reaction to the growing popularity of eugenics, biological reductionism and

---

58 See the papers by Ankermann and Graebner (1905) in the *Zeitschrift für Ethnologie*, 37.
59 Cited by Kluckhohn and Prufer (1959), 'Influences during the formative years', p. 22.

behaviourism. (The new generation of Boasians was also influenced by psychoanalysis – as were some of the older generation, Kroeber, for example, becoming a lay analyst.) Later, when the growing threat of European Fascism and racist theories was recognized, the Boasians concentrated their energies for an assault on an old enemy in a new guise. Boas's own commitment never flagged. In 1942 at the age of eighty-five he was addressing colleagues at the Columbia Faculty Club on the question of racism when he had a sudden heart-attack and fell, dying, into the arms of the man sitting next to him, who was Claude Lévi-Strauss.

CHAPTER 8

Rivers and Melanesian society

Boas's rejection of evolutionism – and of Morgan – were almost inevitable given his German training and the structure of American anthropology. In Britain, however, the new generation of anthropologists carried on from the old. It was only in the second decade of the new century that German diffusionist ideas began to undermine the orthodox evolutionism of the British school. Yet in one important respect the leading figures of the new generation did differ decisively from their predecessors. They were natural scientists rather than classicists or lawyers. Of course, Baldwin Spencer had also been a natural scientist, so perhaps it is more accurate to say that in the new generation a natural science tradition took over at the centre. The consequence was that theory and fieldwork began to be developed as a single procedure, carried out by one individual. And at the same time the physical centre of the discipline moved to the heartland of the natural sciences, the University of Cambridge.

Rivers and Haddon

The founders of the Cambridge school of anthropology were W. H. R. Rivers and Alfred Cort Haddon. In Cambridge they introduced the first undergraduate courses in anthropology in the United Kingdom and built up the first graduate school.

Both men arrived at Cambridge in 1893, to take up insecure and marginal appointments in the natural sciences. Both moved into ethnology, but they always regarded it as a rather undeveloped branch of the natural sciences, sorely in need of better methods – scientific methods. Rivers once expressed their ambitions in uncharacteristically melodramatic fashion, when he told his student

Layard that he hoped his tombstone would bear the inscription, 'He made ethnology a science'.[1]

Rivers[2] died young and was in any case also professionally active for some years in physiological psychology and later in psychiatry. His career in anthropology was consequently a short one, beginning with the Torres Straits expedition in 1898, and stretching effectively only until the publication of his masterpiece, *The History of Melanesian Society*, in 1914. If he ever was a professional social anthropologist, it was only between the ages of thirty-four and fifty. Yet despite the brevity of his career Rivers did become the dominant European anthropologist of his generation.

Born in 1864 into an old Kent family ('solidly middle-class, with Cambridge, Church of England, and Royal Navy associations'[3]), Rivers studied medicine at St Bartholomew's Hospital in London, graduating in 1886 and taking an MD in 1888. Here he began to work on problems of neurology under John Hughlings Jackson, together with Henry Head and Charles Sherrington. Hughlings Jackson was a devotee of Spencer. He propagated an hierarchical view of the structure of the nervous system, which was conceived in almost geological terms as a series of strata deposited at different periods of evolutionary history. This conception was to inform Rivers' neurological work, including his famous experiment with Henry Head between 1903 and 1907 on the peripheral sensory mechanism. When he moved to Cambridge in 1893 it was to lecture on the physiology of the sense organs. His position remained insecure until his appointment to a new Lectureship in Physiological and Experimental Psychology in 1897.

Alfred Cort Haddon,[4] nearly ten years older than Rivers, also arrived in Cambridge in 1893, and in rather similar circumstances. He had been an undergraduate in Cambridge and gone on to Dublin as Professor of Zoology at the Royal College of Science. There he had found himself obliged to lecture on tropical fauna

1 The dedication of Layard's (1942) *Stone Men of Malekula* reads: 'To the memory of Dr. W. H. Rivers who once told me that he would like to have inscribed on his tombstone the words, "he made ethnology a science".'
2 Accounts of Rivers' life can be found in Langham's (1981) *The Building of British Social Anthropology* and in Slobodin's (1978) *W. H. R. Rivers*.
3 Slobodin (1978), *Rivers*, p. 3.
4 For Haddon's career see Quiggin (1942), *Haddon the Head-Hunter* and Urry (1982), 'From zoology to ethnology: A. C. Haddon's conversion to anthropology'.

and coral reefs, which he had never seen ('retailing second-hand goods over the counter', as he described it[5]). With the encouragement of T. H. Huxley he decided to remedy matters by doing fieldwork in the tropics, and settled on the Torres Straits (between Australia and New Guinea). In the summer of 1888 he made his first expedition, and while he was in the Pacific he collected ethnological as well as natural history specimens to sell to museums in order to help meet his expenses. This fostered an interest in local traditions, and on his return he published two ethnological papers which were praised by Frazer. He decided to concentrate in future on ethnology, a decision which made him prepared to accept an insecure position with a very small income in Cambridge.

His mentor, T. H. Huxley, sent him a kindly warning

I admire Mrs Haddon's and your pluck immensely, but after all you know there is an irreducible *minimum* of bread and butter the need of which is patent to a physiologist if not to a morphologist and I declare with sorrow that at this present writing I do not see any way by which a devotee of anthropology is to come at the bread – let alone the butter.[6]

Mrs Haddon remarked that 'You might as well starve as an anthropologist as a zoologist',[7] but in the event Haddon hung on to his post in Dublin, commuting from Cambridge. In these precarious years he used his organizational skills to mount the Cambridge Anthropological Expedition to the Torres Straits and New Guinea, which took place in 1898–9. Shortly after the expedition returned, Haddon was appointed to a new Lectureship in Ethnology at the University. In the following year he was elected to a fellowship at Christ's.

The Torres Straits expedition

The Torres Straits expedition was contemporary with Boas's Jesup expedition, but where Boas had a large subvention and recruited American and Russian scientists, Haddon's expedition was very much a shoestring, Cambridge affair. Its members were drawn in the first instance from among the students to whom Haddon and Rivers were lecturing in anatomy and physiology. Rivers himself

5 Quiggin (1942), *Haddon the Head-Hunter*, p. 77.
6 *Op. cit.*, p. 94.
7 *Op. cit.*, p. 115.

was not initially enthusiastic, but C. S. Myers and William McDougall joined up and, as Haddon later put it:

When Rivers found that his two best students were going he asked whether after all he might come too. Naturally I was very much pleased at this though I own that I felt that the psychological side was rather overweighted. I put the direction of the psychological department entirely into the hands of Rivers and for the first time psychological observations were made on a backward people in their own country by trained psychologists with adequate equipment.[8]

Certainly the 'psychologists' predominated, although a linguist, S. H. Ray (who taught arithmetic in a London elementary school) was recruited on the recommendation of Codrington, and two volunteers signed up, C. G. Seligmann, a pathologist who was a friend of Myers, and Anthony Wilkin, a King's undergraduate, who joined as a photographer and made a speciality of material culture.

Most of the research was carried out in five weeks in September and October 1898 on the island of Mabuiag. Rivers did make some influential psychological experiments, but notwithstanding Haddon's anxieties and despite the provenance of the recruits, the expedition turned out to be concerned as much with 'sociological' as with 'psychological' questions. Haddon subsequently claimed that he had been the decisive influence on Rivers, remarking that 'One of the things of which I am most proud in a somewhat long life is that I was the means of seducing Rivers from the path of virtue ... (for Psychology was then a chaste science) ... into that of Anthropology.[9] For the next sixteen years Rivers was to work on problems of primitive social structure, although even during this period he kept up other professional commitments.

The theoretical models which Rivers and Haddon took into the field can be reconstructed without difficulty. Rivers referred ultimately to Morgan's theory and to commentaries on it, especially Köhler's, but he was clearly most directly influenced by recent British research on the Australian aborigines, particularly the work of Fison and Howitt, and by Tylor's and Frazer's reflections on this work.

The model of primitive social structure current among the few

8 *Op. cit.*, p. 97.
9 *Op cit.*, p. 97, note.

specialists in Britain at the turn of the century can be summarized as follows.

Originally there may or may not have been a period of promiscuity (this was one of the few issues on which the experts were seriously divided). At a very early stage of human social evolution, however, sibling incest was banned and groups of brothers exchanged their sisters with other groups of brothers. Each set of brothers held its wives in common. At it simplest, there were only two such groups. According to Fison, this was the classic Australian system. It was generally assumed that relationships between mothers and children were given special recognition at an early stage, so that an element of matrilineal descent was present in even very primitive societies. The system also unfolded in time. Fison and Tylor pointed out that dual organization could be perpetuated by means of systematic marriage between children of siblings of opposite sex, for whom Tylor invented the term 'cross-cousins'.

Fison had introduced the idea that in Australia the primitive matrilineal dual organization was refined by the introduction of a generation division in each moiety, which yielded four marriage 'classes'. Gradually, more exogamous units developed through fission. At some stage paternity was recognized and a system of patrilineal clans developed. Finally the family-based system replaced the old gentile systems.

The basic tenet of Morgan's methodology was also accepted. Traces of primeval social systems could be found in contemporary kinship terminologies. All the ancient systems were 'classificatory', all the modern, family-based systems 'descriptive'. Methodologically, this was a crucial assumption, since the main evidence for the ancient systems came from 'survivals' in contemporary exotic kinship terminologies.

Finally, although Tylor was already sceptical, it was quite generally believed that the organization of society into exogamous matrilineal descent groups was associated with a specific religion, 'totemism'.

The main competing view was that of McLennan, who denied the significance generally attached to the kinship terminologies. His own alternative model of social evolution had few influential adherents by the end of the nineteenth century but at least one friend of Rivers, Arthur Hocart, shared McLennan's scepticism about the value of kinship terminologies. Rivers, however, seemed to have had no doubts on this score.

Rivers' main ethnological contributions to the report of the Torres Straits expedition cover genealogies, kinship, personal names and (with Haddon) totemism. In keeping with the natural science conception of the expedition, he stressed especially his methodological contribution to these fields; above all, his invention of the 'genealogical method'.[10] Genealogies or pedigrees provided a powerful tool with a variety of uses, but above all they allowed the scientist to record with a new precision the crucial data – terms for kinsmen – which permitted the reconstruction of the social structure.

Nor were the kinship terms merely fossils, devoid of any contemporary significance. On the contrary, the terms regulated etiquette and even entailed norms of behaviour.

While going over the various names which one man would apply to others, I was occasionally told that such and such a man would stop a fight, another would bury a dead man, and so on. When the clues given by these occasional remarks were followed up, it was found that there were certain very definite duties and privileges attached to certain bonds of kinship.[11]

Indeed the system of kin terms 'has a still more important place in the community in that it is the means of regulating marriage'.[12] This was evident from the way in which the terminology classified certain relatives together in a manner which 'would be a necessary result of the Australian and Fijian custom which Tylor has called "cross-cousin marriage", in which the children of brother and sister marry one another'.[13] For example, if a mother's brother is termed 'father-in-law', this is because a man has a claim to marry his mother's brother's daughter.

The model was clear enough, but the data proved to be recalcitrant. Rivers noted that the people of Mabuiag did not in fact go in for cross-cousin marriage (though there were cases of sister-exchange), nor did they show any traces of a system of marriage classes or even of definitely exogamous clans. He and Haddon did claim that there were 'clans' which inherited totems in the male line, but there were problems here too.

---

10 Rivers (1910), 'The genealogical method of anthropological enquiry'.
11 Rivers (1904), *Report of the Torres Straits Expedition*, p. 144.
12 *Op. cit.*, p. 151.
13 *Op. cit.*, p. 141.

There was no doubt that there was considerable confusion in the minds of the Mabuiag people on the subject of their rules of descent, and about two years before our visit the men had a great talk about the totems and had agreed to allow some children to take the totem of the mother, but we do not know of any instance since that time in which this has taken place.[14]

The genealogies provided no clear evidence to show that 'clan' membership affected the pattern of marriage, and there were even cases of marriage between persons with the same 'totem' (although Rivers decided that the persons concerned must have come from clans which had split).

Given this divergence between model and data, Rivers concluded that the Torres Straits people no longer practised group marriage. Their marriages were 'regulated by kinship rather than by clanship'.[15] Marriage had become an individual rather than a class matter. The rules of exogamy now referred to specific categories of consanguines, traced genealogically, where at an earlier stage they had imposed blanket prohibitions on all members of a clan. None the less, 'the system of kinship' (by which Rivers meant no more than the terminological system) 'was of fundamental importance and determined to a large extent the relations of individuals to one another'.[16] The research tradition established by Morgan was therefore vindicated, the criticism of McLennan undermined.

'The Todas'

In a subsequent field-study, of the Todas in South India with whom he spent some months in 1901–2, Rivers again found a 'primitive society' without exogamous clan groups. Marriage restrictions referred to a category of *puliol*, a broad category embracing many non-clansmen. Indeed, Rivers confessed that 'it seemed to me in several cases as if it came almost as a new idea to some of the Todas that his *puliol* included all the people of his own clan'. He concluded 'that the Todas recognise the blood-kinship as the restrictive agency rather than the bond produced by membership of the same clan'.[17] Cross-cousins were, however, frequently married (and Rivers provided statistics to prove this). 'Thus it is obviously

14 *Op. cit.*, p. 160.
15 *Op. cit.*, p. 177.
16 *Op. cit.*, p. 151.
17 Rivers (1906), *The Todas*, pp. 509–10.

not nearness of blood-kinship which in itself acts as a restriction on marriage, but nearness of blood-kinship of a certain kind.'[18] Marriage was regulated by individual genealogical constraints, and particular marriages were strongly influenced by material considerations relating to inheritance.

Yet while Rivers conceded that clans did not regulate marriage, he tried to define a system of Toda 'clans'. However, paternity was a vague matter among the Todas, and the status of the putative patrilineal 'clans' was so uncertain that their neighbours – and previous ethnographers – had supposed them to have a 'five-clan' structure, which Rivers discovered to be a total fabrication. He concluded that neither the 'clan' nor the 'family' was a central Toda institution and that their 'state of social evolution' was 'intermediate' between a clan-based and family-based system.[19]

Relationship systems

The emphasis which Rivers placed on methodological issues was never intended to minimize the central importance of theory. The status of kinship terminologies was significant because they were the golden key to the recovery of ancient social structures. And these structures were vital as clues to man's social evolution.

In general, then, he accepted Morgan's theory, but he was obliged to recognize that it was under siege from various directions. In 1907 he explicitly addressed these questions for the first time in his contribution to Tylor's *Festschrift*.[20] He noted that Starcke, Westermarck, Crawley, Lang and Thomas had attacked the idea of primitive promiscuity. He accepted this criticism,[21] but urged that, for the rest, Morgan's system was supported by the evidence. If a group of brothers did indeed marry collectively a group of sisters (which is what Rivers took 'group marriage' to mean), then

---

18 *Op. cit.*, p. 541.
19 *Op. cit.*, p. 541.
20 Rivers (1907), 'On the origin of the classificatory system of relationships'.
21 Rivers even added a new argument in support of the critics. Morgan's evidence for an original condition of primitive promiscuity depended upon an interpretation of the 'Malayan' terminology. Rivers argued that many relatively advanced peoples had terminologies of this sort, while the most apparently primitive peoples did not. Simplification of terminological distinctions appeared, if anything, to be a mark of sophistication. Consequently one could not assume that 'Malayan' terminologies were the fossils of the most primitive systems of social organization.

father's brothers would be merged with 'father', mother's sisters with 'mother', and their children with one's own brothers and sisters. Mother's brothers, father's sisters and cross-cousins would be distinguished. Many systems of kinship terminology had these features, attesting to the prior existence of systems of group marriage.

If this argument was correct, then kinship terms might signify group membership rather than positions in a genealogy. Rivers accordingly preferred to write about 'relationship systems'. In his jargon, relationship terms referred to 'status', that is, group membership, rather than to genealogically-defined 'kinship'. Admittedly he had discovered that even in the Torres Straits people used relationship terms to refer to genealogical position rather than to clan membership or 'status'. He thought this was probably true even in Australia today, but was simply an index of the progress these peoples had made from the original system of group marriage.

But there was also another, more insidious, assault being mounted on Morgan in the United States, and quite soon Rivers was obliged to take note of it. It is evident that he was not aware of the whole sweep of the Boasian critique, or of its historical roots, but he was so impressed by one prong of the argument that he devoted a series of lectures at the London School of Economics in 1913 to refuting it.[22] This was the point of view which he associated with Kroeber, that relationship terms were psychologically rather than sociologically determined.[23] Rivers wrote that 'the paper of Professor Kroeber is only the explicit and clear statement of an attitude which is implicit in the work of nearly all, if not all, the opponents of Morgan since McLennan'.[24]

Precisely what he – or Kroeber – meant by 'psychological explanations' in this context is far from clear, but broadly this was a label for a variety of possible non-realist theories of semantics. Things were grouped together under one label not because they were objectively similar but because they somehow felt similar or

22 The lectures were published in 1914 under the title *Kinship and Social Organization*.

23 The paper in which Kroeber proposed this view was entitled 'Classificatory systems of relationship', and was published in 1909. For a valuable discussion of this controversy see Schneider (1968), 'Rivers and Kroeber in the study of kinship'.

24 Rivers (1914a), *Kinship and Social Organisation*, p. 95.

because they were united by the internal logic of the system of classification itself. Kroeber seemed to incline to the latter option – systems of classification of kin had an inner logic. They represented alternative combinations of universal semantic principles. Rivers sometimes understood Kroeber to be taking another position, more obviously 'psychological', that if relatives were grouped together into one category it was because one felt the same emotions for them all. Either hypothesis was diametrically opposed to that upon which Rivers had based his own methods, and his lectures met this new challenge head on. As he said, 'the object of these lectures is to show how the various features of the classificatory system have arisen out of, and can therefore be explained historically by, social facts'.[25] The relevant 'social facts' – or, as he also called them, 'social rights'[26] – were obligations and claims between persons, of which the most important were claims to a wife.

The demonstration took the form of establishing that relationship terms and marriage rules covaried. The best-attested example concerned societies in which cross-cousin marriage was practised. Here one might find that mother's brother is equated terminologically with wife's father, his wife with wife's mother, and so forth; which is what one would expect if a man was indeed required to marry his mother's brother's daughter. These correlations could be shown in parts of the Pacific – in Fiji, for example, or the southern New Hebrides. Now one might argue that people in some societies feel the same emotions towards a mother's brother as to a wife's father, and that this would explain why they are classified together. Rivers argued that, on the contrary, any such psychological identification would be a consequence of the social facts. 'If it were not for the cross-cousin marriage, what can there be to give the mother's brother a greater psychological similarity to the father-in-law than the father's brother?'[27]

Rivers then extended the argument, borrowing heavily from Köhler's ingenious elaboration of Morgan, which had been published in German in 1897.[28] Köhler had drawn attention to two variant forms of the 'classificatory type of terminology' which he

25 *Op. cit.*, p. 40.
26 *Op. cit.*, p. 47.
27 *Op. cit.*, pp. 52–3.
28 See Köhler (1897), *On the Prehistory of Marriage*.

named after American Indian tribes, the Omaha and the Choctaw (nowadays the 'Crow' type). These types are characterized by what we now call the 'skewing' of generations. In some systems, for example, one cousin may be termed 'father', while another cousin might be termed 'son'.

What was the logical basis of such bizarre classifications? Fison and Tylor had argued that the Australian and 'Dravidian' terminologies were consistent with a system of cross-cousin marriage or sister-exchange. Köhler argued that the Omaha and Choctaw systems of classification reflected different forms of group marriage. Where kin of different generation were classified together this was because intergenerational marriage was practised. In the Omaha version 'a man also marries his wife's aunt and niece', and in the Choctaw version 'a woman marries both her husband's uncle and his nephew'.[29] If among the Choctaw a man calls his father's sister's son 'father', that is because this cousin is actually married to his mother. When a Choctaw lady marries, she also takes into her marriage bed her husband's mother's brother and his sister's son, who were members of his matrilineage. Rivers' conclusion was that the various classificatory systems were all modes of organizing group marriage.

Evolution and diffusion

But if Rivers remained committed to the central proposition of Morgan's method, that the terminology reflected social arrangements, particularly marriage rules, he was always prepared to question features of the grand evolutionary story which Morgan derived from these data. At an early stage he had discarded the hypothesis that there was an original condition of primitive promiscuity. In 1911, in his opening address as President to Section H of the British Association for the Advancement of Science,[30] he took a far more radical step, announcing that he was no longer wedded to evolutionary explanations in general. This lecture announced a dramatic departure from the orthodoxy of British ethnology.

The shift could be defined – as Rivers in fact defined it – with reference to national traditions of anthropology.[31] He was aban-

---

29 *Op. cit.*, p. 144.
30 Rivers (1911), 'The ethnological analysis of culture'.
31 This lecture makes a fascinating comparison with Boas's lecture in 1904 in St Louis. See pages 141–2, and Stocking (1974), pp. 23ff.

doning the traditional English assumptions that in all human populations customs and institutions progressed through a determined
series of evolutionary stages. In their place he adopted the new
German view that changes were normally a consequence of the
mixtures of peoples and cultures.[32] There was now clear evidence
that in Melanesia the development of culture was crucially influenced by migratory movements. This had been demonstrated by a
young ethnologist at the Berlin museum, Robert Fritz Graebner.[33]

Graebner's diffusionist essays on Melanesian culture probably
precipitated Rivers' change of direction,[34] but he nevertheless
argued that Graebner was too undiscriminating in his use of
evidence. Graebner gave the adoption of a piece of material culture
as much weight as a change in marriage rules. However Rivers
pointed out that material goods could be taken over quite casually.
Even beliefs and languages could be adopted without long or profound intermixture of peoples. The only really reliable evidence
of intermixture was provided by what Rivers called the 'social

---

32 Rivers mentioned the American school only in passing, although it was precisely
    to Boas's department at Columbia University that the German reaction against
    evolutionism was being worked through most systematically within anthro-
    pology.

33 Graebner, 'Kulturkreise und Kulturgeschichten in Ozeanien' (1905) and 'Die
    Melanesische Bogenkultur und ihre Verwandten' (1909). For a good English-
    language account of Graebner see Zwernemann (1983), *Culture History and
    African Anthropology*.

34 It is sometimes suggested that Rivers was converted to diffusionism by Elliot
    Smith. It seems evident, however, that both he and Elliot Smith were inde-
    pendently influenced by the German ethnologists. Smith recalled that when he
    returned to England in 1911 with the manuscript of his book *The Ancient
    Egyptians*, he visited Rivers and told him about his radical diffusionist hypoth-
    eses. Rivers

    told me that my first incursion into ethnology was a flagrant defiance of all the current
    doctrines of that branch of study, and would draw down upon my head the most bitter
    opposition – a prediction that was amply fulfilled. However, he reassured me by telling me
    that he was actually engaged (at the moment when I disturbed his work) on the task of
    writing his Presidential Address for the Anthropological Section of the British Association,
    in which he was making a full and frank recantation of his former acceptance of the orthodox
    ethnological doctrines. Although it was not until seven years later (1918) that Rivers went
    the whole way with me in recognizing the initiative of Egypt in the creation of civilization
    (*Psyche*, vol. 111, 1922, p. 118), the fortunate circumstance of his change of opinion in 1911
    played a very material part in securing any hearing at all for my heresies. (Dawson (1938),
    Sir Grafton Elliot Smith, p. 52)

    This subsequent conversion to Egyptocentric diffusionism – by Smith – gravely
    damaged Rivers' posthumous reputation.

structure'. 'The basic idea which underlies the whole argument of this book', he wrote in volume two of his *History* (1914b) 'is the deeply seated and intimate character of social structure. It seems at first sight impossible that a society can change this structure and yet continue to exist.'[35] This was the aspect of the culture which was least likely to change without 'the intimate blending of peoples'.[36] It followed that studies of social structure would provide the most reliable evidence of diffusion and migration.

Graebner's essays may have precipitated Rivers' change of direction, but he was also part of a broad contemporary movement in scientific thinking which Julian Huxley has called the 'eclipse of Darwinism'. This eclipse lasted for a generation, from the early twentieth century until the evolutionary synthesis of the 1930s and, although it was most marked in Germany, it affected some even in the stronghold of Cambridge, where a rebellious spirit like William Bateson completely rejected Darwinian evolution. 'We go to Darwin for his incomparable collection of facts', he wrote in 1914, but Darwin's 'philosophy' had only an historical interest. 'We read his scheme of Evolution as we would those of Lucretius or of Lamarck.'[37]

Rivers himself insisted that he changed his mind as a consequence of new field discoveries. He had made a further expedition to the Pacific, where he spent about a year in 1907–8 with G. C. Wheeler and Arthur Hocart. This was the Percy Sladen Trust Expedition to the Solomon Islands. Rivers and his companions did some 'intensive work' (as Rivers called it), but most of his research took the form of what he distinguished rather as 'survey-work', 'in which a number of peoples are studied sufficiently to obtain a general idea of their affinities in physique and culture',[38] and he relied largely on missionary intermediaries.[39] But it was not an encounter with a particular island culture or a specific ethnographic discovery to which Rivers attributed his change of mind. Rather his conversion to 'diffusionism' (as it came to be called) occurred while he struggled with the analysis of his materials – and then only at an advanced stage, for he began his book as an evolutionist

35 Rivers (1914b), *History of Melanesian Society*, vol. 2, p. 4.
36 Rivers (1911), 'The ethnological analysis of culture', p. 359.
37 Quoted in Mayr (1982), *The Growth of Biological Thought*, p. 547.
38 Rivers (1914b), *History of Melanesian Society*, vol. 1, p. 1.
39 Slobodin (1978), *Rivers*, pp. 40–3.

account and had originally intended to entitle it *The Evolution of Melanesian Society*.[40] Even in its final form the evolutionary theme is rather untidily welded to the diffusionist story which the book tells.

'The History of Melanesian Society'

It is worth reviewing the argument of the *History* in some detail, not only as the culminating achievement of Rivers' ethnological career but also because the book itself – in its form as much as its content – reveals the intellectual tension between ethnographic description, history and evolutionary theory.

It is characteristic of Rivers' intellectual culture that the issues were presented in methodological terms. In the preface to his *History* he confesses:

It was only in the act of writing this book that I came gradually to realise the unsatisfactory character of current ethnological methods. From that time, method again became my chief interest, and it is primarily as a study in method that this book is put forward.

Some of the basic assumptions of his method remained firm. Relationship systems are 'like fossils, the hidden indications of ancient social institutions and . . . their study is essential for advance in our knowledge of prehistoric sociology'.[41] They can be accurately recorded with the aid of genealogies, although when it comes to interpretation it is also helpful to have other material on marriage, descent and other social institutions.

The new element in Rivers' method was the introduction of geographical comparisons. Originally Rivers had been interested only in structural questions, and he had ignored the geographical distribution of relationship terms. But when he did map out the distribution of particular terms he was forced to recognize that his evolutionary sequences were cross-cut by other patterns and associations. These he now put down to population movements. Melanesian cultures were 'complex' – mixed – and accordingly their histories could not be told in classical evolutionary terms.

---

40 *Op. cit.*, pp. 7–8. Nor was the emphasis in the title on 'society' accidental. 'Again, I have called the book a history of Melanesian society rather than of Melanesian culture, because it is with social forms and functions in the narrower sense that I chiefly deal' (*ibid.*).

41 Rivers (1914b), *History of Melanesian Society*, vol. 1, p. 3.

But this methodological shift did not mean that Rivers was abandoning evolutionism.

> The method of this book ... lies between that of the evolutionary school and that of the modern historical school of Germany. Its standpoint remains essentially evolutionary in spite of its method becoming historical, a combination forced upon me because it was with social structure that I was primarily concerned.[42]

It was possible to combine these approaches since 'the contact of peoples and the blending of their cultures act as the chief stimuli setting in action the forces which lead to human progress'.[43]

Pressing and fundamental though these methodological problems might be, they had to be segregated from the precious data. Inferences must be kept distinct from 'the facts collected in the field'.[44] The *History* is actually divided into two volumes, the first containing summaries of observations, the second, argument. Yet Rivers – and in turn his students – nevertheless insisted upon using a deductive approach. As Rivers emphasized:

> This method has been the formulation of a working hypothetical scheme to form a framework into which the facts are fitted, and the scheme is regarded as satisfactory only if the facts can thus be fitted so as to form a coherent whole, all parts of which are consistent with one another.[45]

This boldly deductive method allowed Rivers to order his argument with great clarity and force.

The first volume is made up of repetitive chapters, each dealing with a specific Melanesian culture. The emphasis is on 'social organisation', which covers the structure of moieties, clans, etc., and the relationship system. Under this heading Rivers provided relationship terms, and also a sketch of the rights and duties of particular relatives. He also described the regulation of marriage, adoption, inheritance and succession.

The second volume turns to theory. Its central concerns are the explanation of cross-cousin marriage, which was widespread in the Pacific, and also what Rivers identified as 'anomalous' marriage forms. These anomalous forms were intergenerational marriages. Their existence was deduced from the terminology, and occasion-

---

42 *Op. cit.*, p. 5.
43 *Op. cit.*, p. 6.
44 *Op. cit.*, p. 5.
45 *Op. cit.*, vol. 2, p. 586.

ally given some further plausibility by other pieces of stray evidence. In Pentecost Island, mother's mother and elder sister were referred to by the same term. This generational confusion Rivers explained on the hypothesis that men married their brother's daughters' daughters (a practice which Howitt had recorded for the Dieri in Australia). In Fiji and Buin there was an apparently patrilineal version of the same system, since father's father is classified together with elder brother. Rivers put this down to marriage with father's father's wife. This would yield the required correspondences if one further hypothesis was introduced – that the system arose in an earlier state of society when Fiji and Buin had matrilineal moieties.

Obviously it was not easy to find evidence in support of such associations. Sometimes the chain of reasoning became very long indeed. For example, Rivers claimed there were faint indications that at one time men in the Banks Islands had sexual access to their wife's sisters and brothers' wives (as would have been the case in a system of group marriage). This was no longer the case. Nor was there any fossilized terminological evidence in favour of such an hypothesis. Indeed, in the Banks Islands terminology which he had recorded himself, wife's sister and brother's wife are classed as 'sisters'. Rivers concluded 'that there is a definite association between the classing of these relatives with the sister and the cessation of such sexual relations'.[46] In other words, if the terms indicated that marriage must have been banned, then it was acceptable to conclude that marriage had once been permitted!

Having identified these 'anomalous and extraordinary' forms of marriage, Rivers had to account for them. In what situation would men marry great-aunts or grandchildren? Inter-generational marriages might make sense if primeval societies were dominated by their old men. These gerontocrats would exploit their power and accumulate wives, marrying women of their own generation, but also women of a younger generation, so long as they belonged to the other matri-moiety.

This recalls the scenarios of Atkinson and Andrew Lang, who had picked up a hint from Darwin and posited an original condition in which a patriarch controlled all the women of his group. Rivers distinguished his own idea from theirs, since his presupposed not

46 *Op. cit.*, p. 76.

only 'the monopoly of women by the old men' but also a moiety system, 'the clear recognition of generations and the existence of the classificatory system of relationship.'[47]

Given these further constraints, the old men would not marry their own daughters, and so they resorted to daughters of their own daughters, or daughters of their brothers' daughters. Nor were the young men left celibate. They would be supplied with the widows and cast-offs of their elders. But a man could only pass on a wife to a member of his own moiety. Therefore his wives went not to his sons or brothers' sons, but to his sons' sons and sisters' sons. Once the balance of power between the generations improved, the young men would begin to press a demand for their mother's brother's daughters rather than their mother's brother's wives. This was the origin of cross-cousin marriage. Infant betrothal was a relic of this struggle for women between men of different generations. Ritual marriage by capture recalled the actual trials of strength between young and old men.[48]

The beauty of the scheme which has been advanced is that the explanations suggested for the four forms of marriage form a coherent whole. A form of marriage such as that with the wife of the mother's brother, which taken by itself seems anomalous and difficult to understand, becomes the obvious consequence of another form of marriage which seems still more anomalous, viz., marriage with the daughter's daughter; and so with the other marriages.[49]

Yet even if one formulated the problem in Rivers' way, there was an obvious alternative solution. These bizarre 'anomalous' marriages might be just a permutation of an Australian-type 'marriage class' system. After all, Howitt had reported marriages between members of alternate generations among the Dieri. On this line of reasoning, Melanesia would fit into place as a natural further stage of development of Australian society. Rivers rejected this possibility on the grounds that marriage with the mother's brother's wife was completely incompatible with any Australian-type marriage class system.

47 *Op. cit.*, p. 68.
48 *Op. cit.*, pp. 64, 246.
49 *Op. cit.*, p. 65.

The essence of [the Australian systems] is that members of contiguous generations belong to different classes; a man and his sister's son could never marry women of the same class, and therefore could never marry the same women.[50]

Even if this argument was accepted, Rivers' new theory raised another problem. Why did dual organization lead to cross-cousin marriage? Dual organization is a system of inter-group marriage; cross-cousin marriage is a genealogically defined system of kin marriage. The answer was that native peoples with a moiety system had been set on the road to social development by more advanced immigrants. Melanesian society is an amalgam.

It seems that a succession of migrant peoples have blended with the indigenous population who were the original possessors of the dual organisation of society, and that the culture we now call Melanesian is the result of the influence of these successive migrations on the indigenous culture.[51]

Patrilineal succession, patrilineal inheritance and chieftainship were all attributable to immigrant influence. So was cross-cousin marriage, which depended upon the recognition of paternity (because then one got individualized genealogies). So was the institution of bride-price, which arose because the immigrants were mainly men, who had to find wives from the local populations. Totemism and ancestor worship both derived from the immigrant 'kava people', who believed in reincarnation in the form of animals and plants. Where they had not managed to impose their own religion, they practised it privately in 'secret societies'.

In these ways, an appeal to diffusion allowed Rivers to account for evolution. The Melanesians went through all the conventional evolutionary stages, but as a result of contact rather than endogenous development. The argument could even be turned back to deal with the very first stages of human society. Could dual organization itself not have been the result of the fusion of two peoples rather than a consequence of fission, as was normally supposed? In the penultimate chapter of the second volume of his history, Rivers argued that this is precisely what had happened.

The differentiation of waves of population movement allowed Rivers also to account for differences in the culture of Melanesia

50 *Op. cit.*, p. 52.
51 *Op. cit.*, p. 292.

and Polynesia; and he suggested that a similar line of argument could be extended to Indonesia, which was probably the source of these immigrations.

CHAPTER 9

The reaction to Rivers

Rivers set the agenda for the study of primitive society in Britain, just as Boas did in the USA. But while Boas's students implemented his research programme and developed his critique of Morgan, Rivers' Cambridge men reacted against his ideas. Rivers had himself ended by rejecting evolutionism in favour of diffusionism, and yet his theory of Melanesian history redeployed the classic elements of evolutionary anthropology. His students for their part accepted the rules of the game which Rivers taught them, although each strained to develop a fresh and more satisfactory arrangement of the old elements of the model of primitive society.

Columbia was perhaps more authoritarian than Cambridge; Boas himself was certainly more paternalistic than Rivers. He was also very much older than his students, whereas Rivers was, for example, less than twenty years older than Radcliffe-Brown. Above all, perhaps, Boas and his students were outsiders, establishing themselves in academic institutions but always insecure. Rivers and his students, in contrast, were all middle-class English scientists who felt perfectly at home in the leading scientific university in the country. Within the university their discipline might have been marginal and rather insignificant, but they operated confidently enough by the norms of the place. Rivers and his students worked essentially as colleagues in the atmosphere of élite egalitarianism which Cambridge fostered.

Rivers' first student, Radcliffe-Brown, inverted his teacher's most general theories of social organization, which were in essence those of Morgan and his Australian followers. Younger men of a later Cambridge vintage took Rivers' theories of Melanesian society apart, and upset his conclusions. All, however, asked the same questions as Rivers, and produced the same species of answer. It was an outsider, a Pole, Bronislaw Malinowski, working from a fragile base in a marginal academic institution, the London School of Economics, who questioned the nature of the game itself, injecting a new kind of data into the argument, challenging the very reality of Rivers' Melanesia, and scorning the 'kinship algebra' on which Rivers and his students alike depended.

Malinowski is known above all for revolutionizing field methods in anthropology. His study of the Trobriand Islands (in the Solomon Sea, Southwestern Pacific) between 1915 and 1918 was to change the rules of fieldwork. Beginning in the late 1920s, his students at the London School of Economics were trained to spend one to two years in a single community, learning the language, participating in everyday life and gathering data by direct observation instead of by interviews which elicited rules and ideologies rather than practice. The institutionalization of the new field methods was part of a change in the power centre of British anthropology which occurred after the death of Rivers; but that happened after the reaction to Rivers, which is the subject of the present chapter. Functionalist field methods were not responsible for the discontents of the Cambridge school.

Radcliffe-Brown made a lengthy peregrination through Australia in 1910–11, surveying a variety of aboriginal communities, but his methods were essentially those which Rivers was employing at the same time in Melanesia. Later, some of Rivers' younger students spent longer periods in single communities, notably Layard in 1914 and Deacon in 1924, but the data they produced was qualitatively very similar to that of Rivers or Radcliffe-Brown. The reaction to Rivers had more to do with debates in classrooms and in letters than with new ethnographic methods or discoveries.[1]

Radcliffe-Brown (1881–1955) and Australia

Like Haddon and Rivers, Radcliffe-Brown started off as a natural scientist, but at Cambridge he switched to moral sciences and became Rivers' first student in social anthropology.[2] After graduating he did fieldwork in the Andaman Islands. His initial analysis

---

1 See Stocking (1983), 'The ethnographer's magic: fieldwork in British anthropology from Tylor to Malinowski'.
2 On Radcliffe-Brown see Chapter 2 of my *Anthropology and Anthropologists* (1983).

of this material was evidently in Rivers' historical vein but around 1910 he adopted a Durkheimian approach.

In 1910–11 Radcliffe-Brown carried out what was essentially survey research in Australia, in the tradition of Rivers' broad and rather superficial collecting expeditions, although compared to Rivers he spent a long period actually in the field. For the next two decades he occupied himself with the analysis of his new material, which he integrated with the mass of published and unpublished data on Australian aboriginal social organization that had accumulated since the heroic days of Fison, Howitt, Spencer and Gillen. Preliminary syntheses published in 1913, 1918 and 1923 influenced Rivers and his students. In 1930–31, while he held the foundation chair in social anthropology at Sydney University, Radcliffe-Brown published a summation of his views, *The Social Organization of Australian Tribes*. This long essay, the most important achievement of Rivers' students, established a paradigm which was to exert a strong influence over the next generation of British social anthropologists.

So while Rivers turned his attention to Melanesia, Radcliffe-Brown was reviewing the classic body of research on 'primitive society', that dealing with the Australian aborigines. The received wisdom on Australian social structure since Fison was that marriage choices were regulated by a system of exogamous matrilineal groups – in the simplest case moieties, in other systems four, eight, or even sixteen 'marriage classes'. In a marriage class system, every member of one specific group (A) had to marry into another specified group (B), and their children would belong to a third group (C), and would have to marry into a fourth group (D). Other social units, notably local groupings, were recent developments, signalling the eclipse of the ancient system. The initial assumption was that these classes were linked through a system of 'group marriage', but by the turn of the century it had become widely accepted that marriage was on an individual basis (though most writers assumed that it had developed from a previous system of thoroughgoing group marriage).

An alternative line of argument could also be traced back to Fison, who had demonstrated that repetitive marriage between two 'classes' produced marriages between cousins who were children of one another's mother's brother and father's sister. Tylor had drawn attention to this type of marriage, and R. H. Matthews, a surveyor who spent many years in the outback, kept the issue alive in the Australian field. Fison and Tylor had argued that cross-cousin marriage was a byproduct of group marriage, but Rivers postulated a sharp break between group-based marriages and individual, genealogically-based marriages with cross-cousins. In his view cross-cousin marriage must have been a late development in social evolution, since it presupposed the recognition of fatherhood and individual genealogical identity.

Radcliffe-Brown turned all these fundamental assumptions around. He argued that the basic elements of Australian social structure were the family and the local group which occupied and owned a definite territory. Following Howitt and Fison, he called this local group the 'horde'. (The horde was autonomous. Beyond it there were loose tribal groupings, within which a common language was spoken but lacking any political identity.)

Even more radically, he denied that moieties, sections, and sub-sections were primary features of Australian society. They were not completely dropped from the model, but were displaced, becoming epiphenomena. Radcliffe-Brown insisted that the 'classes' were derivative functions of the system of kin classification. The system of kin classification itself followed from the marriage rule. The 'classes' were therefore reflections of a system of marriage, not ingredients of it. Finally, the marriage rule had nothing to do with group marriage. It prescribed marriage with a cross-cousin.

Radcliffe-Brown had praised Malinowski's essay on the family among the Australian aborigines,[3] and he took the central importance of the family as given. His aim was to show how the family provided the structural basis of the Australian social systems. Relationships between members of the family were extended to incorporate all members of the tribe. This was achieved by a system of classification which grouped more distant kin with close relatives. The key was the tendency to identify brothers with each other, and to associate brother and sister very closely. The identification of distant relatives had real consequences. One treated a distant kinsman according to the norms governing relations with a close kinsman of the same category.

The marriage rules in all Australian communities were rules of kin marriage, normally cross-cousin marriage. One might marry a

3 See his review in *Man* (1914b), p. 32.

mother's brother's daughter, or father's sister's daughter, or both types of cross-cousin. Indeed, Australian kinship systems could best be divided into two types, depending on the form of cross-cousin marriage which they favoured. In Type I, marriage was with a mother's brother's daughter, and in Type II marriage was with a mother's mother's brother's daughter's daughter ('or some woman who stands to him in an equivalent relation'[4]). A man had to marry a cross-cousin, not a member of a specific group.

Each type of marriage generated an appropriate classification of relatives. If men regularly married matrilateral cross-cousins, for example, then they would classify their relatives in each generation into two sets, roughly speaking 'in-laws' and others. In the parental generation a mother's brother and father's sister would be in-laws, while mother's sister and father's brother would be lumped together with one's own parents. In one's own generation, similarly, cross-cousins would be distinguished from the children of mother's sister and father's brother, who would be classified together with siblings.

From the point of view of any individual, therefore, the world of kin was divided in two; the marriageable on one side, the unmarriageable on the other. This was the true source of the 'class' system. Given the dual classification of kin, all that remained was to give each category a name, and one had a moietey system (at least from the point of view of the individual). If more distant cross-cousins were specified as marriage partners, then extra distinctions were required in the terminology, so that three or more 'descent lines' were distinguished. 'Clans', similarly, were conceptual categories. They might be introduced to draw a boundary around close kin on the father's side, and to distinguish them from more distant patrilateral kin.

The various 'classes' did not in themselves have any effect on the system of marriage. There was no necessary correlation between a particular marriage rule and a particular class structure. 'The fact that a tribe has two or four named divisions tells us nothing whatever about the marriage law of the tribe, which can only be ascertained by a careful study of the system of relationship.'[5]

---

4 Radcliffe-Brown (1913), 'Three tribes of Western Australia', pp. 1901–1.
5 *Op. cit.*, p. 193.

Radcliffe-Brown's presentation of this argument was always extremely formal and spare. His papers were notably brief and devoid of detail. His two types of Australian system were presented as little more than lists of features. The first he identified with the Kariera tribe. In this type of system either cross-cousin was marriageable, although Radcliffe-Brown analysed the Kariera system as one in which mother's brother's daughter marriage was the vital element. This marriage rule was accompanied by a division of all relatives in each generation into two categories (further divided by sex). Relatives of alternate generation were classified together (so, for example, the same term was applied to father's father, brother (and father's brother's son) and son's son).

The second type, which he identified with the Aranda, was a refinement of the Kariera system. Marriage in the Aranda system was with a mother's mother's brother's daughter's daughter. To accommodate such a marriage rule each Kariera kinship category was split in two by the Aranda, yielding four categories for each sex in each generation. Radcliffe-Brown rephrased this contrast by saying that the Kariera system required two 'descent lines' where the Aranda system required four. Each 'line' grouped together patrilineal descendants and ascendants, generating the required number of categories of kin in each generation.

The Kariera system automatically yields four sets of kin (given the combination of alternate generations) while the Aranda system with its four 'lines' yields eight classes in any two successive generations. A man can indeed marry a woman only from one other class – that containing his mother's brother's daughter in a Kariera-type system, or a mother's mother's brother's daughter's daughter in an Aranda-type system – but class membership is not the decisive criterion for the marriage, and there are unmarriageable women in the 'marriage class' within which he seeks a wife. The classic 'marriage classes' were no more than convenient summaries of the consequences of the system of kinship and marriage.

Relationships between the autonomous patrilineal hordes are mainly established by marriage, and often a man marries into his mother's natal horde (where his mother's brother's daughter lives) so reinforcing his links with it. In the Aranda-type system a man is forced into a series of affinal links with at least four other hordes, yielding a more complex social integration and representing a further evolutionary development. Like Fison, Radcliffe-Brown saw the local hordes as the first germ of the state.[6]

Radcliffe-Brown and Rivers

From early in 1912, when Radcliffe-Brown returned from his expedition to Australia, until early in 1914, when both he and Rivers left once more for Oceania, Rivers and Radcliffe-Brown exchanged a series of fascinating letters in which they reviewed their ideas concerning Melanesia and Australia, and debated the state of theory in their subject.[7]

One of the major issues which divided them was the question of diffusion. Specifically, Rivers argued that both Melanesia and Australia were 'complex' societies, which could be understood only if their constituent parts were analysed out.[8] Radcliffe-Brown disagreed and he questioned the methods by which Rivers identified extraneous cultural traits.

Radcliffe-Brown's letters also record his first reactions to Durkheim's *Elementary Forms of the Religious Life*, which originally appeared (in French) in 1912. He thought that Durkheim was fundamentally mistaken in his Australian ethnography, but accepted the principle of his method and agreed that totemism was to be understood as a reflection of forms of social organization. On this question again he came into conflict with Rivers. For Rivers, 'totemism' referred in the first place to a system of social organization – essentially a system of exogamous clans. The form of religious expression was secondary. For Radcliffe-Brown the whole concept of exogamous clans was dubious – so far as he was concerned, the Australian system was based on genealogical rather than group identities. He regarded totemism as a religion, which derived from an earlier 'ritual value' given to economically important foods. As a society became increasingly differentiated, so each grouping adopted one of the valued foods as its special emblem. Where an Australian tribe was dominantly organized in local patrilineal hordes, local totems inherited in the male line would predominate. Where dispersed matrilineal categories were more significant, totems inherited in the female line would be more important.

---

6 He even drew parallels between the Australian tribe and the United States of America! See Radcliffe-Brown, 'Patrilineal and matrilineal succession', p. 289.
7 I have edited these letters and will publish them shortly.
8 See Rivers (1914c), 'Is Australian culture simple or complex?', 1914.

His student's new model of Australia did not directly disturb Rivers. He was concentrating upon Melanesia, and (perhaps in the light of Radcliffe-Brown's conclusions) he decided that Melanesia was inherently different from Australia, and had its own distinctive history. Nor were differences of method yet decisive. Rivers' diffusionist ideas were still developing at the time of this correspondence, and even in his 1914 *History* he did not allow diffusionist reconstructions to take over completely. For his part, Radcliffe-Brown was happy to engage in similar historical and diffusionist speculations for another decade. Rivers' later Cambridge students, however, confronted him directly on his theories about Melanesia, and produced a remarkable series of theoretically driven investigations.

The Ambrym case

The History of Melanesian Society (Rivers, 1914b) was the central point of reference of the students trained at Cambridge immediately after the First World War, and one problem which Rivers constructed came to obsess the next generation of Cambridge kinship specialists. In retrospect there is something almost absurd, certainly quite disproportionate, in the concentration on one question, yet this obsession was logical enough, inevitable almost, in the context of the theory of the day.

The question at issue was extremely technical. To recapitulate, it concerned the fact that, in some Melanesian kinship terminologies, relatives of alternate generations were classed together. Most authorities assumed that kinship classification reflected marriage practices. Two kinds of marriage rule had been invoked to account for the skewing of generations. Rivers believed that it signalled the existence of regular inter-generational marriages. Another possibility was that it indicated the presence of 'marriage classes' of the Australian type, which grouped together grandparents and grandchildren.

The significance of the question, apparently so restricted, was very great if the assumptions of the Rivers school are appreciated. If these Melanesian systems were simply variants of Australian marriage classes, then Rivers' elaborate model of gerontocracy would have to be abandoned. Indeed, his whole history of Melanesian society would lose much of its credibility. On the other hand, if one could demonstrate that there was continuity with Australian systems this would lend plausibility to the original Morgan-Fison model according to which moiety systems developed into marriage class systems (which Fison and Tylor had identified with systems of cross-cousin marriage).

Given River's construction of the problem of Melanesian social organization, the Australian hypothesis (to give it a label) was obviously a most vital challenge. All agreed that the crucial test would be provided by the most primitive Melanesian system, since if there was an Australian connection it would be most evident in the earliest Melanesian examples. On Rivers' reading of Melanesian social history, this meant that the test had to be made in Pentecost, or, ideally, in an even purer version of the classic Melanesian system, which Rivers thought might be found on Ambrym, since its language had what he took to be archaic features. In Ambrym one might still find granddaughter marriage alone, without the subsequent complications of mother's brother's wife or father's father's wife marriage, let alone cross-cousin marriage, which Rivers regarded as a very recent innovation.[9]

It was on his second visit to the New Hebrides in 1914 that Rivers made the first systematic study of the Ambrym system. He did not actually visit Ambrym (which had been devastated by an earthquake in 1913), but he collected informtion from an Ambrym man, William, who was living as a teacher at a Presbyterian mission station in Tangoa. Rivers worked at first in pidgin, and later through an interpreter, a missionary named Bowie.

When Rivers worked up this material in England he sent drafts of his conclusions to Bowie. William was dead by this time, and Bowie discussed Rivers' notes with a man called Lau, who came from a village close to William's. Lau disagreed with William's account on a number of crucial points. Bowie communicated his observations to Rivers, and gave Lau's version his support.

The accounts of William and of Lau put Rivers on the spot. Quite contrary to his expectations, it appeared that the people of Ambrym were patrilineal, living in exogamous patrilineal villages. The other main social institution, the *vantinbul*, which regulated property relations, was also dominantly patrilineal, though it did include the sister's son. Rivers might discern traces of an earlier matrilineal state in certain rituals,[10] but he had to concede that by

9 Rivers (1914b), *History of Melanesian Society*, vol. 2, p. 89.
10 Rivers (1915), 'Descent and ceremonial in Ambrym'.

his own rules there were indications that marriage might be possible with the father's father's wife, since alternate generations in the male line were classed together, just as they were in Fiji and Buin.

Rivers never fully worked up this new Ambrym material, but to his post-war students it was crucial. There was a strong strand of opinion amongst them that the marriage-class hypothesis was a good one, and that the Melanesian systems might turn out to be very like the Australian.

After Rivers' sudden death in 1922, one of his former students, W. E. Armstrong, was appointed to deliver his Cambridge lectures in social anthropology. He concentrated on kinship and social organization, and soon also took over Haddon's lectures on primitive religion.[11] Armstrong deployed abstract models in his kinship lectures and, while he concentrated on the classic Rivers' issues, he exercised a traditional Cambridge independence and scepticism. Like Malinowski and Radcliffe-Brown, he argued that the family was the basis of all kinship systems, and that 'clans' and other kin groups were the product of the classificatory systems, rather than vice versa.

Armstrong believed that class systems did formerly exist in Melanesia, but they were class systems in Radcliffe-Brown's sense, which grew out of cross-cousin marriage. Reversing Rivers' argument, he suggested that their absence in modern Melanesia might have resulted from the introduction of mother's brother's wife marriage. The presence of mother's brother's wife marriage should therefore not be a bar to the acceptance of the Australian hypothesis of Melanesian origins. When the post-war Cambridge anthropologists went into the field to test Rivers' theory of Melanesian culture history they were therefore primed to seek any clues that might point to the existence of a class system, though a class system which might be derived from a form of matrilateral cross-cousin marriage.

A brilliant group of students went out, but they were dogged by quite extraordinary ill-luck. Rivers took John Layard back with him to the New Hebrides in 1914, but war broke out and after a few weeks he had to leave for England, where he was drawn into military psychiatric work. Left behind, Layard had a severe break-

---

11 See Urry (1985), 'W. E. Armstrong and social anthropology at Cambridge'. Armstrong never published these lectures, but the general argument appears as an appendix to his 1928 *Rossel Island*.

down, and was able to write up his material only in the 1940s.[12]

In 1922 T. T. Barnard went to the New Hebrides. Rivers had planned to guide him, but died suddenly a few days before they were to begin work (and when in the middle of a parliamentary election campaign in which he was standing for the London University seat as a candidate for the Labour Party). Nevertheless, in the course of his research Barnard met and collected information from five Ambrym men. Although the data were not very helpful in themselves, the contact led him to ask Professor Elliot Smith, Rivers' literary executor, whether he might examine Rivers' unpublished notes on Ambrym. Permission granted, he stumbled on the correspondence with Bowie. In his thesis he devoted a chapter to the re-analysis of this material.

As a student of Rivers, Barnard looked for clues to the social structure in the system of relationship terms. He therefore argued that, if there were marriage classes, then kin terms would reflect their existence. All kin grouped together under one term would be members of one class. On the basis of the terminology he concluded that the Ambrym social system was based upon six marriage classes. (These were not coextensive with the *vantinbul* discussed by Rivers, for the number of *vantinbul* in different localities was evidently quite variable.)

Members of classes A and B intermarried, classes C and D intermarried, and classes E and F intermarried. Children did not belong to the same class as their parents. The children of A men were C, of B men E and of D men F, and vice versa. Accordingly a man's son's son was a member of his own class. Since the islanders were patrilineal and patrilocal, men and their sons and son's sons lived in the same local community. All the women who were marriageable in Rivers' 'anomalous' marriage types were members of the marriageable class.[13]

12 See Jeremy MacClancy (1986), 'Unconventional character and disciplinary convention: John Layard, Jungian and anthropologist'. When Layard returned to England Rivers treated him, but according to Layard he

 exacerbated his condition of nervous exhaustion by suggesting that he start to write up his field notes ... When Layard, during one of his crises, declared his love for his mentor, Rivers, 'blanching' and 'almost trembling', left the room, never to return. 'Rivers had obviously not recognized the whole homosexual content of our relationship, probably on both sides'. (*Op. cit.*, p. 53)

13 T. T. Barnard (1924), doctoral thesis, Chapter 6. This chapter has recently been reprinted, in G. De Meur (ed.) (1986), *New Trends in Mathematical Anthropology*.

Barnard's thesis was accepted in 1924. Soon afterwards, a brilliant young Cambridge student, Bernard Deacon, went to make a new field study on Malekula in the New Hebrides, where he was to spend over a year. Deacon acknowledged the value of Armstrong's lectures and his notes of these lectures include much material on Radcliffe-Brown's Australian studies.[14] Nevertheless, he could complain with reason that he had not enjoyed an adequate briefing from his predecessors. He wrote to his fiancée from the field:

I have very little idea of what others have done here – Layard in '13, Rivers at the same time, then Barnard in 1921 or so, & Humphries . . . Rivers' theory I begin to find a hindrance, I was brought up on it at Cambridge, and now it clogs me . . . I am very much puzzled to know what Rivers really thought about certain things . . . More particularly I want to know what Barnard thinks of Rivers' ideas. There must be more coordination of ethnological work in the field – it's useless letting people just float out & grope in the dark where they want.[15]

Nevertheless, he had enough information to realize that the acid test for Rivers' culture history was the social system of Ambrym. He wrote to his fiancée:

Rivers of course had an elaborate theory, still the best, but his work in Ambrym later (with Layard in Malekula) seems to me to raise very great objections to its acceptance. I have never seen however, any paper of Rivers' attempting to reconcile the two, or at least stating how far he considered his Ambrym work modified his 1908 expedition work. Then in 1922 or so Barnard suggested a scheme which, so far as I understood it from hurried reading of his thesis, was almost the exact reverse of Rivers'.[16]

Deacon's own detailed fieldwork on Malekula was heartbreakingly difficult and yielded very little relevant information on social structure, but he had known all along that the crucial test of Rivers' hypothesis would have to be made on Ambrym. 'I determined, therefore, when I came out, to seek an opportunity of visiting Ambrym and going more deeply into the marriage regulations in that island.'[17]

14 Urry (1985), 'W. E. Armstrong', pp. 427 and 430, note 18.
15 Gardiner (1984), *Footprints on Malekula*, p. 47.
16 *Op. cit.*, p. 45.
17 Deacon (1927), 'The regulation of marriage in Ambrym', p. 327.

He eventually spent six weeks on Ambrym early in 1928 and made what he considered a major discovery – 'something rather valuable', he wrote to his fiancée, with the proper modesty of a gentleman, 'a class system of marriage of the type of those among the Central Australian aborigines – it clarifies the whole series of problems here, besides being, I think, of considerable importance in relation to Melanesian culture in general'.[18] When he communicated his findings to Radcliffe-Brown in Sydney, Brown wrote to say it was 'one of the most important discoveries made in Melanesia',[19] and urged him to publish his report immediately. By the time the paper appeared, later in 1927, Deacon was dead. He had a sudden and fatal attack of blackwater fever, dying just short of his twenty-fourth birthday. He had been on the point of going to Sydney as a lecturer in Radcliffe-Brown's department.

Deacon's paper began with powerful criticisms of Rivers' fundamental assumptions. Rivers posited three anomalous marriages in Melanesia – with the father's father's wife, with brother's daughter's daughter, and with the mother's brother's widow. Marriage with the father's father's wife – if at all systematic – argued a marriage class system on the Australian model. This implied that the rule referred to a classificatory grandmother. It might have been possible to explain marriage with a classificatory granddaughter in a similar way, but Deacon questioned the very existence of 'granddaughter marriage'. Rivers had seized upon the observation of one man about an island he had not even visited, to the effect that there men married their 'granddaughters'. Deacon pointed out that in some of the terminologies in the area mother's brother's children are classified as children, and their children as grandchildren. What was at issue was really marriage with the daughter of the cross-cousin, a form of marriage which Deacon had recorded in practice in the region. This was another pointer in favour of an Australian hypothesis, since Radcliffe-Brown had recently concluded that all the Australian systems were variant forms of matrilateral cross-cousin marriage.

The real stumbling block in the way of the Australian hypothesis was mother's brother's widow marriage, since in any moiety system a man's mother's brother's widow would be drawn from his own

---

18 Gardiner (1984), *Footprints on Malekula*, p. 47.
19 *Op. cit.*, p. 53.

moiety. Deacon argued that this form of marriage was an individual genealogical entitlement comparable to the levirate, and that it was part of a complex of matrilineal inheritance. These traits all indicated a fairly advanced type of social institution. If mother's brother's widow marriage was shown to be a late development (as Armstrong had also argued) then the Australian hypothesis could be salvaged. It only remained to find evidence of a Melanesian system where men could marry cross-cousins and classificatory grandmothers but not the mother's brother's widow – and according to Deacon, Ambrym was such an area.[20]

During his weeks in Ambrym, Deacon collected relationship systems, genealogies and statements of marriage rules, but his decisive evidence came, he wrote, 'from the remarkably lucid exposition of the class-system by the natives themselves'.[21] This is slightly misleading, however. Judging from the indications in his paper, his informants told him that marriage involved the regular alignment of three parties in an exchange system. One informant placed three stones in a triangular pattern, and explained that 'if a woman of A married a man of C, her daughter in C would marry a man of B, her daughter's daughter in B would marry a man of A again, a man of her M.m.F.'s "line"'.[22] A second informant provided a slightly more complex version of the same model; three lines intermarried, but women went both clockwise and counter-clockwise round the circle.

Deacon complicated the models by introducing six 'lines' in place of the three elements, in order to accommodate the genealogical complexities needed to discriminate mother's mother's father's line as a separate source of marriage partners. Reading this paper in the context of Armstrong's lectures and Radcliffe-Brown's Australian researches, it seems obvious that the six 'lines' derived from the lecture-rooms of Cambridge rather than the informants of

---

20 It seemed to me, then, that if an area could be found where F.Sis.D.D. and M.B.D.D. marriage were practised, but not with the M.B.W., it would be in this area that the class-system which might have given rise to F.Sis.D.D. and M.B.D.D. marriage should be sought. Ambrym is such an area. (Deacon (1927), 'The regulation of marriage in Ambrym', p. 328)

Evidently he attributed greater independent significance to the classes than did Radcliffe-Brown or Armstrong.

21 *Ibid.*

22 *Op. cit.*, p. 329.

Ambrym. This is probably why his model ended up looking so very much like Barnard's, despite his very different data.

Marriage with the mother's brother's widow did not exist in Ambrym, though it had been recorded by Deacon in Malekula. Deacon accordingly concluded that it emerged after the collapse of dual organization and the arrival of a new immigrant culture. In sum, properly understood, Rivers' anomalous marriages could be derived historically from a class system (though not precisely the Australian class system). Rivers' theory of Melanesian geron-tocracy was no longer tenable.

Deacon's 1927 paper in the *Journal of the Royal Anthropological Institute* was followed by a long comment from Radcliffe-Brown, in which he concluded that the Ambrym system was a variant of the Australian Type II system (which, it will be recalled, was based on MMBDD marriage). More broadly, it fitted into 'a single general type of kinship organization (the Dravidian-Australian type) found over a large area of South India and Ceylon ... and perhaps over the whole of Australia, and in certain parts of Melanesia', a type, Radcliffe-Brown speculated, 'possibly dating back to the first peopling of Australia and Melanesia'.[23] Within five years of Rivers' death, and thirteen years after the publication of his *History* (1946), his outstanding student had succeeded finally in reversing even the conjectural history of Melanesia which had been his monument.

The debate on Ambrym illustrates perfectly the procedure of Rivers and his Cambridge students. They were sceptical and daring, but within the limits of the narrow tradition of research which derived from Morgan; and they were rigorous, but without doubting the value of their basic data, the kinship terms.[24] In all

23 Radcliffe-Brown (1927), 'The regulation of marriage in Ambrym', quotation from p. 345. Radcliffe-Brown further speculated that there might be matrilineal clans in Ambrym. Together with the patrilineal local moieties, they could generate marriage classes. In a later paper ('A further note on Ambrym') he triumphantly recorded that Rivers had reported the existence of clan-like structures in Ambrym, vindicating his guess.

24 They all operated with a sophisticated idea of scientific procedure, which empha-sized the value of deduction. Rivers had insisted on the necessity of combining objective description and deductive reasoning, and both Armstrong and Layard proceeded by deduction. Radcliffe-Brown typically welcomed Deacon's dis-covery in Ambrym, 'particularly by reason of the way in which it was made as the confirmation of acute reasoning that something of the sort should be there' (Radcliffe-Brown (1927), 'The regulation of marriage in Ambrym', p. 343). He

its transformations the identity of the model remains unmistakable. Boas led his students away from the traditional obsessions of Anglo-American anthropology, but in Britain only Westermack and Malinowski escaped its domination before the 1930s. And it was largely due to Malinowski that a fresh agenda was set for the British anthropologists.

Malinowski's Melanesia

Malinowski's Australian book developed Westermarck's critique of classical theory, but its materials were pieced together from available ethnographies. In 1914, however, he began to do fieldwork on his own account, first in New Guinea and then in the Trobriand Islands. In due course he delivered the most vivid firsthand ethnographic descriptions which had yet been published.[25] The distance in purely descriptive terms between the Melanesia of Malinowski and Melanesia of Rivers or Deacon was very great indeed. Nevertheless, there were continuities with some of the classical preoccupations.

Carrying on the argument of his earlier work, Malinowski insisted that individual family relationships existed in every society. Parents were always bound up with their children. Yet he accepted that there were generally also group bonds, as the whole tradition of anthropology had supposed. According to the authorities, from Maine and Morgan to Durkheim and Rivers, group bonds were primeval, individual family relationships a product of civilization. It had now been established that individual family relationships were found in even the most primitive society, coexisting with group bonds. Indeed, Malinowski supposed that the clan was an outgrowth of the family, an extension of relationships with the

later claimed on his own account and in almost identical terms that

> The discovery of the Kariera system by myself in 1911 was the result of a definite search, on a surmise made before visiting Australia, but after a careful study of the Australian data in 1909, that some such system might very well exist and that Western Australia would be a reasonable place in which to look for it. (Radcliffe-Brown (1931), *The Social Organization of Australian Tribes*, note 5)

This particular note led to a flurry of criticism nearly half a century later. See especially Needham (1974), *Remarks and Inventions*, and Isobel White (1981), 'Mrs Bates and Mr Brown: An examination of Rodney Needham's allegations'.

25 For a general introduction to Malinowski's career see Chapter 1 of my *Anthropology and Anthropologists* (1983). For an introduction to Malinowski's Trobriand studies see M. Young (1979), *The Ethnography of Malinowski*.

mother or the father. But in that case a new question arose. How were family relationships and 'clan' relationships reconciled with each other?

Malinowski argued that family ties had to do with individual self-interest. Clan ties were a public, political imposition on the individual. Accordingly, individual family ties were structurally in conflict with these group relationships. Private sentiments tugged against public rules. People were driven by a healthy regard for their own interests rather than by automatic submission to any authority, including the authority of tradition. But they did not generally come clean about their real interests. They paid lip-service to the public morality of the clan, while doing their best to further the private interests of their families. They said one thing and did another.

This realist credo was illustrated above all by the contrast (drawn on many occasions by Malinowski) between the corporate social duty a man had to his sister's son – his heir – and the personal love which he felt for his own son. He had to leave his main estate to his sister's son, but he passed on what he could to his son. His sister's son succeeded him if he held office – but if he could marry his own son to the daughter of his sister, then his son's son would eventually succeed.

In this fashion Malinowski incorporated but transformed the classic opposition between family and clan.[26] He also milked it ingeniously for further theoretical points. For example, he argued against the Freudians that the Oedipus complex did not occur in the Trobriand Islands. A young man had no hidden resentments against his father. Instead he loathed his mother's brother because of his hold on him.[27]

For the rest, however, he scorned the issues which had pre-occupied Rivers. They were apparent, not real. The data on which they were based were misleading. Ethnographers should concern themselves with what people really did, not with vague ideological constructions. Kinship terminologies and 'kinship algebra' lost all interest when one recognized that words were really used to change social situations, not to describe them. Marriage rules were not some lifeless obligation. They were the consequences of self-inter-

26 For an interesting critique of Malinowski's procedure see Fortes (1957), 'Mali-
    nowski and the study of kinship'.
27 Malinowski (1927), *The Father in Primitive Psychology*.

est. If men married cross-cousins, as the Trobriand chiefs did, this was because it profited them to do so.

In 1930 Malinowski published a polemical article in *Man* in which he decared that an impasse had been reached in the study in kinship. Conjectural history and bastard algebra had debased the field, and even among experts there was confusion on fundamental issues. 'As a member of the inner ring', he wrote,

> I may say that whenever I meet Mrs Seligman or Dr Lowie or discuss matters with Radcliffe-Brown or Kroeber, I become at once aware that my partner does not understand anything in the matter, and I end usually with the feeling that this also applies to myself. This refers also to all our writings on kinship, and is fully reciprocal.

The impasse was due

> to the inheritance of false problems from anthropological tradition. We are still enmeshed in the question as to whether kinship in its origins was collective or individual, based on the family or the clan ... Another false problem is that of the origins and significance of classificatory systems of nomenclature.[28]

In the 1930s the leading school of social anthropology in Britain was at the London School of Economics, and that was dominated by Malinowski. Westermarck and Seligman taught there as well as Malinowski, but Malinowski proved to have enormous appeal as a teacher, and his weekly postgraduate seminars attracted and formed the young men and women who were to staff British social anthropology for the next thirty years.[29] At University College London, Elliot Smith and Perry promulgated their extreme diffusionism, but they had little influence. Elsewhere there was no real competition. Rivers had died in 1922, and although Haddon remained at Cambridge he lacked Rivers' intellectual power. He retired in 1926 and was replaced by an uninspiring ex-India Civil Service officer, T. C. Hodson. Armstrong was not given a tenured position and in the 1930s he became an economist.[30] At Oxford, anthropology remained marginal and uninspired.

---

28 Malinowski (1930), 'Kinship'. Quotations from p. 28 and p. 21.
29 See my *Anthropology and Anthropologists* (1983), Chapter 3.
30 See Urry (1985), 'W. E. Armstrong', p. 414. In 1939 Armstrong moved to University College, Southampton, as lecturer in economics. He ended his career as Professor of Economic Theory at what was by then the University of Southampton.

Malinowski's critique of Rivers became entrenched, part of the received wisdom of the discipline, alongside his new way of doing fieldwork and the theoretical assumption on which it was based, that reality was to be found in deeds rather than words (unless words themselves were deeds). But at the end of the 1930s Malinowski left for the USA, where he died soon after. At precisely the same moment Radcliffe-Brown returned to Britain to occupy the first chair in social anthropology at Oxford.

Radcliffe-Brown also pitched his arguments in opposition to Rivers, but his discourse admitted more of the traditional assumptions. His main lieutenants at Oxford were reacting against Malinowski, but they were unwittingly to demonstrate the continuity of Radcliffe-Brown's thought with the entrenched deep theory of social anthropology. Imagining that they were serving the revolution of Radcliffe-Brown, they revived the old anthropology in a new form.

CHAPTER 10

Descent theory: a phoenix from the ashes

At the worst possible time, in 1940, early in World War Two, three books were published which announced the advent of a new model in social anthropology. The texts were *African Political Systems*, edited by Meyer Fortes and E. E. Evans-Pritchard, and two monographs by Evans-Pritchard, *The Nuer* and *The Political System of the Anuak*. When peace came a second series of books appeared, which completed the establishment of the new paradigm. These were Meyer Fortes's two monographs on the Tallensi (1945 and 1949), Evans-Pritchard's 1951 monograph on Nuer kinship, and a second symposium, edited by Radcliffe-Brown and Forde, *African Systems of Kinship and Marriage*. By 1953, when Fortes published a review in the *American Anthropologist* entitled 'The structure of unilineal descent groups', he was able to refer to what was already a distinct and influential new paradigm, which had come to be known as 'lineage theory' or 'descent theory'.

Descent theory was by no means an inevitable development from the writings of Radcliffe-Brown and Malinowski. Its leading proponents, Meyer Fortes and E. E. Evans-Pritchard, were young Africanists, who had completed long periods of field research. Both had studied loosely-organized tribes without centralized authorities, and both were concerned to understand the way in which such political systems operated. Their field experience was therefore quite different from that of the earlier functionalists.

Yet it is significant that both Evans-Pritchard and Fortes had been directly influenced by Malinowski and Radcliffe-Brown. They had both been trained at the London School of Economics, where Malinowski was the dominant influence. Later, when they were formulating descent theory, they worked together at Oxford, where Radcliffe-Brown had been appointed to the new chair in

1937. Both were in reaction against Malinowski, and both drew upon the ideas of Radcliffe-Brown as they developed their own positions.

Three central assumptions of descent theory nevertheless derived from Malinowski. One was negative; the descent theorists followed Malinowski in ignoring kinship terminologies. (These only became respectable again when they were revived by alliance theorists who, following Rivers, called them relationship terminologies.)

The second, much more significant, assumption was that the family was a universal domestic institution. In virtually all societies, children were raised in families by two parents. The father always had a crucial role, even if physiological paternity was obfuscated. Only men had public roles, and the father was needed to legitimize a child – to attach it to the broader society.

Finally, the descent theorists took over Malinowski's ideas about the relationship between the family and the clan. Malinowski denied that the family developed out of the clan. If anything, the reverse was true. Where the clan existed, it was an outgrowth of elements of the family. If family and clan coexisted, each had specific functions and distinct spheres of operation. Family relationships created personal networks of individual, person-to-person ties. The clan in contrast was a political unit. Clan relationships were group relationships. Rivers and others had made a similar contrast, but they had mistaken it for an evolutionary series. Malinowski insisted that group ties based on clans could coexist with individual ties based on families.

Despite their obvious debts to Malinowski, Evans-Pritchard and Fortes appointed Radcliffe-Brown as the godfather of the new movement, but it is less easy to specify his contribution to their thinking. Fortes had difficulties when he tried to place Radcliffe-Brown in the genealogy. Writing towards the end of his life he recalled:

Evans-Pritchard states in his review of my *Dynamics* ... that the suggestion of how to handle the data of Nuer descent groups came from a conversation with Radcliffe-Brown in 1931 ... I was present on this occasion. Evans-Pritchard was describing his Nuer observations, whereupon Radcliffe-Brown said, as he stood in front of the fireplace: 'My dear Evans-Pritchard, it's perfectly simple, that's a segmentary lineage system, and you'll find a very good account of it by a man called

Gifford'. Thereupon Radcliffe-Brown gave us a lecture on Gifford's analysis of the Tonga system.[1]

His attempt to forge a link not only to Radcliffe-Brown but beyond to Gifford, one of Boas's students, is a tribute to Fortes' loyalty, but it is not persuasive as history. Fortes and Evans-Pritchard did adopt the term 'lineage' which Gifford preferred to 'clan', but that is the limit of their debt. Gifford's model of Tonga society was no more than the vaguest sketch and certainly did not inspire the models of Fortes and Evans-Pritchard.

Radcliffe-Brown's Australian models were more directly influential, but descent theorists referred most often to a paper he had published in 1935 – on the eve of his return to Britain – entitled 'Patrilineal and matrilineal succession'. The argument of this paper was in the tradition of Rivers and even of Maine, but Radcliffe-Brown's central proposition was more modern. He began from the assumption that the family was the core of the kinship system, whatever the form of descent. However, it was essential that rights could be transmitted between generations. Unilineal forms of organization were efficient mechanisms for transmitting social status and ordering the distribution of rights and duties in a community. Most primitive societies were therefore based on an association of such corporate descent groups. But kinship systems are outgrowths of the family, and so they are always bilateral, even though one line of descent is picked out for such organizational purposes.

Some elements of status will derive from a person's father, others from his or her mother. Normally these rights and duties are of contrasting kinds. Where the socially critical rights – the corporate rights – are transmitted through the father, one has a patrilineal form of organization; where they are transmitted through the mother, a matrilineal form. The differences between patrilineal and matrilineal systems (so central to the old evolutionists) were secondary. Functionally they were very similar.

Another element of descent theory derived from Durkheim's notion that primitive society was 'segmentary'. It was made up of equivalent parts which hung together because of shared values, or common sentimental attachments to symbolic foci, or (in the

---

1   Fortes (1979) in a preface to Holy (ed.), *Segmentary Lineage Systems Reconsidered.* Fortes referred to Gifford's *Tongan Society*, though an earlier paper by Gifford, 'Miwok lineages', was equally relevant.

formulation of Durkheim's nephew Mauss) through a system of exchanges. Durkheim had termed these segments 'clans'. Fortes and Evans-Pritchard equated them with the corporate descent groups of Radcliffe-Brown.[2] This Durkheimian perspective yielded a global view of 'primitive society' from the whole to the parts. It was markedly more structural than Malinowski's individualist perceptions, or even than Radcliffe-Brown's structural-functionalism, for he focused on role and status.

The model

The first published account of modern lineage theory is the introduction by Fortes and Evans-Pritchard to a symposium published in 1940 with the title *African Political Systems*. This volume brought together the initial reports of the new generation of Africanists who had been trained in Malinowski's seminar in the 1930s, and who had been financed by the International African Institute to make the first functionalist field studies of African societies. The editors and the contributors discussed a variety of issues, but what made the deepest impression was the classification they proposed of African political systems.

The basic dichotomy with which they worked went back to Maine and Morgan. It was between states and stateless societies. What the editors called Group A societies had 'centralized authority, administrative machinery and judicial institutions – in short a government'. Group B societies were those 'which lack centralized authority, administrative machinery, and constituted judicial institutions – in short which lack government'.[3] Societies without government were in turn divided into two categories. In some very small societies all members of the community are related to each other 'so that political relations are coterminous with kinship relations and the political structure and kinship organization are completely fused'.[4] In other societies, the organizational framework is provided by the segmentary lineage system.

The classification therefore preserved the conventional oppo-

---

2 Durkheim's formulation had been influenced by Robertson Smith's description of ancient Semitic societies. Robertson Smith's writings were also a direct source of inspiration for Evans-Pritchard.
3 Introduction to Fortes and Evans-Pritchard (1940), *African Political Systems*, p. 4.
4 *Op. cit.*, pp. 6–7.

sition between the primitive, stateless societies and the state. The stateless societies were still ordered by kinship rather than territory. Lineages provided the basis for settlements. Kin came before kith.

Membership of the local community [is] ... acquired as a rule through genealogical ties, real or fictional. The lineage principle takes the place of political allegiance, and the interrelations of territorial segments are directly co-ordinated with the interrelations of lineage segments.[5]

'The Nuer'

The new model came alive in the monographs by Evans-Pritchard on the Nuer and by Fortes on the Tallensi. These paradigmatic case-studies gave the first plausible account of how quite large societies could operate in the absence of central authorities. The secret lay in the structure of segmentary lineages.

Evans-Pritchard's monograph, *The Nuer* (1940), was the first volume of what was to be a trilogy on a dispersed Sudanic people, transhumant pastoralists and agriculturalists on the banks of the lower Nile. The first volume dealt with 'social structure', a term which Evans-Pritchard used in a very specific and restricted sense: 'By structure we mean relations between groups of persons within a system of groups'.[6] The units of this structure among the Nuer were unilineal descent groups. A second volume dealt with individual, person-to-person relationships of 'kinship'.

In Evans-Pritchard's account, the largest territorial and political community among the Nuer was the tribe, the unit within which homicide should be compensated for by blood-wealth rather than by vengeance. The tribal territory was divided into segments. At each successive level of segmentation the local groups were smaller and more cohesive. These territorial segments had no absolute political identity. They provided the context for communal action only in specific situations, and then only in opposition to like units. If a man in one village killed a man in another, the two entire villages would be forced into confrontation. If a man in either of these villages killed a man in another district, then all the villages in his district would unite against all the villages in the other district.

These processes of 'fission and fusion', which Evans-Pritchard

5 *Op. cit.*, p. 11.
6 Evans-Pritchard (1940b), *The Nuer*, p. 262.

identified as the dynamic of the segmentary political system, operated through the blood feud. Its 'function', Evans-Pritchard wrote, was 'to maintain the structural equilibrium between opposed tribal segments which are, nevertheless, politically fused in relation to large units'.[7]

But it was only when viewed from the outside that Nuer politics seemed to operate in territorial terms. The secret of Nuer society lay elsewhere. A series of descent groups provided the framework for the local community organization. These descent groups were based on patrilineal ties ('agnation'). The tribe, the largest territorial association, was built around a dominant clan whose members claimed to be descended in the male line from the clan founder. The clan was divided into smaller descent goups, formed by the patrilineal descendants of more recent ancestors. Within the clan there were several levels of 'nesting' segments, which in *African Political Systems* (1940) Fortes and Evans-Pritchard called maximal, major and minor lineages. These segments of the clan – various orders of lineages – were each associated with lower levels of local organization. They were real groups since they could be called into action through the mechanism of the feud.[8]

In Evans-Pritchard's exposition the lineage system was the expression, in a particular idiom, of the system of local organization; but equally the territorial system was an expression of the descent system. Indeed, he wrote:

The assimilation of community ties to lineage structure, the expression of territorial affiliation in a lineage idiom, and the expression of lineage affiliation in terms of territorial attachments, is what makes the lineage system so significant for a study of political organization.[9]

Though this correspondence might not be exact, the two systems could be represented in a single diagram (see Fig. 10.1). Blood and soil were two sides of a single coin.

The model's clarity and power were immediately apparent. One

---

7 *Op. cit.*, p. 159.
8 Evans-Pritchard's central argument could be restated in the words of Robertson Smith, writing about ancient Arabia:

> The key to all divisions and aggregations of Arab groups lies in the action and reaction of two principles: that the only effective bond is a bond of blood, and that the purpose of society is to unite men for offence and defence. These two principles meet in the law of the blood-feud. (Robertson Smith (1885), *Kinship and Marriage in Early Arabia*, p. 56)

9 Evans-Pritchard (1940b), *The Nuer*, p. 205.

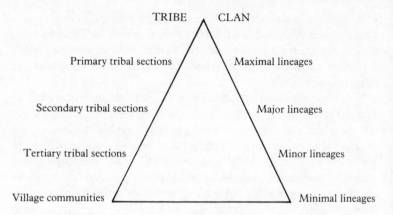

Figure 10.1   Blood and soil: Evans-Pritchard's model of Nuer social structure (from Evans-Pritchard (1940b), *The Nuer*, p. 248).

of the first critics of the book, the Africanist Audrey Richards – a loyal pupil of Malinowski – suggested, however, that the clarity was bought at the expense of verisimilitude. She remarked that her own field experience in Africa had taught her that:

> nothing is more remarkable than the lack of permanence of particular lineages or 'segments'; the infinite variety there is in their composition, their liability to change owing to historic factors, the strength of individual personalities and similar determinants. Such societies, in my experience, are not divided into distinct and logical systems of segments, but rather owe their being to the existence of a number of different principles of grouping.[10]

One of Evans-Pritchard's loyal young Oxford men, Max Gluckman, responded that Evans-Pritchard's detailed case materials would soon provide the empirical underpinnings for the model.[11] However, this was a line of defence which could not be sustained for long, particularly after the publication of Evans-Pritchard's

10 Richards' review of *The Nuer* in *Bantu Studies* (1941), p. 51.
11 Gluckman's Preface to Evans-Pritchard's *Some Aspects of Marriage and the Family Among the Nuer* (1945).

second Nuer monograph, *Kinship and Marriage among the Nuer*, which appeared in 1951. That book contained detailed information on the composition of local communities, and it became apparent that the relationship between the Nuer ethnography and the Nuer model was rather complicated. To appreciate just how complicated, it is worth considering briefly Evans-Pritchard's earlier essays on the Nuer, which appeared in *Sudan Notes and Records* in the 1930s.

In these earlier essays Evans-Pritchard noted that the system of territorial political groups did not actually mesh neatly with the system of clans and lineages. Far from brushing off this lack of fit, Evans-Pritchard specifically drew attention to it. It showed, so he suggested, that the Nuer were in a state of transition from a pure lineage system to a territorially-based polity. Generations of war and expansion 'broke up clans and lineages to an extent which must have greatly impaired the unifying influence of kinship'. As a result clans were diffused. They broke up into 'small lineages' which were

in frequent feud with their relatives and neighbours. This means that community of living tended to supplant community of blood as the essential principle of social cohesion though in a society based upon ties of kinship change took place by assimilating symbiotic [i.e. territorial] ties to kinship ties.[12]

This was precisely what an adherent of the classical model might have anticipated. Originally the Nuer had been organized into clans. Now they were advancing, developing a political system based upon territorial groups. This seems to have been Evans-Pritchard's own view, since he suggested that the remnants of the clan system now constituted 'the main obstacle to political development'.[13]

Five years later, however, *The Nuer* makes no mention of a possible movement from a clan system to a territorial system. In this book Evans-Pritchard adopts a functionalist model, in which the two modes of organization are treated as contemporary. Just as family and clan coexisted in Malinowski's ethnography, so here clan and territory, blood and soil, operated in tandem. But this formulation raised in a particularly acute form the problem of why

12 Evans-Pritchard (1933–5), 'The Nuer: tribe and clan', *Sudan Notes and Records*, Pt 3, pp. 86–7.
13 *Ibid.*

the lineage segments did not in fact neatly match the territorial segments. Evans-Pritchard did not attempt to argue along the lines suggested by Gluckman, that the model captured the empirical form of actual groups out there, camped across the flood-plains of the White Nile. However, the empirical discrepancies could no longer be attributed to the inevitably untidy processes of historical transition. Evans-Pritchard's solution was to argue that the lineage system existed on a different level of reality from the territorial system. It was 'a system of values linking tribal segments and providing the idiom in which their relations can be expressed and directed'.[14] The lineage system was an ideological construct, a way of thinking and talking about the actual camps and villages and their relationships with each other. It was assumed to be primary, since values were primary; but it need not match any particular concrete praxis.

Given this new formulation, the contrasts between the model and what Evans-Pritchard and Fortes sometimes termed 'the actualities' were no longer a source of embarrassment. Evans-Pritchard, indeed, came to glory in the lack of fit between the rules and values (which constituted the reality for Radcliffe-Brown), and the practice (on which Malinowski insisted). 'The underlying agnatic principle is ... in glaring contrast to social actualities. But the actualities are always changing and passing while the principle endures'.[15] He even seemed to suggest that the more the Nuer diverged from the model, the more fundamental were the values encapsulated in the model.

I suggest that it is the clear, consistent, and deeply rooted lineage structure of the Nuer which permits persons and families to move about and attach themselves so freely, for shorter or longer periods, to whatever community they choose by whatever cognatic or affinal tie they find it convenient to emphasize; and that it is on account of the firm values of the structure that this flux does not cause confusion or bring about social disintegration. It would seem it may be partly because the agnatic principle is unchallenged in Nuer society that the tracing of descent through women is so prominent and matrilocality so prevalent. However

14 Evans-Pritchard (1940b), *The Nuer*, p. 212.
15 Evans-Pritchard (1945), *Some Aspects of Marriage and the Family among the Nuer*, p. 63.

much the actual configurations of kinship clusters may vary and change, the lineage structure is invariable and stable.[16]

As Glickman commented, 'This statement implies that if the principles were challenged, descent through women would be less prominent and matrilocality less prevalent.'[17] It seemed an unlikely claim. In a similar vein Evans-Pritchard could suggest that the wide cognatic range of Nuer marriage prohibitions was also somehow a proof of their patrilineal bias. 'Nuer make any kind of cognatic relationship to several degrees a bar to marriage, and, at least so it seems to me, it is a bar to marriage because of the fundamental agnatic principle running through Nuer society.'[18] Social scientists have from time to time been accused of evading empirical tests of their theses. Evans-Pritchard went one better; every disproof somehow consolidated his faith. The model was about values, and if the values were sufficiently powerful then they would permit great divergences of practice. The appeal was to faith, not to acts. Malinowski was firmly put in his place.

Some critics, however, pointed out that the model does not capture basic Nuer values. Indeed, certain Nuer values appear to contradict it. This is the vital issue in the assessment of the model, but it cannot be simply resolved by an appeal to ethnography. Once again it is instructive to trace the development of Evans-Pritchard's thought.

In an early essay in *Sudan Notes and Records*, Evans-Pritchard remarked on the difficult fieldwork conditions he had to endure, and on the rapid changes in Nuer society. In consequence, he confessed:

I was more successful, for these reasons, in grasping their kinship system and the daily contacts of cattle camp life than the organization of the less tangible clan and tribal groups ... in the case of the second I had to rely largely upon what little information could be dragged out of the occasional informants by question and answer methods of enquiry. I am therefore compelled to generalise upon what may sometimes be insufficient data and to regard some of my conclusions as working hypotheses though I feel that I have drawn the outlines correctly.[19]

16 Evans-Pritchard (1951), *Kinship and Marriage Among the Nuer*, p. 28.
17 M. Glickman (1971), 'Kinship and credit among the Nuer', p. 309, note.
18 Evans-Pritchard (1951), *Kinship and Marriage Among the Nuer*, p. 47.
19 Evans-Pritchard (1933–5), 'The Nuer: tribe and clan', *Sudan Notes and Records*, Pt 3, p. 76.

Whatever the reasons, Evans-Pritchard's difficulty with the 'less tangible clan and tribal groups' were apparently shared by the Nuer themselves. 'What exactly is meant by lineage and clan?' he asked rhetorically. 'One thing is fairly certain, namely, that the Nuer do not think in group abstractions called clans. In fact, as far as I am aware, he has no word meaning clan and you cannot ask a man an equivalent of 'What is your clan?'[20]

These scrupulously-recorded uncertainties suggest that the Nuer would have had difficulty in constructing a way of life upon the values of clan and lineage. But some years later, in *The Nuer*, although no further fieldwork had supervened, Evans-Pritchard gave a very different impression, writing that:

it is only when one already knows the clans and their lineages and their various ritual symbols, as the Nuer does, that one can easily place a man's clan through his lineage or by his spear-name and honorific salutation, for Nuer speak fluently in terms of lineage. A lineage is *thok mac*, the hearth, or *thok dwiel*, the entrance to the hut, or one may talk of *kar*, a branch.[21]

Apparently, the Nuer had achieved a fresh precision by abandoning a 'clan' model for a 'lineage' model, just as Radcliffe-Brown, or perhaps Gifford, had advocated. But what was their idea of 'lineages' of which they 'speak fluently'?

A Nuer rarely talks about his lineage as distinct from his community, and in contrast to other lineages which form part of it, outside a ceremonial context. I have watched a Nuer who knew precisely what I wanted, trying on my behalf to discover from a stranger the name of his lineage. He often found great initial difficulty in making the man understand the information required of him, for Nuer think generally in terms of local divisions and of the relationships between them, and an attempt to discover lineage affiliations apart from their community relations, and outside a ceremonial context, generally led to misunderstanding in the opening stages of an inquiry.[22]

When Evans-Pritchard elicited a Nuer diagram of 'clan' or 'lineage' relations, it was not at all like the tree-and-branch imagery which he favoured. On the contrary, the Nuer drew a focus, with lines radiating out from it. As Holy has pointed out, this was a map of

20 *Op. cit.*, Pt 1, p. 28.
21 Evans-Pritchard (1940b), *The Nuer*, p. 195.
22 *Op. cit.*, p. 203.

a particular set of territorial relations.[23] Evans-Pritchard in fact conceded that this particular informant visualized the social system 'primarily as actual relations between groups of kinsmen within local communities rather than as a tree of descent'.[24]

The Nuer do not seem to have even the basic vocabulary for a folk model which would correspond however loosely to the model of the segmentary lineage system. And even if the Nuer could be shown to value a unilineal descent group structure, it is hardly credible that their commitment to agnatic values *explains* the loose, cognatic pattern of relationships which is found on the ground. It is more reasonable to conclude that the Nuer model provides reliable guidance neither to Nuer behaviour nor to Nuer values. Even the Nuer are not like *The Nuer*. The model must be read as an attempt to translate the classic evolutionist stages of political development into aspects of a single structure. Blood and soil are different dimensions of a single system, time and space two ways of conceptualizing the same social reality. It is a brilliant synthesis, subtly defended.

The Tallensi

Fortes' analysis of the segmentary structure of Tallensi society provides an instructive counterpoint to Evans-Pritchard's Nuer model. Less elegant, less hermetic, Fortes' account is even more revealing of the problems which arose when descent theory was applied. He shared Evans-Pritchard's view that the social structure depended on a system of values: 'the centre of gravity of the equilibrium characteristic of a stable and homogeneous primitive society lies in its scheme of cultural values'.[25] But Fortes was not prepared to retreat entirely to a world of values. Rather than indulging in the Father Brown paradoxes which so delighted Evans-Pritchard, he tried to stretch the model, to make it more accommodating. The price was a sacrifice of precision and, at worst, fuzziness.

The Tallensi, a scattered population of farmers in northern Ghana, were like the Nuer to the extent that they lacked kings and

---

23 Fortes (1979), 'The segmentary lineage structure', in Holy (ed.), *Segmentary Lineage Systems Reconsidered*, pp. 5–6.
24 Evans-Pritchard (1940b), *The Nuer*, pp. 202–3.
25 Fortes (1945b), 'An anthropologist's point of view'.

chiefs. (Actually there were chiefs of a sort, but Fortes paid little attention to their role.) Like the Nuer again, family relationships were very important, and patrilineal ties provided a means of ordering political affiliations. Following Evans-Pritchard, Fortes treated the putative system of unilineal descent groups separately from the network of individual kinship relations. Like Evans-Pritchard again, he devoted a separate monograph to each type of organization.[26]

The Tallensi population was divided between the autochthonous Talis and the immigrant Namoos, who assumed a position of political superiority. Fortes' most detailed descriptions of a clan structure actually deal with the dominant section of the Namoos. However, he argued that the Namoo-Tali stratification was secondary. Tallensi society was an egalitarian and uncentralized congeries of local communities. These local communities were organized on the basis of unilineal descent groups, and were linked to other unilineal descent groups in 'fields of clanship'.

These associations of lineages did not produce a coherent structure like the Nuer pattern of 'nesting' segments. Nor were they mechanically ordered by genealogical connection, however fictitious. Clan ties were constituted in all sorts of ways. They might be based upon simple spatial proximity, without any genealogical basis; on periodic ritual collaboration; on a shared rule of exogamy; or even occasionally on a pattern of intermarriage. Some clans, however, were ordered upon principles so uncertain that Fortes was obliged to distinguish a further category of 'extra-clan ties of clanship'.

It was especially difficult to distinguish clan ties from the effects of neighbourhood relations. Fortes also recorded that 'lineages belonging to the same clan, or to a series of linked clans . . . do not have completely congruent fields of clanship'.[27] 'Clanship ties cut across clans.'[28] Once again a less rigid specification was required: 'a clan is the region where the fields of clanship of two or more lineages have the maximum overlap'.[29]

The lineages within (or overlapping) the clan were elaborately

---

26 Fortes, *The Dynamics of Clanship Among the Tallensi* (1945a) and *The Web of Kinship Among the Tallensi* (1949a).
27 Fortes (1945a), *Dynamics of Clanship*, p. 63.
28 *Op. cit.*, p. 63.
29 *Op. cit.*, p. 63.

distinguished into levels. 'We thus have a hierarchy of lineage segments: the effective minimal lineage or segment, the nuclear lineage or segment, the inner lineage or segment, the medial lineage or segment, the section or major segment, the maximal lineage'.[30] These segments, however, were not easy to distinguish in operation, being relative and situationally variable. 'As usual in Tali social organization no rigorous criterion can be found.'[31]

Having reached this point, Fortes must have been tempted to follow Evans-Pritchard and beat a retreat to the level of values. But he conceded that the Tallensi did not articulate these supposedly fundamental principles. 'These distinctions are not made by the natives ... it should be noted that the Tallensi have no term for the lineage.'[32]

Fortes paid especial attention to the function of non-lineal kinship. If the Nuer and the Tallensi were organized politically into unilineal descent groups based on agnation, what was the significance of cognatic kinship? Why were ties through the mother so vital? For Evans-Pritchard they were simply an area of play which could be exploited with safety precisely because the central structure was so secure. Fortes argued, like Malinowski, that domestic relations of kinship had a very specific set of functions; they had to do with moral sentiments, with emotional attachments. Domestic relationships also stretched beyond the clan, setting up networks of cross-cutting ties that linked individuals across political boundaries and so helped sustain the political structure itself. He contrasted relationships of 'descent' and 'complementary filiation'. Among Malinowski's Trobrianders the father provided sympathy and support while the public political relationships of the matrilineage were typically full of tension. Among the patrilineal Tallensi relationships on the mother's side of the family had a similar supportive function.

Fortes' most subtle and powerful presentation of this thesis occurred in an essay on another West African society, the Ashanti. The Ashanti were in many respects a 'matrilineal society', but Rattray, the early ethnographer (a correspondent of Frazer), had reported that they were moving on to a patrilineal condition, and that they exhibited a dual system of descent. Moreover, the family

---

30 *Op. cit.*, p. 205.
31 *Op. cit.*, p. 203.
32 Fortes (1949a), *The Web of Kinship Among the Tallensi*, p. 10.

group was emerging, signalling the passage to a more advanced system. Fortes applied the Malinowskian principle that 'clan' and 'family' coexisted, but in tension with each other. Moreover, this tension worked itself out in different ways during the life-cycle. When a young couple first married, they were still attached to the matrilineages. As they had children and these children began to grow up, so the ties of the children to the father became more significant, and the individual family tended to form a single residential unit. Then the children left home to live with their mother's brother, and the mother followed them to her brother's home. The family had its own specific functions, but these were particularly important as the children were growing up.[33]

In his essay 'The structure of unilineal descent groups' Fortes generalized the argument:

It appears that there is a tendency for interests, rights and loyalties to be divided on broadly complementary lines, into those that have the sanction of law or other public institutions for the enforcement of good conduct, and those that rely on religion, morality, conscience and sentiment for due observance. Where corporate descent groups exist the former seem to be generally tied to the descent groups, the latter to the complementary line of filiation.[34]

Elaboration and reaction

In the 1950s British social anthropology entered a period of sudden institutional growth. At least from the outside, it appeared also to become a coherent school. Every recruit had to do a spell of field-work on the Malinowskian model (and for a while it seemed that this fieldwork had to be in Africa); and the resulting materials had to be processed in the mould of the new descent theory.

Segmentary lineage systems now turned up virtually everywhere. A new symposium, edited by Middleton and Tait, *Tribes Without Rulers*, brought together the work of a whole cadre of 'lineage theorists' working in Africa. The systems they described seemed astonishingly uniform; indeed, virtually indistinguishable from each other. Further, it now appeared that these lineage structures explained all sorts of apparently unrelated phenomena. Gluckman appealed to the lineage structure to account for differential divorce

---

33 Fortes (1949b), 'Time and social structure'.
34 Fortes (1953), 'The structure of unilineal descent groups', p. 34.

rates.[35] Marwick used it to explain the incidence of witchcraft accusations.[36] Ancestor worship, burial rituals, the position of women, all came down to the structure of unilineal descent groups.

And if a fieldworker came across what seemed incontrovertibly to be a state, he defined it in opposition to segmentary lineage systems. Southall, working in East Africa, invented a new type, the segmentary state, to bridge the gap between lineage-based societies and the state.[37] Kirchhoff – an American-based devotee of Engels – proposed an equivalent construct, the hierarchically-ordéred clan, which he called the 'conical clan'.[38] Leach apparently found something of the sort in the Kachin hills in Burma, where stratified clans consolidated into states or collapsed into segmentary lineages.[39]

By the 1960s, however, a coherent critique of lineage theory began to be formulated within British social anthropology. One strand of this critique was ethnographic, but it derived from work carried out in New Guinea rather than in Africa. In New Guinea, anthropologists trained or influenced directly by the British descent theorists were studying societies which were on the face of it perfect candidates for the orthodox treatment. There were no powerful central authorities in the Highlands. Patrilineal descent was emphasized. And indeed one of the first and most influential monographs, by Meggitt, had applied the Africanist model with little modification to a Highland tribe, the Mae-Enga.[40] Yet although Meggitt's study was at least as sophisticated as the best of the Africanist descent studies, it provoked an immediate reaction among other fieldworkers.

The reaction was crystallized by a British Africanist descent theorist, John Barnes, who had recently been appointed to a chair at the Australian National University, which was the centre of the new wave of New Guinea studies. On board ship, travelling out to Australia, without the resources – and distractions – of a library,

35 Gluckman (1950), 'Kinship and marriage among the Lozi of Northern Rhodesia and the Zulu of Natal'.
36 Marwick (1965), *Sorcery in its Social Setting*.
37 Southall (1953), *Alur Society*.
38 See Fried (1957), 'The classification of corporate unilineal descent groups', pp. 4–6.
39 Leach (1954), *Political Systems of Highland Burma*.
40 Meggitt (1965), *The Lineage System of the Mae-Enga of New Guinea*.

he reflected on the contrasts between Africa and New Guinea and wrote a brief but extremely influential paper.

The people of the New Guinea Highlands first became accessible for study at a time when anthropological discussion was dominated by the analyses of political and kinship systems that had recently been made in Africa. Ethnographers working in New Guinea were able to present interim accounts of the polysegmentary stateless systems of the Highlands with less effort and greater speed by making use of the advances in understanding already achieved by their colleagues who had studied similar social systems in Africa. Yet it has become clear that Highland societies fit awkwardly into African moulds.[41]

To begin with, descent principles did not provide the foundation of community organization. Local groups often included large numbers of non-agnates, and some of these might be powerful members of the community. Status distinctions within the local community did not depend on descent. Barnes contrasted the variety of affiliations of typical individuals with the apparently solidary group structures of the Tallensi. A corollary was the absence of 'predictability or regularity in the segmentary pattern'.[42] In sum, as his colleague Paula Brown complained:

we may be hard put to decide, for example, whether descent groups are mainly agnatic with numerous accretions, or cognatic with a patrilineal basis. We find that people are more mobile than any rules of descent and residence should warrant, that genealogies are too short to be helpful, that we don't know what 'corporate' means when applied to some groups, that local and descent groups are fragmented and change their alignments.[43]

Some authors suggested that the problem was one of level of abstraction. As Langness put it, 'the comparisons made are often between jural rules (ideologies) of the lineal-segmentary societies of Africa, and presumed (but not actual) statistical norms of New Guinea'.[44] This suggested that the New Guinea studies might be comparable to the African, if all concerned restricted themselves to the level of values. But Highland values seemed very different from the values which were described by Evans-Pritchard and

---

41 Barnes (1962), 'African models in the New Guinea Highlands', p. 5.
42 *Op. cit.*, p. 9.
43 Brown (1962), 'Non-agnates among the patrilineal Chimbu', p. 57.
44 Langness (1964), 'Some problems in the conceptualization of Highlands social structures', p. 163.

Fortes. Locality was generally emphasized. There was even a widespread belief that living in the same place and eating the same food created kinship. These difficulties drove some to suggest that there need be no necessary connection between ideology and practice in descent systems. 'In major territorial descent groups, there is no particular relation between the descent ideology and group composition', Sahlins argued. 'A descent doctrine does not express group composition but imposes itself upon the composition.'[45]

In any case, far from seeking safety in the world of values, the Australian-based students of New Guinea were inclined to concentrate upon actions. And if one looked at the situation on the ground, then perhaps New Guinea was not so peculiar after all, since even the Tallensi and the Nuer did not rigidly follow the precepts of the descent model when it came to the organization of local groups. Kaberry wrote that 'an analysis of some Nuer communities reveals that they have a number of the characteristics attributed by Barnes to many Highland societies'.[46]

It may have been the distance from the English universities that fed the scepticism of anthropologists working in New Guinea. They were well aware of the Africanist descent models, but they were to a certain extent free of the weight of the orthodoxy. Within Britain other non-Africanists, particularly loyal former students of Malinowski, were also less committed to descent theory. Some followed Firth and questioned the universal superiority of unilineal descent groups; in Oceania, apparently, descent groups could be set up in a perfectly satisfactory way on the basis of 'cognatic descent'.[47] Among the Malinowskians there was also a nagging feeling – first enunciated by Audrey Richards – that the descent models were too neat, too abstract to capture the realities of social action, and that the anthropologist should not ignore the 'actualities'.

The leading home-based dissident was Edmund Leach, a former student of Malinowski and a close associate of Raymond Firth.[48] In a monograph on a Sri Lankan village, *Pul Eliya*, published in 1961, Leach turned the classic arguments of descent theory on their head. In essence, he put the Malinowskian case.

45 Sahlins (1965), 'On the ideology and composition of descent groups', p. 104.
46 Kaberry (1967), 'The plasticity of New Guinea kinship'.
47 See, e.g., Firth (1963), 'Bilateral descent groups: an operational viewpoint'.
48 See my *Anthropology and Anthropologists* (1983), Chapter 6.

To begin with, descent theorists preferred illusion to reality.

In Evans-Pritchard's studies of the Nuer and also in Fortes's studies of the Tallensi unilineal descent turns out to be largely an ideal concept to which the empirical facts are only adapted by means of fictions. Both societies are treated as extreme examples of patrilineal organization. The evident importance attached to matrilateral and affinal kinship connections is not so much explained as explained away.[49]

Moreover, the descent theorists looked for explanations in quite the wrong places and represented behaviour in a completely unrealistic manner. People's behaviour was not governed by principles of kinship and descent, and their strategies could not be captured by the rigid models of descent theory. Social systems all had to allow room for manoeuvres and manipulation.[50] Normal people were motivated by self-interest. Communities were not elaborate ideological constructions: they were competitive associations of individuals making a living as best they could in a particular landscape. A community was 'simply a collection of individuals who derive their livelihood from a piece of territory laid out in a particular way'.[51]

The classic anthropological opposition was between blood and soil. Lineage theory assumed that blood was paramount. On Leach's argument everything in Pul Eliya revolved around the soil. 'Pul Eliya is a society in which locality and not descent forms the basis of corporate grouping; it is a very simple and perhaps almost obvious finding, yet it seems to me to have very important implications for anthropological theory and method'.[52] Admittedly, the villagers did talk a lot about kinship, but this was their way of wrapping up the reality. Kinship was an idiom, a way of talking about property relationships; and if kinship relationships did not conform with the real dispositions of property and power, they were massaged into appropriate patterns.

Leach's critique suffered to some extent because he manifestly underplayed the real, independent significance of at least certain kinship relationships in Pul Eliya. The attack had another obvious weakness. His case-study dealt with a village in Sri Lanka. Who

---

49   Leach (1961b), *Pul Eliya*, p. 8.
50   Leach (1962), 'On certain unconsidered aspects of double descent systems'.
51   Leach (1961b), *Pul Eliya*, p. 300.
52   *Op. cit.*, p. 301.

would have expected these Asian peasants to operate African-style segmentary lineages? Indeed, in making Pul Eliya a test of descent theory he was paying a massive tribute to its influence. By the same token, however, the critique stung, since the pretensions of lineage theory had become very great indeed. And in essence his critique was independent of the case-study. His claim was that descent theory distracted attention from fundamental features of social organization. Increasingly, it concerned itself with ideological constructs. And were these the constructs of the actors – or of the anthropologists? 'It might even be the case that "the structure of unilineal descent groups" is a *total* fiction; illuminating no doubt, like other theological ideas, but still a fiction.'[53]

Later Leach revived another issue. Descent theorists had ignored 'exogamy'. This had, however, been put on the agenda once again by Lévi-Strauss. In a widely-read polemical exchange in *Man*, Leach claimed that Fortes, 'while recognizing that ties of affinity have comparable importance to ties of descent, disguises the former under his expresssion "complementary filiation"'.[54] These questions are discussed in the following chapter.

By the 1970s descent theory was in retreat. It had failed to establish significant bases outside the British school, and even within Britain it was beset by opponents, old and new: the die-hard Malinowskians; the new 'alliance theorists', who followed Lévi-Strauss; and the non-Africanists, who had always been uneasy about the dominance of the Africanist model. There was a moment when it seemed that a revival was possible. A new wave of neo-Marxist theorists emerged, who tried to resuscitate the ideas of Engels with the help of the British models. The segmentary lineage system was transformed into the 'lineage mode of production', in which old men exploited young men and women.[55] This translation of Fortes' and Evans-Pritchard's models into the language of class analysis did not catch on, however, though it did briefly produce a market for reprints of Morgan.

---

53 Leach (1961b), *Pul Eliya*, p. 302.
54 Leach (1957), 'Aspects of bride wealth and marriage stability'. Cf. Fortes' (1959) response, 'Descent, filiation and affinity: a rejoinder to Dr Leach'.
55 See Meillassoux (1981), *Maidens, Meal and Money*; and Rey (1975), 'The lineage mode of production' and (1979), 'Class contradiction in lineage societies'.

CHAPTER 11

A short history of alliance theory

Descent theory was a transformation of the leading ideas in British social anthropology. Developed by young ethnographers on the cutting edge of the discipline, it was immediately applied to fresh field-data. Its main rival in post-war anthropology was alliance theory, but alliance theory was invented by a man with no training in anthropology and with a minimum of field experience.

Alliance theory is very much the creation of Lévi-Strauss. He developed it out of his own reading, and this reading took him into the world of anthropology as it had been in the first decades of the twentieth century. Lévi-Strauss has himself singled out two influences on the development of his ideas on kinship: one is that of Roman Jakobson and so of linguistics; the other that of the school of Durkheim, and in particular Marcel Mauss's ideas about reciprocity and exchange.[1] I shall, however, suggest that these influences were less directly important than that of James George Frazer. Writing the history of alliance theory, I shall therefore have to retrace my steps and begin almost at the beginning of my story again.

Lévi-Strauss was born in Brussels, of French parents, in 1908.[2] He was educated in France and took a teacher's qualification in philosophy at the Sorbonne in 1931. For a time he taught philosophy at high schools, but he became intrigued by ethnology –

---

1 See Lévi-Strauss (1983), *Introduction to the Work of Marcel Mauss* and Part 1 of his *Structural Anthropology* (1963).

2 There is little biographical information available on Lévi-Strauss. His *Tristes Tropiques* (1973) is a memoir but has little personal informaton. Pouillon's entry in *The Social Science Encyclopaedia* (edited Adam Kuper and Jessica Kuper) is brief but useful. See also D. Pace (1983) *Levi-Strauss, The Bearer of Ashes*.

largely for philosophical reasons, and through his reading. Between 1935 and 1939 he served with a French university mission in São Paulo, in Brazil, and made several short ethnographic expeditions in the Mato Grosso and the Amazon.

When Germany invaded France he was mobilized. After the defeat of the French army he escaped to the United States, where he spent the last years of the war as part of a circle of exiled continental intellectuals in New York. During this period he made contact with Boas and with Lowie, but he was particularly inspired by another exile, the Russian structural linguist, Roman Jakobson. Under the influence of Jakobson he came to believe that cultural systems were informed by unconscious structures, mental grids, which constrained the ways in which people thought and communicated. He was also persuaded that linguistics should provide a model for anthropology. It was the most successful of the human sciences, and the first to break through the barrier dividing the humanities from the natural sciences.[3]

While he was in New York Lévi-Strauss seems to have devoted much of his time to his researches, spending many hours in the famous New York City Library. After the war ended he served briefly as cultural attaché in the French mission in Washington, DC, but he then returned to France and in 1949 published his massive book on kinship theory, *The Elementary Structures of Kinship* (1969).

It would be interesting to know precisely what he read in that alien library, and to what extent his reading was guided by others. My guess is that he read a great deal, with very little outside advice (although Lowie read the final manuscript for him[4]); and that his starting-point, or at least his main point of reference, was Volume 2 of Frazer's *Folklore in the Old Testatment*, a book (first published in 1918) which is discussed again and again in the course of the *Elementary Structures*.

---

3 See Part 1 of Lévi-Strauss's *Structural Anthropology* (1963).
4 Lévi-Strauss remarked in his preface to the second edition that Lowie had returned the manuscript to him with the ambiguous observation that it was 'in the grand style' (Lévi-Strauss (1969), *Elementary Structures of Kinship*, p. xxvii).

Frazer's theory of cross-cousin marriage

Chapter 4 in Volume 2 of Frazer's *Folklore in the Old Testament* is entitled 'Jacob's Marriage'. In characteristic Frazerian style, a classical episode is described – here Jacob's marriages to Laban's daughters, who were his cousins – and the question is posed whether the apparently strange actions of the protagonists can be explained as primitive customs. In this case:

The customs in question may conveniently be distinguished as three in number, namely; first, marriage with a cousin, and in particular the marriage of a man with his mother's brother's daughter, or, to put it conversely, the marriage of a woman with her father's sister's son; second, the marriage of a man with two sisters in their lifetime, the elder sister being married before the younger; and third, the practice of a son-in-law serving his father-in-law for a wife.[5]

In fact Frazer was mainly concerned with cross-cousin marriage and the other customs were dealt with only cursorily. He followed his usual method, which was to search for parallels in 'primitive societies', and, having assembled comparative material, to seek an explanation for the custom which he was investigating. The pursuit was characteristically leisurely and thorough, and the final product, the chapter on Jacob's marriage, would make a substantial modern book – it runs to almost 300 printed pages.

The sources of this interest in cross-cousin marriage have already been described. Fison, in his reflections on Australian marriage classes, had demonstrated that sister-exchange between moieties was congruent with the identification of two kinds of cousin. Children of the father's sister and of the mother's brother were never members of one's own moiety, and were therefore marriageable. They were distinguished in the terminology from parallel cousins and siblings. Tylor had coined for them the term 'cross-cousins'.[6] He had also stated as a general proposition that cross-cousin marriage was one of the simplest forms of exogamy, deriving directly from dual organization. Whether moieties were matrilineal or patrilineal, they always excluded cross-cousins. The same indeed was true if a system of patrilineal moieties was superimposed upon a system of matrilineal moieties. Tylor's argument implied that dual

5 Frazer (1918), *Folklore in the Old Testament*, vol. 2, p. 97.
6 Tylor (1889), 'On a method of investigating the development of institutions'. This paper was discussed in Chapter 5 of this book.

organization made cross-cousins marriageable almost by accident. Nevertheless, the effect – marriage with cross-cousins – persisted after the moiety framework itself had been abandoned.

In his usual fashion, Frazer began by trying to define the 'custom' involved. In many societies there was a curious opposition between 'cross-cousins' and other cousins, whom he proposed to call 'ortho-cousins'. Cross-cousins were marriageable, ortho-cousins were not. Moreover, he noted that in some societies one but not the other type of cross-cousin was marriageable; usually, where such a distinction was made, one could marry a mother's brother's daughter but not a father's sister's daughter.

The next step was to establish the distribution of this custom. In India cross-cousin marriage was common in the south, being particularly conspicuous among the Dravidians. In the Aryan north it was rare. Elsewhere in Asia it was prominent among the Chin and Kachin of Burma and the Gilyaks of Siberia. There were also traces of the custom in America, Africa, Indonesia, New Guinea and Australia.

The next question was, 'Why is the marriage of cross-cousins favoured?'[7] Following established tradition, Frazer looked for an answer first of all in Australia. Here he discovered an economic rationale for the exchange of women in marriage. In Australia a man acquired a wife in exchange for a sister or a daughter, for he had nothing else to offer.

Thus it appears that among the Australian aborigines a woman is prized not merely as a breeder of children, a nurse, a labourer, and a porter, but also as an article of barter; for in this last capacity she possesses a high commercial value, being exchangeable, either temporarily or permanently, for another woman or for other valuable commodities such as rugs and boomerangs. Hence a man who is rich in daughters or sisters is rich indeed. In truth, among these savages the female sex answers in some measure the purpose of a medium of exchange; they are the nearest native representative of the coin of the realm.[8]

In short, the exchange of sisters or daughters was a form of barter in a society 'where women had a high economic value as labourers, but where private property was as yet at so rudimentary a stage

---

7 This question provides the heading for a section of the chapter in Frazer's book; see Frazer (1918), p. 193.

8 *Op. cit.*, p. 198.

that a man had practically no equivalent to give for a wife except another woman'.[9]

If this exchange was satisfactory, it might be repeated by the offspring of the married couples. They would then be marrying double cross-cousins – mother's brother's children who were at the same time father's sister's children. So sister exchange might lead to cross-cousin marriage. As Frazer explained, 'The same economic motive might lead the offspring of such unions, who would be cross-cousins, to marry each other, and thus in the easiest and most natural manner the custom of cross-cousin marriage would arise and be perpetuated'.[10] Although the economic motive for cross-cousin marriage could only be demonstrated in a few specific cases, it must explain the custom of cross-cousin marriage wherever it was to be found, 'for under the surface alike of savagery and of civilization the economic forces are as constant and uniform in their operation as the forces of nature, of which, indeed, they are merely a peculiarly complex manifestation'.[11]

Even if Frazer were right, he had to recognize that he had dealt only with one part of the puzzle. Although economic motives might explain a preference for cross-cousin marriage, why was marriage with ortho-cousins generally forbidden?[12] Like Tylor before him, Frazer argued that where marriage was prohibited with ortho-cousins, this was a relic of a former moiety system. Moieties had been introduced to stop men marrying their sisters, but a consequence of their establishment was that marriage with ortho-cousins was also made impossible, since they were always members of one's own moiety.

The ban on ortho-cousin marriage might go back to the moiety structure, but Frazer was reluctant to adopt Tylor's deduction that cross-cousin marriage was also a relic of a former moiety form of organization. If this were the case, then his economic explanation for the custom was at best redundant. Accordingly he concluded that sister-exchange had been introduced even before brother-sister marriage was forbidden. Since cross-cousin marriage derived directly from sister-exchange, 'it is possible and indeed probable

9 *Op. cit.*, p. 220.
10 *Ibid.*
11 *Ibid.*
12 *Op. cit.*, p. 221.

that the practice of cousin marriage and the preference for it long preceded the two-class system of exogamy'.[13]

This left Frazer with two quite separate explanations for clearly related phenomena: one dealt with the prohibition on ortho-cousin marriage; the other with the preference for cross-cousin marriage. This was clearly unsatisfactory, and at times Frazer implied that the preference for cross-cousin marriage and the ban on ortho-cousin marriage could both be traced back to an original moiety structure. 'Hence wherever the dual organization exists or has formerly existed, we may expect to find the preference for the marriage of cross-cousins and the prohibition of the marriage of ortho-cousins.'[14] In consequence, he argued, cross-cousin marriage is found in very much the same areas as those in which dual organization has been reported. Moreover, if there are any traces of a former state of dual organization – totemic exogamy or a classificatory kinship terminology – then one should expect to find a system of cross-cousin marriage.

An alternative economic explanation of some forms of cross-cousin marriage had been proposed by F. E. Richards, according to whom cross-cousin marriage was a way of evading inconvenient rules of inheritance.[15] For example, a man in a matrilineal society, who had to accept that his possessions would pass to a nephew, might marry his daughter to a sister's son in order to allow her to share in his estate after his death. Frazer admitted this explanation as a special case, and Malinowski put forward a variant of this idea in his analysis of patrilateral cross-cousin marriage in Trobriand chiefly families.[16]

Rivers had of course proposed a much more radical alternative theory concerning the origin of cross-cousin marriage. According to Rivers, it derived from a previous rule whereby a man might marry the wife of his mother's brother in a gerontocratic society. Frazer objected that marriage with the mother's brother's wife 'appears to have been rare and exceptional in other parts of the

---

13 *Op. cit.*, p. 235.

14 *Op. cit.*, p. 240.

15 F. J. Richards (1914), 'Cross-cousin marriage in South India'.

16 Frazer remarked that Richards' hypothesis posited 'a sort of compromise between matrilineal succession and Brahmanic law' (*Folklore* (1918), pp. 220–1, footnote). Malinowski clearly echoed this formulation in his account of Trobriand cross-cousin marriage; see, e.g., his 1935 *Coral Gardens*, vol. 1.

world'.[17] Moreover, if Rivers was correct, then cross-cousin marriage must have been a late development in the evolution of kinship systems, following even the recognition of paternity. Tylor and Frazer believed on the contrary that it was very primitive. According to Tylor, it was a byproduct of the first arrangements which were made to impose exogamy.

But how had exogamy arisen? Tylor believed that exogamy had beneficial social consequences since it generated alliances, but he did not insist that these consequences explained the adoption of the rule. For Frazer the ban on marriage with kin followed from a general improvement in moral character, but the sources of this refinement remained obscure.

The general cause which I have assumed for the successive changes in marriage customs which we have now passed under review is a growing aversion to the marriage of persons nearly related to each other by blood. Into the origin of that aversion I shall not here inquire; the problem is one of the darkest and most difficult in the whole history of society.[18]

Elaborating the thesis

As happened each time Frazer published one of his magisterial surveys, this review of cross-cousin marriage stimulated various authors to suggest additional considerations. In India, Hodson pointed to an association between cross-cousin marriage and the existence of more than two intermarrying groups.[19] Fortune showed that each type of cousin marriage resulted in a different pattern in which women were transmitted.[20] The work of Radcliffe-Brown and Rivers in Oceania also continued to generate new case-studies, most notably Warner's study of matrilateral cross-cousin marriage among the Murngin of Australia.[21]

On the continent there was also interest both in Tylor's ideas and in those of Durkheim and Mauss, on which Lévi-Strauss was to draw. In Leiden a group of Indonesia specialists under the leadership of J. P. B. de Josselin de Jong began to publish analyses

---

17 Frazer (1918), *Folklore*, p. 251.
18 *Op. cit.*, pp. 245–6.
19 Hodson (1925), 'Notes on the marriage of cousins in India'.
20 Fortune (1933), 'A note on some forms of kinship structure'.
21 Warner (1937), *A Black Civilization*.

which on some points anticipated ideas of Lévi-Strauss.[22] In 1935 one of de Josselin de Jong's associates, van Wouden, published a thesis on Indonesian marriage systems,[23] for which he borrowed Tylor's term 'connubium'. He concentrated on systems of cross-cousin marriage, which he associated in the classical fashion with dual organization. He also assumed (with Durkheim) that cross-cousin marriage was rooted in a system of dual descent. The combination of matrilineal and patrilineal descent isolated cross-cousins and proclaimed their marriageability, since they were the closest relatives to fall outside both kinds of groups.

Van Wouden also drew on Durkheim and Mauss's classic essay, *Primitive Classification*. They had argued that a society with dual organization, that is, with moieties, would develop a matching dual classification of the universe. Accordingly, he and other Leiden anthropologists were inspired to seek systematic series of dual oppositions in the structure of various Indonesian artifacts and ideologies.

Lévi-Strauss developed a similar argument. Dual organization – or cross-cousin marriage – will be linked to a dualistic world view based, for instance, on right/left oppositions.[24] In Lévi-Strauss's hands, however, this form of thinking was related to a universal binary 'logic of the concrete'. Where Durkheim and Mauss argued that the social forms determine the intellectual categories, Lévi-Strauss rejected sociological determinism. Rather, both the classification of groups and the classification of the natural world derive from the unconscious binary mode of categorization with which all human beings operate, and which had first been made evident by Jakobson. When Lévi-Strauss later returned to the classic problem of 'totemism', he presented it as a way of thinking rather than a religion. Using binary oppositions, totemism created social and natural categories, and linked them to each other.[25]

---

22 For accounts of the Leiden school see P. E. de Josselin de Jong's Introduction to his 1977 *Structural Anthropology in the Netherlands*; A. de Ruijter (1978), 'The Leiden school of anthropology'; and S. Jaarsma (1984), *Structuur: Realiteit*. Lévi-Strauss was unaware of the work of this school until after the publication of his *Elementary Structures*, but the convergences are readily explained by the fact that they all drew on the same sources.
23 van Wouden (1935), *Sociale structuurtypen*.
24 The most recent version of the argument is to be found in R. Needham (1973), *Right and Left*.
25 Lévi-Strauss (1962), *Totemism*.

In the same year as van Wouden's thesis was published, in 1935, de Josselin de Jong attempted to define a characteristic Indonesian culture area, which was characterized by double descent, cross-cousin marriage and oppositional classificatory forms.[26] His immediate model was Radcliffe-Brown's analysis of the various Australian systems, seen as variations on a single theme.[27]

Also in the mid-1930s, a French scholar, Granet, tried to show that the Chinese had followed the same evolutionary route as the Australians. Beginning with a four-section system rather like that of the Kariera, but based upon matrilocal marriage, they had later developed an eight-class patrilineal system in which marriage was preferred with the mother's brother's daughter.[28] As Leach remarked, Granet 'must have been familiar with the work of both Radcliffe-Brown and Warner'. Lévi-Strauss drew heavily on Granet and acknowledged him generously, but Leach is surely correct that his 'lavish praise of [Granet's] originality' was 'unwarranted'.[29]

Frazer's work therefore brought into focus a number of studies which had already appeared. By bringing order into the published materials he prepared the ground for others to add their reports and speculations. Yet although there was an established tradition of studies it is fair to say that Lévi-Strauss was the first to offer a full-blown alternative to Frazer, albeit an alternative which was essentially a transformation.

Lévi-Strauss's theory of marriage exchange

Lévi-Strauss acknowledged that 'Frazer must be given credit for being the first to call attention to the structural similarity between marriage by exchange [of sisters] and cross-cousin marriage, and for establishing the real connection between the two'.[30] However,

---

26 De Josselin de Jong's inaugural lecture *De Maleische archipel als ethnologisch studieveld* is available in English translation in P. E. de Josselin de Jong (1977), *Structural Anthropology in the Netherlands*.

27 P. E. de Josselin de Jong identifies the influence of Radcliffe-Brown. See his essay, 'A field of anthropological study in transformation', in P. E. de Josselin de Jong (1984), *Unity in Diversity*, p. 2.

28 Granet (1939), 'Catégories matrimoniales et relations de proximité dans la Chine ançienne'.

29 Leach (1951), 'The structural implications of matrilateral cross-cousin marriage'.

30 Lévi-Strauss (1969), *The Elementary Structures of Kinship*, p. 134.

Frazer had failed to establish a *necessary* connection between the practice of cross-cousin marriage and the prohibition on marriage with an ortho-cousin.

Lévi-Strauss argued that Frazer's failure came down to his mistaken notion of what exchange is about. Frazer's savage had 'the mentality of *Homo Oeconomicus* as conceived of by nineteenth-century philosophers'.[31] But economic calculation and barter are not primitive social practices. One must grasp exchange 'as a mere aspect of a total structure of reciprocity which ... was immediately and intuitively apprehended by social man'.[32] This gnomic observation can only be understood by referring it back to its inspiration in the work of Marcel Mauss.

In 1925 Mauss had published a brief essay on 'the gift' (*le don*), which was subtitled 'The form and cause (*raison*) of exchange in archaic societies'. The theme of the essay is that exchange in primitive societies is not directly comparable to 'economic' transactions in contemporary societies. Primitive peoples have an ethic of reciprocity. This has been destroyed in capitalist systems and must be recovered if a socialist society is to be possible.

In the systems of the past we do not find simple exchange of goods, wealth and produce through markets established among individuals. For it is groups, and not individuals, which carry on exchange, make contracts, and are bound by obligations; the persons represented in the contracts are moral persons – clans, tribes, and families ... Further, what they exchange is not exclusively goods and wealth ... They exchange rather courtesies, entertainments, ritual, military assistance, women, children, dances, and feasts ... Finally, although the prestations and counter-prestations take place under a voluntary guise they are in essence strictly obligatory, and their sanction is private or open warfare. We propose to call this the system of *total prestations*.[33]

What is immediately relevant here is his conclusion that the exchange of women in marriage is only a special case of a general structure of inter-group exchanges, and that these are grounded in the principle of reciprocity, not in any desire for gain.

Lévi-Strauss took the argument even further. The principles of exchange and reciprocity are burned into the human unconscious.

31 *Op. cit.*, p. 138.
32 *Op. cit.*, p. 137.
33 M. Mauss (1954), *The Gift*, p. 3.

They are 'fundamental structures of the human mind'.[34] Mauss's principle of reciprocity becomes an unconscious but universal rule, like a rule underlying a grammatical structure or defining a phoneme; in short like the principles which were described in Jakobson's linguistics. According to Lévi-Strauss, it could be observed even in the thinking of Western children.[35]

It will be appreciated that this notion of reciprocity is very different from Frazer's straightforward principle of economic rationality which might lead, for example, to the barter of women. Beginning with this imperative to exchange, Lévi-Strauss proposed a single explanation not only for cross-cousin marriage but also for sister-exchange, dual organization and rules of exogamy (including the prohibition on marriage with ortho-cousins). All these kinship institutions are simply different mechanisms for ensuring the exchange of women in marriage.

Reciprocity and so exchange are crucial. A man must not marry his sister, because she is his ticket of entry into social life. Marrying her to another man, he enters into relations of reciprocity. Lévi-Strauss explained,

as soon as I am forbidden a woman, she thereby becomes available to another man, and somewhere else a man renounces a woman who thereby becomes available to me ... [The rule of exogamy] is instituted only in order to guarantee and establish, directly or indirectly, immediately or mediately, an exchange.[36]

The rule of exogamy is therefore the necessary precondition for exchange, and it is instituted precisely in order to promote exchange.

Lévi-Strauss generally assumes that 'primitive' peoples operate in groups, and that marriage exchanges will therefore be between descent groups operating as units. In its simplest form, the exchange of women may follow one of two modes. Women may be exchanged directly between two groups. This direct give-and-take Lévi-Strauss calls restricted exchange. It may take the form of sister-exchange or lead to a full-blown system of dual organization.

34 Lévi-Strauss (1969), *Elementary Structures*, p. 84.
35 Lévi-Strauss devoted Chapter VII of his monograph to an examination of 'the relationship between primitive and infant thought' about reciprocity. He discusses Piaget but pays special attention to the work of the psychologist S. Isaacs.
36 Lévi-Strauss (1969), *Elementary Structures*, p. 51.

Alternatively, women may be indirectly exchanged between three or more groups. This leads to what Lévi-Strauss calls generalized exchange. 'Generalized exchange establishes a system of operations conducted "on credit". A surrenders a daughter or a sister to B, who surrenders one to C, who, in turn, will surrender one to A. This is its simplest formula.'[37]

In either sister-exchange or dual organization, both kinds of cross-cousin are marriageable. In generalized exchange, only the mother's brother's daughter may be married. The father's sister's daughter is forbidden. (If a systematic series of mothers' brother's daughter marriages are drawn in a model, it will be seen that women are circulating in one direction between fixed lines of men.)

There are other critical differences between the two systems. One had been central to Rivers' theory. Dual organization allocates women according to 'class' membership. These classes are the expression of a dual descent principle – a matrilineal moiety system is cross-cut by a patrilineal system of local groups. Since the principle of residence is different from the principle of group membership, it is a 'disharmonic' system in Lévi-Strauss's jargon. In contrast, a system of generalized exchange (roughly equivalent to a system of matrilateral cross-cousin marriage) uses a genealogical calculus. Moreover, generalized exchange is necessarily based on an 'harmonic' system whereby residence and descent are ordered in the same fashion. Finally, the two systems are contrasted in terms of their social effectiveness; here generalized exchange is judged far more efficacious, since it can join an unlimited series of groups in a single exchange cycle, while dual organization is restricted to the integration of two primary social units.[38]

Lévi-Strauss believed that dual organization was most common in Australia, while the most important concentration of systems of generalized exchange was in Asia. Following Frazer, he identified the Burmese tribes and the Gilyak of Siberia as the most prominent contemporary exponents of this form of marriage exchange, and

---

37 *Op. cit.*, p. 375.
38 Radcliffe-Brown had argued similarly that different Australian marriage rules had the effect of joining together a greater or smaller number of groups depending on the cross-cousin designated for marriage, and that consequently some cross-cousin marriage systems were more effective in maintaining a large field of social contacts. (See the final section of Radcliffe-Brown's (1931) *The Social Organization of the Australian Tribes.*)

suggested that they represent the remnants of a widespread system which once spanned the whole of China.

India, particularly South India, is both geographically and structurally intermediate between these two centres of kinship structures. Generalized exchange (or at least matrilateral cross-cousin marriage) is indeed widespread in South India, as Frazer had noted, but Lévi-Strauss identified a recurrent temptation to break down the long speculative cycles of exchange and to demand a more immediate return. This may lead back to dual organization (as Rivers had suggested for Melanesia), but in India it was more likely to resurrect the hidden possibility of marriage with the father's sister's daughter. This form of marriage implies a deferred but direct return; I give you my sister, and you give your daughter to my son. It is, Lévi-Strauss wrote, 'the Cheap-Jack in the scale of marriage transactions',[39] appropriate in a state of political uncertainty when people are reluctant to gamble on the long term. It is poorly adapted to the integration of a series of social groups. In terms which Frazer might well have used, he argued that 'marriage with the father's sister's daughter contrasts with other forms of cross-cousin marriage as an economy based on exchange for cash contrasts with economies permitting operations on deferred terms'.[40]

Lévi-Strauss's book is dedicated to Lewis Henry Morgan, and he accepted Morgan's principle that the kinship terminology provides definitive evidence of the system of marriage. Any system of dual organization or cross-cousin marriage is based upon a dichotomization of the world of kin. On the one hand there are affines – wife-givers and wife-takers; on the other hand, there are unmarriageable relatives. This opposition between kin and affines persists from generation to generation. The kinship terminology will therefore characteristically oppose cross-cousins to parallel cousins and siblings. It is also likely to identify the parents of cross-cousins with affines. The term for mother's brother, for example, will often be the same as the term for wife's father.

By the time Lévi-Strauss was writing, mainstream anthropologists had finally rejected the classic thesis that the family had evolved late in human history. The leading anthropologists in

---

39 Lévi-Strauss (1969), *Elementary Structures,* p. 449.
40 *Ibid.*

Britain and America, Malinowski, Radcliffe-Brown, Lowie and Kroeber, believed that the nuclear family was universal. Moreover, it was the main generating force behind all kinship systems and kinship terminologies. Lévi-Strauss rejected this family-centric orthodoxy, but he did not revert to the classic evolutionist model. Instead, arguing from the primacy of exchange, he insisted that the basic unit of any kinship system included a nuclear family *plus a wife-giver*. It linked not simply a man, his wife and their child, but also included his wife's brother, his affine. The 'atom of kinship' could be further analysed into two opposed principles. It was built about the combination of consanguinity and affinity, and this distinction was in turn the product of the principle of reciprocity.[41]

By opposing a mental structure of 'reciprocity' to Frazer's very earthy notion of barter, Lévi-Strauss offered a deductive, unitary theory which accounted at one stroke for exogamy, dual organization and cross-cousin marriage. In the central chapters of his book he also developed a new model of how systematic matrilateral cross-cousin marriage could order social groups in a whole society. Moreover, he provided a number of detailed case-studies in which complex kinship systems were reanalysed in terms of his theory.

All this was certainly most impressive, and yet there was an obvious danger that Lévi-Strauss's theory was actually too powerful. If the generative principles of reciprocity and exchange were universal, burned into the human mind, why were not all kinship systems based upon cross-cousin marriage or dual organization? Yet many, including our own, were not. Did we lack the primitive drive towards reciprocity (as Mauss, indeed, had hinted)? On the other hand, if Lévi-Strauss's theory applied only to a small group of primitive societies, then how could cross-cousin marriage and dual organization express universal principles of human mentality?

Lévi-Strauss recognized that he had dealt with only a category of human marriage systems. He termed these 'elementary structures' or 'closed systems' and opposed them to 'complex structures' or 'open systems', in which the choice of a wife was governed by principles which did not derive from the kinship system at all, but had to do with such considerations as the wealth or power of her relatives, or simply with her personal attractions. These systems

---

41 This argument was first advanced by Lévi-Strauss in an article published in 1945, which is republished as Chapter 11 of *Structural Anthropology* (1963).

were still governed by the negative rule of exogamy, and so in some sense reciprocity and exchange might be at work, although it was not easy to specify quite how they operated. But his dialectical cast of mind suggested that the binary oppositions might be mediated. Crow-Omaha systems were an intermediate type. In these systems the rules of exogamy were extremely wide-ranging. Typically a man could not marry into the clans of any of his four grandparents. Moreover, these rules operated in rather small societies, with few clans, so that there were not many women whom a man could marry. In this way, the negative rules might produce a statistical pattern of choice not unlike that which might be imposed by positive marriage preferences.[42]

Leach and the Kachin

Lévi-Strauss's remarkable solution to Frazer's puzzle immediately stimulated a series of critiques and responses. The first major critical reaction to Lévi-Strauss's thesis was Edmund Leach's essay, published in 1951, entitled 'The structural implications of matrilateral cross-cousin marriage'.

Leach was a student of Malinowski. This meant that he was conditioned to expect that rules were there to be broken, and that individuals pursue their own interests regardless. Moreover, he had actually spent the best part of the previous decade with the Kachin, first as ethnographer and later as a guerrilla. The Kachin provided Lévi-Strauss with his main example of Burmese cross-cousin marriage, but Leach was immediately aware that he had got the Kachin material very wrong – even mixing up reports on the Kachin with data on neighbouring groups – and that even where he had got it right, he was dealing only with Kachin ideology. Nevertheless Leach admitted that Lévi-Strauss had obliged him to see the Kachin data in a new way, and in his essay he provided an analysis of the Kachin which took as its point of departure Lévi-Strauss's model of a society based on systematic matrilateral cross-cousin marriage.

But if Lévi-Strauss's model was suggestive, the goal was very different. Leach was concerned not with ultimate mental universals and unconscious principles of reciprocity. He was interested rather in a concrete, historical society and with the way in which real

---

42 Lévi-Strauss (1965), 'The future of kinship studies'.

individuals within it conducted their affairs and thought about their world. The Kachin ideology, according to Leach, depicted a classic system of groups which married in a circle. In practice, however, the system was radically unbalanced; there was a built-in status difference between wife-givers, who were equals or superiors, and wife-takers, who were equals or inferiors. The system was therefore not driven by a principle of Maussian reciprocity. The flow of wives was just one aspect of a broader series of unequal exchanges. To get a wife a man was obliged to pay a brideprice, and often also to occupy what was virtually the position of a feudal inferior. The marriage system was therefore to be understood as a facet of a broader structure of political and economic transactions between people of different status. As he summarized the situation:

1   From a *political* aspect, chief is to headman as feudal Lord of the Manor is to customary freeholder.
2   From a *kinship* aspect, chief is to headman as *mayu* to *dama*, that is as father-in-law to son-in-law.
3   From a *territorial* aspect, the kinship status of the headman's lineage in respect to that of the chief is held to validate the tenure of land.
4   From an *economic* aspect the effect of matrilateral cross-cousin marriage is that, on balance, the headman's lineage constantly pays wealth to the chief's lineage in the form of bridewealth.[43]

In 1954 Leach published an ambitious monograph on the Kachin, *Political Systems of Highland Burma*, in which he linked this analysis of alliance relationships to the Africanists' opposition between state systems and apparently egalitarian lineage-based systems. The Kachin vacillated between Fortes' and Evans-Pritchard's famous Types A and B. Some Kachin communities seemed to Leach very like segmentary lineage systems (though with systematic cross-cousin marriage). Others were hierarchical states. He argued that in fact they lurched from feudal hierarchy to radical republicanism because they were constructed upon a fundamental contradiction between a lineage system – in which all lineages must be equal – and a system of unilateral transmission of wives, which implied hierarchy.

This was an extraordinary dialectical synthesis of the dominant

---

43   Leach (1951), 'The structural implications of matrilateral cross-cousin marriage', p. 89.

models of the day, yet there was a fundamental ambiguity about Leach's real objective. In his original 1951 essay he had contrasted the ideal model of the Kachin to the political realities. In *Political Systems* he flirted with an idealist vision of the anthropologist's task. Was his book about what Kachin politicians did, or about the way in which the Kachin thought about what their politicians did? Increasingly he took a very un-Malinowskian point of view on this question, and in his preface to the 1964 reprint of his monograph he wrote that 'my own attempt to find systemic ordering in historical events depends upon the changing evaluation of verbal categories and is, in the final analysis, illusory'.[44] It may be that even a sceptical adoption of Lévi-Strauss's approach imposed a certain idealism; certainly the other main transformation of Lévi-Strauss's theory was to take a radically idealist path.

Leiden, Needham and Dumont

In the academic year 1950–1 de Josselin de Jong's anthropology seminar in Leiden worked its way through Lévi-Strauss's massive book which had just recently appeared.[45] In 1952 de Josselin de Jong published the first extended appreciation of *Les Structures* (and since his essay was published in English, it served for nearly twenty years as the main source on Lévi-Strauss's ideas for anthropologists unable to read French[46]).

Rodney Needham, a young British social anthropologist specializing in Indonesia, was a member of this de Josselin de Jong seminar. On his return to Britain he became one of the leading promoters of Lévi-Strauss's monograph, which he described in the most effusive terms as 'a masterpiece, a sociological classic of the first rank'.[47] True, like de Josselin de Jong himself, he was not a blind advocate. Although *The Elementary Structures* was 'a great book', Needham wrote:

I do not by any means think it is perfect. There is much in it that I would dispute or recast on theoretical grounds, it suffers from serious lacks as regards sources, and it contains a number of ethnographic errors and

44 Preface to the 1964 reprint of Leach (1954), *Political Systems of Highland Burma*.
45 The participants in the seminar are listed in P. E. de Josselin de Jong (1977), *Structural Anthropology in the Netherlands*, p. 10.
46 J. P. B. de Josselin de Jong (1952), *Lévi-Strauss's Theory on Kinship and Marriage*.
47 Needham (1962), *Structure and Sentiment*, p. 2.

misinterpretations of facts ... in spite of the quality of Levi-Strauss's insights it cannot be said that he has employed them to their proper effect in the analysis of any single system.[48]

However, it was not his reservations which were to get him into hot water; it was rather his innocent attempt to make the argument clearer.

It seemed obvious to Needham that Lévi-Strauss had not propounded a universal theory of kinship. Rather, he had identified a specific type of primitive society, in which marriage was prescribed within a particular marriage class. What Lévi-Strauss had done was to demonstrate that societies of this type had characteristic forms of classifying relatives (basically, into two sets, marriageable and unmarriageable). He had nothing to say about 'preferential' kinship systems, in which people might actually show a bias in favour of marrying (for example) a mother's brother's daughter, as among the Tswana common people, or a father's brother's daughter, as among Tswana aristocrats.[49]

Unlike Leach, Needham was a formalist. The Malinowskian concern with practice was foreign to him. He believed that people would be obliged to follow the rules in prescriptive systems. That was why, after all, the rules were called prescriptions. In societies which prescribed, for example, matrilateral cross-cousin marriage, men would have to marry women who fell into the appropriate terminological category.

Needham fostered Lévi-Strauss's reputation and undertook to oversee the preparation of the English translation of his masterpiece. At the last moment, Lévi-Strauss contributed a new preface for this translation. With an insouciance that would have been admired by de Gaulle himself, he devoted the preface to the repudiation of Needham's interpretation of his thesis.

---

48 *Op. cit.*, p. 3.
49 Needham, himself, instanced the Tswana case, but wrote that: 'among the nobles [marriage with] the father's sister's daughter is clearly preferred to mother's brother's daughter, while among commoners the mother's brother's daughter is the most frequent choice' (*Structure and Sentiment*, 1962, p. 9). In fact, first-cousin marriage with father's sister's daughter is very rare, even among nobles: much less common than with mother's brother's daughter. His source, Schapera, clearly shows, however, that the most common preference of nobles is for marriage with a father's *brother's* daughter. Evidently Needham simply assumed that a preferential marriage was bound to be with a cross-cousin. This is a good example of how preconceptions get in the way of ethnographic accuracy.

Following Needham, several writers today assert that my book is only concerned with prescriptive systems, or, to be more exact (since one need only glance through it to be assured of the contrary), that such had been my intention had I not confused the two forms. But if the champions of this distinction had been correct in believing that prescriptive systems are few and far between, a most curious consequence would have resulted: I would have written a very fat book which since 1952 [the year in which J. P. B. de Josselin de Jong published his commentary] has aroused all sorts of commentaries and discussions despite its being concerned with such rare facts and so limited a field that it is difficult to understand of what interest it could be with regard to a general theory of kinship.[50]

The notions of preference and prescription were relative: 'a preferential system is prescriptive when envisaged at the model level; a prescriptive system must be preferential when envisaged on the level of reality'.[51]

From now on there was no more implacable enemy of Lévi-Strauss's thesis than Rodney Needham. He even tried to revive the reputation of Rivers's friend Hocart, because he had followed McLennan and cast doubt upon the significance of kinship terms. But Needham was mainly a polemicist. He never published an ethnographic monograph or a substantial book on kinship theory. A more significant challenge came from the French scholar Louis Dumont, who also developed an austerely idealist version of Lévi-Strauss's thesis.

In 1953 Dumont had published an essay on Dravidian kinship terminology, arguing that it divided the universe of kin into consanguineal relatives on the one hand and permanent affines on the other.[52] In 1957 he developed his ideas in a long essay, *Hierarchy and Marriage Alliance in South Indian Kinship*, which he dedicated to Lévi-Strauss. Although he insisted that his analysis was 'quite in accordance with Professor Lévi-Strauss's broad view of South Indian kinship',[53] its effect was to give priority to the system of categories generated by the terminology. The key proposition was that 'the terminology provides a common, regional conceptual

---

50 Lévi-Strauss (1969), *Elementary Structures*, p. xxxi.

51 *Op. cit.*, p. xxxiii.

52 Dumont (1953), 'Dravidian kinship terminology'.

53 Dumont (1957), *Hierarchy and Marriage Alliance in South Indian Kinship*. Both this and the former essay are reprinted in Dumont (1983), *Affinity as a Value*. The citation is on p. 70 of that book.

framework, making affinity the equal of consanguinity'.[54] The expression of this terminology in actual marriage choices, in cross-cousin marriage, was evidently only a potentiality, of subsidiary importance to the semantic structure.

Faced with these arguments Radcliffe-Brown affected total incomprehension,[55] but Dumont's idealism was obviously attractive to Needham, and later to his students. Seeking support for their version of alliance theory they appealed to the authority of Dumont. Yet a thoroughgoing idealist or semantic interpretation of alliance theory was hopelessly constricted. Lévi-Strauss had expressed concern about the way in which Needham limited the application of his theory, but he could hardly have anticipated the final apotheosis of the Needham line. In the hands of the radical idealists, alliance theory had to do only with so-called 'prescriptive alliance'; but soon it was claimed that prescriptive alliance had nothing directly to do with marriage. Alliance was just a conceptual possibility; prescriptive alliance no more than a form of classification. 'This type of organization is defined by the terminology', Needham proclaimed, 'and the terminology is constituted by the regularity of a constant relation that articulates lines and categories'.[56]

Héritier and African lineages again

Given the vehement rejection of Lévi-Strauss's kinship theory by the very people who had been instrumental in promoting it in the English-speaking world, it was left with few adherents in Britain or America in the 1970s. In Paris, Godelier, Terray and others tried to marry Lévi-Strauss's structuralism with Marxist concerns, but the only recent and fairly orthodox attempt to pursue Lévi-Strauss's programme in his own terms is a monograph by his successor at the Collège de France, Françoise Héritier, entitled *L'exercise de la parenté*. Héritier reports a study of a community in Upper Volta, the Samo. The Samo have all the conventional attributes of an 'Omaha' system, and yet despite the elaborate

---

54 Dumont (1983), *Affinity as a Value*, p. 171.
55 See Radcliffe-Brown (1953), 'Dravidian kinship terminology', and Dumont's (1953) 'Dravidian kinship terminology' (reply to A. R. Radcliffe-Brown). Both were published in *Man*, but Dumont's reply and later reflections on the matter were reprinted in his *Affinity as Value* (1983).
56 Needham, 'Remarks on the analysis of kinship and marriage', in Needham (1971), *Rethinking Kinship and Marriage*.

armoury of prohibitions they apparently do engage in systematic marriage alliances with (distant) relatives. This is what Lévi-Strauss had predicted. Yet despite elaborate computer manipulation of the data it remains uncertain whether the Samo actively prefer to marry kin, or whether (given a small population and many prohibitions) they simply have no alternative.

It was also not clear what the prohibitions actually amounted to. They were first presented in conventional terms as prohibitions on marriage with women from particular lineages, but Héritier later demonstrated a sophisticated uncertainty about the significance or even the reality of these lineages. 'From the point of view of their function with respect to marriage,' she wrote, 'the principle of unilineality, so apparent in the semi-complex systems of the Crow-Omaha type, is not really fundamental; it is above all a principle of order and simplification.'[57] In other words, 'lineages' were just ways of tidying up descriptions. They become epiphenomena, like Australian classes in Radcliffe-Brown's theory, where they are similarly presented as rough and ready summaries of the kinship terminology, which is what really determines marriage choices. But if that is the case, then presumably Samo 'lineages' are not exogamous groups, any more than Australian marriage classes regulate marriage.

Héritier's work probably will not salvage Lévi-Strauss's theory, but it does demonstrate how profoundly alliance theory must depend upon descent theory. They have a common ancestry, and, very probably, the same destiny.

57 Héritier (1981), *L'exercise de la parenté*, p. 127, my translation.

CHAPTER 12

Conclusion

The idea of primitive social structure which crystallized in the late nineteenth century was remarkably simple. Primitive society was originally an organic whole. It then split into two or more identical building blocks – exogamous, corporate descent groups. There were no families in the accepted sense. Women and goods were held communally by the men of each group. Marriage took the form of regular exchanges between them. The groups worshipped ancestor spirits. These social forms, no longer extant, were preserved in the languages (especially in kinship terminologies) and in the ceremonies of primitive peoples. After countless generations this system gave way to a form of society based on territorial units, the family and private property and, eventually, the state.

From prototype to model

For the past 130 years, social anthropologists have been engaged in the manipulation of this elementary conception. Each major anthropologist developed his particular version. The elements were generally stable, though one or another might be given special prominence; but these elements were reordered in every conceivable pattern, the relationships between them systematically transformed to produce a succession of prototypes, ideal types and models.

Maine's starting-point was the radical theory that the original human society was a free and egalitarian community into which individuals had contracted. He inverted Rousseau's assumptions, and represented the original society as a totalitarian patriarchal despotism based on family groups. The family groups gradually became larger and more complex, eventually becoming patrilineal corporations. At last territorial ties replaced blood ties as the basis of the community, and the state emerged as the typical form of political organization.

McLennan introduced the extraordinary idea that the family was the end product of a developmental process, not the source of human social organization. He preferred to begin with sets of brothers along with their wives. There was no dominant patriarch but rather a fraternity and, since no child recognized an individual father but was attached to a particular mother, matrilineal groups formed.

Morgan introduced the idea that each set of brothers married a set of sisters (after an initial phase in which they bred with their own sisters). This again led to matriliny, as in McLennan's argument, since the only individual tie was between mother and child. He postulated a complicated hierarchy of family forms, ending with the nuclear family. Its emergence coincided with the development of private property and the beginnings of the territorial state.

Morgan's antipodean disciple, Fison, suggested on purely formal grounds that if an original society was made up of two groups of brothers who exchanged sisters, this would in time yield a set pattern of marriage with specific cousins, children of siblings of opposite sex. Tylor coined the term cross-cousin marriage for this phenomenon.

By the end of the century these inventive lawyers had created a new tradition of intellectual speculation. The first appraisals were written – the most pointed by Tylor, the most systematic by Frazer. Asserting the authority of established scholars, they adjudicated the claims of their predecessors and established an orthodoxy. Matriarchy was prior to patriarchy. Group marriage and cross-cousin marriage was characteristic of early societies. Classificatory kinship terminologies reflected a state of affairs in which exogamous descent groups exchanged wives in a systematic fashion. It was also accepted that the most nearly primitive extant societies were to be found in Australia. Australian aborigines were organized into two or four matrilineal classes which practised group marriage by exchange.

Rivers accepted the traditional characterization of Australian social structure, but he argued that Melanesia was very different. Australia was based upon group marriage between 'classes', while in Melanesia marriages were with specific relatives, traced genealogically, and particularly with cross-cousins. Nor did the Melanesian type of marriage system emerge from the Australian type. Indeed, there was no fixed line of social evolution. Societies changed as a consequence of contacts and migrations. Australia did not represent the starting-point of all primitive societies, and specifically it was not the source of Melanesian systems of social organization.

Rivers' most important student, Radcliffe-Brown, tried to demonstrate that Australian systems were variants on a theme, and that Melanesian social systems belonged to the same family of variants. Where Rivers believed that Melanesia and Australia represented two distinct historical trajectories, Radcliffe-Brown insisted that they were no more than local variants within a huge Australian-Dravidian set of social structures which extended into South India. But Radcliffe-Brown had taken note of Malinowski's critique, and his image of Australia conformed to Rivers' picture of Melanesia at its most advanced stage. Marriage was an individual matter, yielding nuclear families; and the typical rule was that one married a matrilateral cross-cousin.

When Radcliffe-Brown became professor of social anthropology at Oxford shortly before the outbreak of World War Two, his lieutenants were Evans-Pritchard and Fortes. They reintroduced Maine and Morgan's opposition between blood and soil, states and stateless societies, but in their hands this became a classification in space rather than in time. African political systems were organized into kin-based bands, segmentary lineages or states. The segmentary lineage was an intermediate form, combining blood and soil, descent and territoriality. This typology did not imply succession in time, or superiority.

Evans-Pritchard tried to persuade his readers that the Nuer themselves conceived of territory in terms of descent and of space in terms of time. Fortes, for his part, introduced an idea of cyclical time into his conception of social structure. The Ashanti were not a society in transition from matriliny to patriliny; rather, each domestic group went through a developmental cycle, and if it became rather patriarchal at one stage, it began and ended as a minor cell in a matrilineage. The apparently various forms of domestic group on the ground represented stages in the cycle through which all passed.

Their outstanding continental contemporary, Lévi-Strauss, produced a global typology. Australian, South Asian and Chinese forms of society represented the modalities of 'elementary' structures of social organization. These were in turn opposed as a set to the 'complex' structures of modern society. Where Fortes and Evans-Pritchard argued that different modes of descent generated characteristic types of society, Lévi-Strauss (more faithful to the Victorian tradition) insisted that it was different types of cross-cousin marriage which produced various types of social structure.

In the next generation Leach tried to show that communities in the Kachin hills oscillated between state systems and segmentary lineage systems. Later he married this version of lineage theory to Lévi-Strauss's model, and suggested that the alternation between *gumlao* and *gumsa* was generated by a contradiction within lineage systems. Were lineages equal or ranked? The system of matrilateral cross-cousin marriage bred inequality between the partners, since some lineages would succeed in accumulating more wives than would others.

In short, each major author transformed the model of his predecessor, reversing the postulated order of development, inverting the relationship between the elements, or negating their initial premises.

The notion of totemism went through its own series of changes, though in this case theories developed through a process of specialization rather than structural transformation. Tylor had originally suggested that the earliest human societies worshipped animistic spirits. McLennan patented the idea that there was a variant of 'animism', which he called 'totemism', in which certain species of animals or plants were sacred to particular social groups. Totemism was the religion of societies organized into exogamous matrilineal clans. Robertson Smith tried to anchor this fantasy in ancient Arabia, so that it could serve him in his attempt to contextualize the Biblical texts and underpin his critique of superstitious relics in Christian belief. Durkheim and Freud were fascinated by Robertson Smith's notion that primitive religion mirrored features of social organization, and they were both particularly intrigued by the apparent link between the taboo on eating the totem and the incest taboo on women in the clan.

Tylor had always been sceptical of this version of his own idea of the original 'animism', however. Frazer, for his part, was soon ready to distance himself from his mentor, Robertson Smith, who had been the most notable exponent of 'totemism'. They stimulated and publicized ethnographic findings and soon established that 'clans' and 'totems' were not generally found together. Accordingly, Rivers proposed using the term 'totemism' to apply only to a type of social structure – an organization into exogamous descent groups. Radcliffe-Brown immediately proposed that it refer only to a kind of religion. Fortes elided totems with ancestors, and argued that ancestor worship was the characteristic form of worship in societies based on lineages. Lévi-Strauss suggested that both the descent corporation and the totemic species existed in the mind, were forms of classification and were related as metaphors of each other.

Theories of the origin of the state changed least of all over the century. From Maine and Morgan to Engels and Childe, the basic assumptions were that kin-based communities gave way to ter-ritorially-based associations, which developed into states. The Marxist version of this thesis was particularly influential. It linked technological development and the evolution of private property and the family to the political revolution which the state represented. In the USA Steward, White and their students and associates took the Marxist framework for granted. Since this theory promises that political forms can be deduced from tech-nological organization, it has naturally been particularly attractive to archaeologists.[1] In Britain, where the Marxist ideas were least influential, Fortes and Evans-Pritchard were content to retain the opposition between the two basic systems of government without developing a more general evolutionary thesis; and Leach developed the startling idea that in the Kachin hills 'states' emerged from lineage systems and collapsed back into them.

It has been a long story, I fear, but the development is obvious enough. What began as an attempt to specify the characteristics of 'primitive society' became something rather more complicated and sophisticated. The prototype became an ideal type and finally a model. The original set of ideas survived either as an orthodoxy (like the ideas about the early state), or as a special case (like totemism) or, most flamboyantly, as a series of elaborate structural transformations, as in the case of kinship theory. It is tempting to speculate that where the ideas were most closely associated with a political ideology – the early state and Marxism – there was least flexibility and greatest stagnation. Where one or two scholars

---

1 See Lowie (1927), *The Origin of the State* and Service (1985), *A Century of Controversy*, Chapters 12 and 13.

became established as synthesizers and critics, there was a process of specialization and involution (as in the case of totemism). The free range of transformations in the field of kinship studies may, however, also be due to the greater range of variables involved, and to the invention of technical tools. The history of study of kinship terminologies illustrates how technical complexity can tempt initiates to play with endless structural variations.

Dissenters

The persistence of the old theories is somewhat surprising when one recalls that these prototypes were increasingly set against ethnographic descriptions. Reality sometimes seemed to match up (most famously in Evans-Pritchard's account of the Nuer), but more often a particular society could be presented as an interesting exception, a local variant, a transitional form. Genuinely alternative conceptions were developed, nevertheless, by the two most original anthropologists of the century, Boas and Malinowski.

Boas's critique can be seen as part of a German reaction against Darwin, an application in a new sphere of arguments which Boas took over from his teacher Virchow. The specific target was Morgan's model, which had become institutionalized as the American orthodoxy in the Bureau of American Ethnology at the Smithsonian Institution. He and his students at Columbia attacked the Smithsonian people with a barrage of ethnographic counter-examples. Boas himself tried to demonstrate a movement on the Northwest coast from patriliny to matriliny. Speck showed that the Algonkian hunter-gatherers were organized into nuclear families, and that the bands had territorial identities. Kroeber produced a brilliant critique of Cushing's orthodox view of the Zuni as a 'gentile society'. He also rejected the use of kinship terminologies to reconstruct social forms. Goldenweiser published what we would now call a deconstruction of the idea of totemism. Lowie's textbooks, published in the 1920s,[2] summed up a generation of criticism from the Boas school: the family was universal; early societies were based in part on territory; totemism was a fantasy. A cautious man, he hung on to some of the older ideas (notably the reflectionist theory of kin terms), but he wrote as a successful revolutionary.

At the London School of Economics, Westermarck had entren-

---

2 *Primitive Society*, 1920; *Primitive Religion*, 1924; *The Origin of the State*, 1927.

ched a very different critique of Victorian theories of the family. Unlike Boas, Westermarck wrote as a Darwinian – indeed, his major work was endorsed by Wallace. He rejected Morgan and McLennan not as evolutionists but as false evolutionists. However, the effect was similar, and when Malinowski took up the cudgels, he combined the substantive elements of Westermarck's critique with a rejection of traditional evolutionist explanations.

Malinowski's first English monograph, published under the aegis of Westermarck, demonstrated the presence of the family amongst the Australian aborigines. When he came to write up his fieldwork in Melanesia he turned particularly on Rivers. (For Malinowski, Rivers and the Pacific ethnologists represented the enemy, much as the Bureau of American Ethnology did for the Boasians.) Rivers stood for a diffusionist variety of the classic model, and he had developed perhaps the most sophisticated analyses of systems of kinship and marriage. Malinowski ridiculed his study of relationship terminologies as arid exercises in bogus algebra. Terms of relationship were to be understood pragmatically, in the context of their use. Informal practices constantly pulled against the rules. To understand what was going on it was vital to understand individual motives and tactics, not official formulae. Even among the matrilineal Trobrianders, relationships between fathers and children counted in practice for a great deal, despite the fact that the people evidently denied the father's role in procreation. Nor were religious ideologies much developed. What mattered was practical magic, which alleviated anxieties.

By the early 1920s the classic American model had been very badly mauled. When it was taught in the new university departments of anthropology, it was presented only to be demolished. The parallel British tradition had been shaken by the iconoclasts of the London School of Economics. The critique, evidently grounded in superb scientific ethnographic studies, seemed to carry all before it.

Plus ça change

And yet while the old orthodoxy was down, it was not out. Both Boas and Malinowski died during World War Two. In Britain, Radcliffe-Brown, Fortes and Evans-Pritchard resuscitated Maine and Durkheim, and restored the substantive model of the Victorians, although they disclaimed its evolutionist cast. In effect, they retained the prototype, but used it as a model.

In the USA, White, Steward and Murdock revived Morgan's theory and found support in the coming generation. White and Steward were essentially Marxist writers, but like the British archaeologist Childe (whom they much admired) they tended towards technological and ecological determinism. Their main purpose was to identify the evolution of what more orthodox Marxists might have called 'modes of production'. There was a 'band' type of society, a 'peasant' type, and so on, in each of which a particular kind of technology generated appropriate forms of social and political relationship. The features which were emphasized were again rather traditional; kin-groups were contrasted with territorial groups, the mode of descent was regarded as crucial, and (in the more Marxist examples) special attention was paid to the emergence of social stratification.[3]

Another evolutionist was the American George Peter Murdock, but he was concerned purely with the evolution of social structures. His methods and assumptions were a combination of those of Morgan and Tylor. Kinship and residential groups were the building blocks of social structure. The combination of these elements produced certain types of social structure, and they were matched with types of kinship terminology. Types of social structure succeeded each other in a regular fashion. Following Tylor he developed a large sample of societies which allowed for 'statistical tests' of his evolutionary hypotheses. His main innovation was to put 'soil' before 'blood'. When a couple married they had to live alone or with a relative. This choice of residence determined the form of local kinship groupings and gave rise to a particular type of social structure.[4]

Together, these three American scholars effectively continued

---

3 For general statements see Steward (1955), *Theory of Culture Change*, and White (1959), *The Evolution of Culture*. White's *The Social Organizaton of Ethnological Theory* (1966) is an attack on the 'schools' of Boas and Radcliffe-Brown for not being evolutionists. Marvin Harris's *The Rise of Anthropological Theory* (1968) is essentially a history of anthropology written as advocacy for this school of thought.

4 Murdock's most famous book was his *Social Structure*, which appeared in 1949, in the same year as Fortes' *Web of Kinship* and Lévi-Strauss's *Elementary Structures*. John Barnes has devoted an interesting book to the explication and comparison of their theories – see his *Three Styles in the Study of Kinship* (1971).

the old tradition of American anthropology, blocking out the Boasian intervention. In Britain the subversive ideas of Malinowski were neglected in favour of Radcliffe-Brown's more orthodox concerns.

How can this strange continuity be explained? The fact that Morgan's theory had been adopted by Engels and institutionalized in the USSR was certainly significant. A number of the American revisionists were Marxists, intent on restoring a credible evolutionism to anthropology. Murdock was no Marxist, however, and nor were most of the British lineage theorists. Clearly there were also more general factors at work.

One problem with the criticisms of the Boasians and of Malinowski was that, however cogent their objections to the orthodox theory, they did not seem to offer any coherent alternative. To some it appeared that they replaced order with chaos. Boas was criticized as atheoretical and merely negative. Malinkowski was damned for lacking any notion of a social system, any model of kinship. It was a reaction which Kroeber had anticipated. Reviewing one of Lowie's textbooks, he had warned that, however successful the exposure of past errors might be, readers would be left a little dissatisfied – they would want to know *why*.[5]   Malinowski did sometimes argue that the questions themselves were wholly misleading. To the extent that he imposed new questions he encouraged some of his students to produce novel accounts of how particular exotic communities were organized, but these studies could not function as paradigmatic cases. Their authors could not claim that these communities were typical of anything but themselves. At best they might show that people everywhere were wilful and scheming. But societies structured like the Nuer (or at any rate like *The Nuer*) could apparently be found all over the world. In the end, therefore, the critiques of Boas and Malinowski were not decisive because they could not displace the terms of reference which had been established within the anthropological tradition.

The persistence of a myth is usually explained in terms of its political functions, but I have tried to show the variety of public purposes which were served by these ideas. The idea of primitive society served imperialists and nationalists, anarchists and

---

5 Kroeber (1920), Review of Lowie's *Primitive Society*. Cf. Fortes' essay on Malinowski's theory of kinship in Firth (1957), *Man and Culture*.

Marxists. There were certainly some constants. The underlying message was that all societies were based either on blood or on soil. These principles of descent and territoriality were clearly related to ideas of race and citizenship, which were central to political discourse.

The relativism of the anthropological account also carried the message that social forms were not fixed, Reform was possible, indeed inevitable. The idea of primitive society therefore provided an idiom which was ideally suited for debate about modern society, but in itself it was neutral. It could be used equally by right or left, reactionary or progressive, poet and politician. The most powerful images of primitive society were produced by very disparate political thinkers – Maine, Engels, Durkheim and Freud. Yet all were transformations of a single basic model. What each did, in effect, was to use it as a foil. They had particular ideas about modern society and constructed a directly contrary account of primitive society. Primitive society was the mirror image of modern society – or, rather, primitive society as they imagined it inverted the characteristics of modern society as they saw it.

The most influential writers offered a view of the present and a contrasting vision of the past, but subordinated both (implicitly or explicitly) to an ideal which they located in the future. Nowadays images of the ancient past are less potent than images of the future, and seem even to be less real. Instead of constructing new models of primitive society, intellectuals project images of the global village, the international political organization, the 'post-industrial' society. Each is once again a transformation of their images of their own societies.

These ideological functions explain the power and persistence of the idea of primitive society to some degree, but other factors came into play once primitive society became an object of study within academe. University departments of anthropology may have been influenced by ideological pressures – indeed, they certainly were. But they were also swayed by academic considerations, and in many cases these were obviously dominant. Maine and his contemporaries had constituted the object of social anthropology – primitive society. They posed the strategic questions about the origin of the family, the state and religion. But above all, so far as the academics were concerned, they prepared a specialized set of tools. They promised that primitive society could be understood in terms of a new technical discipline, kinship studies.

'Kinship is the central discipline of anthropology,' Robin Fox has remarked. 'It is to anthropology what the nude is to art.[6] It is the technical core of social anthropology, the insiders' special field, the least accessible, the most jargon-ridden, the most susceptible to abstract, quasi-mathematical models. Its invention was an accidental byproduct of Morgan's philology. It depended on the extraordinary idea that kinship terminologies were systematic, readily classified in a few broad types, and that they reflected long-dead practices, in particular, marriage forms. This idea has lasted even longer than the other elements of the model of primitive society, and perhaps predictably, for it was its most sophisticated component.

Once established, this kind of thinking was sustained by social inertia, like any other orthodoxy. At the same time it was never static. It lent itself to the most dazzling transformations. And it certainly helped that it could be accommodated to virtually any theoretical or political discourse. Boas could construct an alternative to Morgan, Radcliffe-Brown to Rivers, Leach to Lévi-Strauss, simply by realizing a new transformation of the basic model. In the same way, Maine had inverted the assumptions of Rousseau and Bentham, and Engels and Durkheim had turned the assumptions of the conservatives upside down.

The classic idea of primitive society therefore had three sources of strength. It referred to ultimate social concerns – the state, citizenship, the family and so on; it generated a specialized tradition of puzzle-solving; and it yielded an endless succession of transformations which could accommodate any special interests.

Refutation

Was there no possibility of escape? Could no ethnographer have found that a particular case-study completely refuted the theory? Evidently not. At best an ethnographer might persuade his or her colleagues that a special case had been discovered. No single exception could shake the theory. Moreover the orthodox models provided convenient short-cuts to analysis, and most students gratefully accepted their help.

David Schneider, an American scholar, has given a fascinating example of how the established ideas constrained ethnographic

6 Robin Fox (1967), *Kinship and Marriage*, p. 10.

analysis. He was brought up in the post-war orthodoxy of descent theory, and made a study of the Pacific island society of Yap. In a series of papers published in the 1950s and 1960s he described Yap in 'descent' terms, and to such effect that it became a well-known instance of 'double descent'. In his account the central institutions in Yap were landholding exogamous patrilineal lineages. A person inherited rights in land by way of membership of his or her father's patrilineal corporation. Wives were given temporary rights in their husband's corporations, but divorced wives returned to their brothers and reasserted more substantial claims based on descent. There were also dispersed, exogamous matrilineal clans.

Then in the 1970s – stirred partly by fresh fieldwork done by others, but more by changes in his theoretical perspective – Schneider returned to the Yap material and interpreted their institutions very differently. Crucially, he now began with the Yap conceptions. That put a completely fresh complexion on matters. Consider, for example, succession and inheritance within the *tabinau*, which Schneider had first rendered 'patrilineage':

> The right to succeed to the position of head of the *tabinau*, the right to the products and resources of the land, the right to use the land, are established by work which the child's mother first does and continues to do for the *tabinau*, and which her children take an increasingly greater role in doing. It is described by the Yapese as a simple exchange: the woman and her children (one *genung*) work for husband and mother's husband on his land, and this establishes the right for her children (another *genung*) to hold that *tabinau* when their mother's husband is dead, provided that they too do the work required of them, and the right to its products and its protection while the mother's husband is alive.[7]

Clearly this was something rather different from a patrilineal corporation, traditionally conceived.

Schneider was led to change his initial view of Yap society when he was confronted by new data collected by another ethnographer, which contradicted his earlier account. Nevertheless he stressed that a change of theory had been needed before he could understand the significance of the new material. He had in the intervening years developed a radical cultural strategy for research, and applied it to the study of American kinship. It was only then that his understanding of Yap kinship changed. As he explained, his initial

7 David Schneider (1984), *A Critique of the Study of Kinship*, p. 28.

account of Yap was guided by a theory which judged certain uncomfortable facts to be 'of minimal relevance, irrelevant, or put those data in an ambiguous or anomalous position'. Because the theory had defined the significance of his data he had ignored some of his own observations.

I had a fairly clear paradigm in mind of what kinship was and what a kinship system could be built like, and then sorted the Yapese materials to see which particular form, of all known forms, the Yapese form took. It is not that I failed to appreciate the significance or relevance of these materials; the paradigm of the traditional wisdom of kinship studies defined their significance for the task in hand for me.[8]

Anthropology without the primitive

If the idea of primitive society were finally rejected, would social anthropology disappear with it? Perhaps that has happened already, though one can still track down a few twilight refuges where the familiar debates continue. But what seems to be happening is something different; social anthropology is changing its object of study. It is no longer about the primitive, and no longer particularly or necessarily about 'the other'. More surprisingly, perhaps, it is no longer centrally concerned with social relations. Mainstream cultural and social anthropology today has abandoned primitive society and, with it, society itself. Instead it is embracing the second tradition of anthropology, the anthropology of Tylor and Frazer rather than Morgan and Rivers, the anthropology of culture. Meanwhile, on the margins, there is the third tradition of anthropology, which has at its heart the theory of biological evolution. It too has imperial designs, and may colonize some of the deserted strongholds of the theory of primitive society. Perhaps the notion of transformations will help us to guess the next move.

My own hope is that, although certain things have been done badly in the past, we may still aspire to do them better in the future. However this book represents a historical critique rather than a programme for future research in kinship studies. My aim has been to free us from some of our history by making one particular tradition explicit and demonstrating the way in which it has held us in its grip. If we liberate ourselves we may also be able to free others. Anthropologists developed the theory of primitive society,

8 *Op. cit.*, p. 7.

but we may make amends if we render it obsolete at last, in all its protean forms.

Bibliography

Ackerknecht, Erwin. H. (1953), *Rudolf Virchow: Doctor, Statesman, Anthropologist*, Madison, University of Wisconsin Press.

Ackermann, Robert (1975), 'Frazer on myth and ritual', *Journal of the History of Ideas*, 36, pp. 115–34.

Acton, J. F. E. (1907), *Historical Essays and Studies*, London, Macmillan.

Ankermann, B. (1905), 'Kulturkreise und Kulturschichten in Afrika', *Zeitschrift für Ethnologie*, 37, pp. 54ff.

Armstrong, W. E. (1928), *Rossel Island: an Ethnological Study*, Cambridge, Cambridge University Press.

Atiyah, P. S. (1979), *The Rise and Fall of Freedom of Contract*, Oxford, Clarendon Press.

Atkinson, J. J. (1903), *Primal Law*, London, Longman (bound with Andrew Lang, *Social Origins*).

Bachofen, J. (1861), *Das Mutterrecht*, Basel, Schwabe.

Bailey, Anne M. and Llobera, Josep (eds) (1981), *The Asiatic Mode of Production: Science and Politics*, London, Routledge & Kegan Paul.

Balfour, H. *et al.* (1907), *Anthropological Essays Presented to Edward Burnett Tylor*, Oxford, Clarendon Press.

Barnard, T. T. (1924), *The Regulation of Marriage in the New Hebrides*, unpublished doctoral thesis, University of Cambridge.

Barnes, J. A. (1962), 'African models in the New Guinea Highlands', *Man*, 52, pp. 5–9.

Barnes, J. A. (1971), *Three Styles in the Study of Kinship*, London, Tavistock.

Beidelman, T. O. (1974), *W. Robertson Smith and the Sociological Study of Religion*, Chicago, University of Chicago Press.

Besnard, P. (ed.) (1983), *The Sociological Domain: The Durkheimians and the Founding of French Sociology*, Cambridge, Cambridge University Press.

Bieder, R. E. (1980), 'The Grand Order of the Iroquois: influences on Lewis Henry Morgan's ethnology', *Ethnohistory*, 27, 4, pp. 349–61.

Black, John S. and Chrystal, George (1912), *The Life of William Robertson Smith*, London, Black.

Boas, Franz (1889), 'First general report on the Indians of British Columbia', *Report of the BAAS*, pp. 801–93.

Boas, Franz (1890), 'Second general report on the Indians of British Columbia', *Report of the BAAS*, pp. 562–715.

Boas, Franz (1897), 'The social organization and the secret societies of the Kwakiutl Indians', *Report of the US National Museum for 1895*, Washington, DC.

Boas, Franz (1920), 'The social organization of the Kwakiutl', *American Anthropologist*, 22, pp. 111–26.

Boas, Franz (1940), *Race, Language and Culture*, New York, Free Press.

Bowler, Peter J. (1975), 'The changing meaning of "evolution"', *Journal of the History of Ideas*, XXXVI, pp. 95–114.

Bowler, Peter J. (1983), *The Eclipse of Darwinism: Anti-Darwinian Evolution Theories in the Decades Around 1900*, Baltimore, Johns Hopkins Press.

Brown, P. (1962), 'Non-agnates among the patrilineal Chimbu', *Journal Polynesian Soc.*, 71, pp. 57–69.

Bunsen, C. C. J. (1854), *Outlines of the Philosophy of Universal History Applied to Language and Religion* (2 vols), London, Longman.

Burrow, J. W. (1966), *Evolution and Society: A Study in Victorian Social Theory*, Cambridge, Cambridge University Press.

Burrow, J. W. (1967), 'The uses of philology in Victorian England', in R. Robson (ed.), *Ideas and Institutions of Victorian Britain*, London, Bell.

Burrow, J. W. (1974), 'The "village community" and the uses of history in late nineteenth-century England', in N. McKendrick (ed.), *Historical Perspectives: Studies in English Thought and Society*, London, Europa.

Burrow, J. W. (1981), *A Liberal Descent: Victorian Historians and the English Past*, Cambridge, Cambridge University Press.

Campbell, G. (1852), *Modern India: A Sketch of the System of Civil Government*, London, John Murray.

Cave-Brown, J. (1857), *Indian Infanticide: Its Origin, Progress and Suppression*, London, W. H. Allen.

Cohen, I. Bernard (1980), *The Newtonian Revolution: With Illustrations of the Transformation of Scientific Ideas*, Cambridge, Cambridge University Press.

Cohen, I. Bernard (1985), *Revolution in Science*, Cambridge, Cambridge University Press

Cole, D. (1983), '"The value of a person lies in his *Hetzenbildung*": Frank Boas' Baffin Island Letter-Diary, 1883–1884', in G. Stocking (ed.), *Observers Observed*, Madison, Wisconsin, University of Wisconsin Press.

Collini, S., Winch, D. and Burrow, J. (1984), *That Noble Science of*

Politics: A Century of Intellectual History, Cambridge, Cambridge University Press.

Corning, P. A. (1982), 'Durkheim and Spencer', *British Journal of Sociology*, 33, 3, pp. 359–82.

Daniel, Glyn E. (1950), *A Hundred Years of Archaeology*, London, Duckworth.

Darwin, C. (1859), *The Origin of Species by Means of Natural Selection*, London, John Murray.

Darwin, C. (1871), *The Descent of Man, and Selection in Relation to Sex*, London, John Murray.

Dawson, Warren R. (1938), *Sir Grafton Elliot Smith*, London, Cape.

Deacon, Bernard (1927), 'The regulation of marriage in Ambrym', *Journal of the Royal Anthropological Institute*, 57, pp. 325–42.

De Meur, G. (ed.) (1986), *New Trends in Mathematical Anthropology*, London, Routledge & Kegan Paul.

Dewey, C. (1972), 'Images of the village community: a study in Anglo-Indian ideology', *Modern Asian Studies*, 6, 3, pp. 291–328.

Dickenson, Robert (1969), *The Makers of Modern Geography*, London, Routledge & Kegan Paul.

Downie, R. A. (1970), *Frazer and the Golden Bough*, London, Gollancz.

Dumont, L. (1953), 'The Dravidian kinship terminology as an expression of marriage', *Man*, 53, pp. 34–9.

Dumont, L. (1957), *Hierarchy and Marriage Alliance in South Indian Kinship*, Royal Anthropological Institute Occasional Paper no. 12, London, Royal Anthropological Institute.

Dumont, L. (1966), 'The "village community" from Munro to Maine', *Contributions to Indian Sociology*, IX, pp. 67–89.

Dumont, L. (1983), *Affinity as a Value: Marriage Alliance in South India with Comparative Essays on Australia*, Chicago, University of Chicago Press.

Durkheim, E. (1893), *De la division du travail social: étude sur l'organisation des sociétés supérieures*, Paris, Alcan.

Durkheim, E. (1898), 'La prohibition de l'inceste et ses origines', *L'Année sociologique*, 1, pp. 1–79.

Durkheim, E. (1907), Lettres, *Revue néo-scolastique*, XIV, pp. 606–7, 612–14.

Durkheim, E. (1915a), *The Elementary Forms of the Religious Life*, London, Allen & Unwin (first French edition, 1912).

Durkheim, E. (1915b), *The Division of Labour in Society*, London, Macmillan.

Durkheim, E. (1938), *The Rules of Sociological Method*, Chicago, University of Chicago Press (original French edition, 1895).

Durkheim, E. (1951), *Suicide: A Study in Sociology*, London, Routlege & Kegan Paul (original French edition, 1897).

Durkheim, E. and Mauss, M. (1963), *Primitive Classification*, London, Cohen & West (French original, 1903).

Engels, Frederick (1972), *The Origin of the Family, Private Property and the State*, London, Lawrence & Wishart (originally published in 1884).

Evans-Pritchard, E. E. (1933–5), 'The Nuer: tribe and clan', *Sudan Notes and Records*, Pt 1, 16, 1 pp. 1–53; Pt 2, 17, 1, pp. 51–7; Pt 3, 18, pp. 37–87.

Evans-Pritchard, E. E. (1940a), *The Political System of the Anuak of the Anglo-Egyptian Sudan*, LSE Monograph No. 4, London, Lund.

Evans-Pritchard, E. E. (1940b), *The Nuer: A Description of the Modes of Livelihood and Political Institutions of a Nilotic People*, Oxford, Clarendon Press.

Evans-Pritchard, E. E. (1945), *Some Aspects of Marriage and Family Among the Nuer*, Lusaka, Rhodes-Livingstone Institute, Paper no. 11.

Evans-Pritchard, E. E. (1951), *Kinship and Marriage among the Nuer*, Oxford, Clarendon Press.

Evans-Pritchard, E. E. (1981), *A History of Anthropological Thought*, London, Faber & Faber.

Feaver, G. (1969), *From Status to Contract: A Biography of Sir Henry Maine 1822–1888*, London, Longman

Firth, Raymond (1957), 'Malinowski as scientist and as man', in Raymond Firth (ed.), *Man and Culture: An Evaluation of the Work of Bronislaw Malinowski*, London, Routledge & Kegan Paul.

Firth, Raymond (1963), 'Bilateral descent groups: an operational viewpoint', in I. Schapera (ed.), *Studies in Kinship and Marriage*, Royal Anthropological Institute Occasional Paper no. 16, London, Royal Anthropological Institute.

Fison, Lorimer and Howitt, A. W. (1880), *Kamilaroi and Kurnai: Group-marriage and Relationship and Marriage by Elopement*, Melbourne, George Robinson.

Fortes, M. (1945a), *The Dynamics of Clanship Among the Tallensi*, Oxford, Oxford University Press.

Fortes, M. (1945b), 'An anthropologist's point of view', in Rita Hinden (ed.), *Fabian Colonial Essays*.

Fortes, M. (1949a), *The Web of Kinship Among the Tallensi*, Oxford, Oxford University Press.

Fortès, M. (1949b), 'Time and social structure: an Ashanti case study', in M. Fortes (ed.), *Social Structure*, Oxford, Clarendon Press.

Fortes, M. (1953), 'The structure of unilineal descent groups', *American Anthropologist*, 55, 1, pp. 17–41.

Fortes, M. (1957), 'Malinowski and the study of kinship', in Raymond Firth (ed.), *Man and Culture: An Evaluation of the Work of Bronislaw Malinowski*, London, Routledge & Kegan Paul.

Fortes, M. (1959), 'Descent, filiation and affinity: a rejoinder to Dr Leach', *Man*, 59, pp. 193–7, 206–12.

Fortes, M. (1979), Preface to L. Holy (ed.), *Segmentary Lineage Systems Reconsidered*, Department of Social Anthropology, Queen's University, Belfast.

Fortes, M. and Evans-Pritchard, E. E. (eds) (1940), *African Political Systems*, Oxford, Oxford University Press.

Fortune, R. F. (1933), 'A note on some forms of kinship structure', *Oceania*, 4, pp. 1–9.

Foucault, M. (1972), *The Archaeology of Knowledge*, New York, Pantheon Books (original French edition, 1969).

Fox, Robin (1967), *Kinship and Marriage*, Harmondsworth, Penguin.

Frazer, J. G. (1887), *Totemism*, Edinburgh, Adam & Charles Black (reprinted in Frazer, 1910).

Frazer, J. G. (1890), *The Golden Bough: A Study in Comparative Religion*, London, Macmillan (2nd edition, 1900).

Frazer, J. G. (1894), 'William Robertson Smith', *The Fortnightly Review*, IV, pp. 800–7.

Frazer, J. G. (1899), 'The origin of totemism', *The Fortnightly Review*, pp. 71 (reprinted in Frazer, 1910).

Frazer, J. G. (1909), 'Howitt and Fison', *Folk-Lore*, 20, 2, pp. 144–80.

Frazer, J. G. (1910), *Totemism and Exogamy: a Treatise on Certain Early Forms of Superstition and Society* (4 vols), London, Macmillan.

Frazer, J. G. (1918), *Folklore in the Old Testament* (3 vols), London, Macmillan.

Freud, Sigmund (1918), *Totem and Taboo*, London, Hogarth Press (German original, *Totem und Tabu*, 1913).

Fried, M. H. (1957), 'The classification of corporate unilineal descent groups', *Journal of the Royal Anthropological Institute*, 87, 1, pp. 1–29.

Fuller, L. (1967), *Legal Fictions*, Stanford, Stanford University Press.

Fustel de Coulanges, N.-D. (1984), *La Cité Antique: Étude sur le culte, droit, les institutions de la Grèce et de Rome*, Paris, Durand.

Gardiner, Margaret (1984), *Footprints on Malekula: A Memoir of Bernard Deacon*, Edinburgh, Salamander Press.

Gifford, E. W. (1926), 'Miwok lineages and the political unit in Aboriginal California', *American Anthropologist*, 28, pp. 389–401.

Gifford, E. W. (1929), *Tongan Society*, Honolulu, Bishop Museum Bulletin, no. 61.

Giraud-Teulon, A. (1867), *La mère chez certains peuples de l'antiquité*, Paris, Thorin.

Glickman, M. (1971), 'Kinship and credit among the Nuer', *Africa*, 41, 4, pp. 306–19.

Gluckman, M. (1950), 'Kinship and marriage among the Lozi of Northern

Rhodesia and the Zulu of Natal', in A. R. Radcliffe-Brown and Daryll Forde (eds), *African Systems of Kinship and Marriage*, Oxford, Oxford University Press.

Goldenweiser, A. (1910), 'Totemism, an analytical study', *Journal of American Folklore*, XXIII, pp. 179–293.

Goldman, Irving (1980), 'Boas on the Kwakiutl: the ethnographic tradition', in Stanley Diamond (ed.), *Theory and Practice*, The Hague, Mouton.

Goldschmidt, Walter (ed.) (1959), *The Anthropology of Franz Boas*, memoir no. 89 of the American Anthropological Association, Washington, D.C.

Graebner, F. (1905), 'Kulturkreise und Kulturgeschichten in Ozeanien', *Zeitschrift für Ethnologie*, 37, pp. 28–53.

Graebner, F. (1909), 'Die Melanesische Bogenkultur und ihre Verwandten', *Anthropos*, 4, pp. 726–80, 998–1,032.

Granet, M. (1939), 'Catégories matrimoniales et relations de proximité dans la Chine ançienne', *Annales sociologiques*, Series B, vols 1–3.

Grey, G. (1841), *Journals of Two Expeditions of Discovery in North-Western Australia*, 2 vols, London, Boone.

Grote, George (1851) (3rd edition), *History of Greece*, London, John Murray.

Haddon, A. C. (1904), Preface to *Reports of the Cambridge Anthropological Expedition to Torres Straits*, vol. V, Cambridge, Cambridge University Press.

Haddon, A. C. and Rivers, W. H. R. (1904), 'Totemism', in *Reports of the Cambridge Anthropological Expedition to Torres Straits*, vol. V, Cambridge, Cambridge University Press, pp. 151–93.

Harris, Marvin (1968), *The Rise of Anthropological Theory*, New York, Thomas Y. Crowell.

Haven, Samuel F. (1856), 'Archaeology of the United States', *Smithsonian Contributions to Knowledge*, VIII, pp. 1–168.

Héritier, F. (1981), *L'exercise de la parenté*, Paris, Gallimard.

Herskovits, M. (1953), *Frank Boas: The Science of Man in the Making*, New York, Scribner.

Hinsley, Curtis M., Jr (1981), *Savages and Scientists: The Smithsonian Institution and the Development of American Anthropology, 1846–1910*, Washington, DC, Smithsonian Institution Press.

Hodson, T. C. (1925), 'Notes on the marriage of cousins in India', *Man in India*, V, pp. 163–75.

Howitt, A. W. and Fison, L. (1885), 'On the deme and the horde', *Journal of the Anthropological Institute*, 14, pp. 142–69.

Hudson, Winthrop S. (1965), *Religion in America*, New York, Scribner.

Jaarsma, S. R. (1984), *Structuur: Realiteit, Kernelementen van de Leidse Anthropologie in Theorie en Praktijk Tussen de Jaren Twintig en Vijftig*,

ICA Publication no. 66, Institute of Cultural and Social Studies, Leiden University.

Jakobson, Roman (1944), 'Frank Boas' approach to language', *International Journal of American Linguistics*, 101, pp. 188–95.

Jhering, R. (1852–64), *Geist des Römischen Rechts auf den Verschiedenen Stufen seiner Entwicklung* (4 vols).

Jones, R. A. (1977), 'On understanding a sociological classic', *American Journal of Sociology*, 83, pp. 279–319.

Jones, R. A. (1981), 'Robertson Smith, Durkheim, and sacrifice: an historical context for *The Elementary Forms of the Religious Life*', *Journal of the History of the Behavioral Sciences*, 17, pp. 184–205.

Jones, R. A. (1985), 'Durkheim, totemism and the *Intichiuma*', *History of Sociology*, 5, 2, pp. 79–89.

Jones, R. A. (1986), 'Durkheim, Frazer and Smith: the role of analogies and exemplars in the development of Durkheim's theory of religion', *American Journal of Sociology*, 92, 3, pp. 596–624.

de Josselin de Jong, J. P. B. (1935), *De Maleische Archipel als Ethnologisch Studieveld*, London, Ginsburg (a translation has been published in P. E. de Josselin de Jong (1977), *Structural Anthropology in the Netherlands*).

de Josselin de Jong, J. P. B. (1952), *Lévi-Strauss's Theory on Kinship and Marriage*, Leiden, Brill (reprinted in P. E. de Josselin de Jong (1977), *Structural Anthropology in the Netherlands*).

de Josselin de Jong, P. E. (ed.) (1977), *Structural Anthropology in the Netherlands*, The Hague, Martinus Nijhoff.

de Josselin de Jong, P. E. (ed.), (1984), *Unity in Diversity: Indonesia as a Field of Anthropological Study*, Dordrecht, Foris.

Kaberry, Phyllis (1967), 'The plasticity of New Guinea kinship', in M. Freedman (ed.), *Social Organization*, London, Cass.

Kantorowicz, H. (1937), 'Savigny and the historical school of law', *The Law Quarterly Review*, L111, pp. 330–43.

Karady, V. (red.) (1969), *Marcel Mauss, Oeuvres*: vol. 3, *Cohésion sociale et division de la sociologie*, Paris, Les éditions de Minuit.

Karady, V. (red.) (1975), *Emile Durkheim, Textes*: vol. 2, *Réligion, morale, anomie*; vol. 3, *Functions sociales et institutions*; Paris, Les éditions de Minuit.

Karady, V. (1981), 'French ethnology and the Durkheimian breakthrough', *Journal of the Anthropological Society of Oxford*, XIII, 3, pp. 165–76.

Karady, V. (1983), 'The Durkheimians in academe. A reconsideration', in Besnard (1983).

Kemble, J. M. (1849), *The Saxons in England* (2 vols), London, Longman.

Kluckhohn, Clyde and Prufer, Olaf (1959), 'Influences during the formative years', in Goldschmidt (1959, pp. 4–28).

Koepping, Klaus-Peter (1983), *Adolf Bastian and the Psychic Unity of*

Mankind: The Foundations of Anthropology in Nineteenth Century German, St Lucia, University of Queensland Press.

Köhler, Josef (1897), 'Zur Urgeschichte der Ehe: Totemismus, Gruppenehe, Mutterrecht', *Zeitschrift für vergleichende Rechtswissenschaft*, 12, pp. 187–353, English translation (1975), *On the Prehistory of Marriage: Totems, Group Marriage, Mother Right*, Chicago, University of Chicago Press.

Krader, Lawrence (1974), *The Ethnological Notebooks of Karl Marx*, Assen, Van Gorcum.

Krader, Lawrence (1975), *The Asiatic Mode of Production*, Assen, Van Gorcum.

Kroeber, Alfred (1909), 'Classificatory systems of relationship', *Journal of the Royal Anthropological Institute*, 39, pp. 77–84.

Kroeber, Alfred (1919), 'Zuni kin and clan', *Anthropological Papers of the American Museum of Natural History*, 18, pp. 39–205.

Kroeber, Alfred (1920), Review of Robert Lowie's *Primitive Society*, *American Anthropologist*, 22, pp. 377–81.

Kroeber, Theodora (1970), *Alfred Kroeber: A Personal Configuration*, Berkeley, University of California Press.

Kuhn, Thomas (1977), *The Essential Tension*, Chicago, University of Chicago Press.

Kuper, Adam (1982), 'Lineage theory: a critical retrospect', *Annual Review of Anthropology for 1982*, 11, 71–95.

Kuper, Adam (1983), *Anthropology and Anthropologists: The Modern British School*, London, Routledge & Kegan Paul.

Kuper, Adam (1985), 'Durkheim's theory of primitive kinship', *The British Journal of Sociology*, 36, 2, pp. 224–37.

Kuper, Adam (1986), 'An interview with Edmund Leach', *Current Anthropology*, 24, pp. 375–82.

Kuper, Adam and Kuper, Jessica (1985), *The Social Science Encyclopedia*, London, Routledge & Kegan Paul.

Lang, Andrew (1903), *Social Origins*, London, Longman.

Langham, Ian (1981), *The Building of British Social Anthropology: W. H. R. Rivers and his Cambridge Disciples in the Development of Kinship Studies, 1898–1931*, Dordrecht, Holland, D. Reidel.

Langness, L. L. (1964), 'Some problems in the conceptualization of Highlands social structures', *American Anthropologist*, 66, 3, Pt 2, pp. 162–82.

Layard, John (1942), *Stone Men of Malekula*, London, Chatto & Windus.

Leach, E. R. (1951), 'The structural implications of matrilateral cross-cousin marriage', *Journal of the Royal Anthropological Institute*, 81, pp. 54–104.

Leach, E. R. (1954), *Political Systems of Highland Burma*, London, Athlone Press.

Leach, E. R. (1957), 'Aspects of bride wealth and marriage stability among the Kachin and Lakher', *Man*, 57, pp. 50–55.

Leach, E. R. (1961a), *Rethinking Anthropology*, London, Athlone Press.

Leach, E. R. (1961b), *Pul Eliya*, Cambridge, Cambridge University Press.

Leach, E. R. (1962), 'On certain unconsidered aspects of double descent systems', *Man*, 62, pp. 130–4.

Leopold, J. (1980), *Culture in Comparative and Evolutionary Perspective: E. B. Tylor and the Making of Primitive Culture*, Berlin, D. Reimer.

Lévi-Strauss, C. (1962), *Totemism*, London, Merlin Press (French original, *Le totémisme aujourd'hui*, Paris, 1962).

Lévi-Strauss, C. (1963), *Structural Anthropology*, Boston, Basic Books (original French edition, Paris, 1958).

Lévi-Strauss, C. (1965), 'The future of kinship studies', *Proceedings of the Royal Anthropological Institute for 1965*, pp. 13–22.

Lévi-Strauss, C. (1966), *The Savage Mind*, London, Weidenfeld & Nicolson (French original, *La pensée sauvage*, Paris, 1962).

Lévi-Strauss, C. (1969), *The Elementary Structures of Kinship*, Boston, Beacon Press (original French edition, *Les Structures élémentaires de la parenté*, Paris, 1949; the translation is based mainly on the second French edition, published in 1967).

Lévi-Strauss, C. (1973), *Tristes tropiques*, London, Cape (original French text, Paris, 1955).

Lévi-Strauss, C. (1981), *The Naked Man*, London, Cape (original French text, Paris, 1971).

Lévi-Strauss, C. (1983), *Introduction to the Work of Marcel Mauss*, London, Routledge & Kegan Paul; original French text, introduction to G. Gurvitch (ed.) (1966), *M. Mauss, Sociologie et anthropologie*, Paris, Presses Universitaires de France.

Lowie, Robert (1914), 'Social organization', *American Journal of Sociology*, 20, pp. 68–97.

Lowie, Robert (1915), 'Exogamy and the classificatory systems of relationships', *American Anthropologist*, 17, pp. 223–39.

Lowie, Robert (1920), *Primitive Society*, New York, Boni & Liveright.

Lowie, Robert (1924), *Primitive Religion*, New York, Boni & Liveright.

Lowie, Robert (1927), *The Origin of the State*, New York, Harcourt Brace.

Lowie, Robert (1947), 'Franz Boas', *Biographical Memoirs*, National Academy of Science, 25, pp. 303–22.

Lowie, Robert (1948), *Social Organization*, New York, Rinehart & Co.

Lowie, Robert (1956), 'Reminiscences of anthropological currents in America half a century ago', *American Anthropologist*, 58, pp. 955–1016.

Lubbock, J. (1870), *The Origin of Civilization and the Primitive Condition of Man*, London, Longman.

Lubbock, J. (1865), *Prehistoric Times*, London, Williams & Norgate.

Lukes, S. (1973), *Émile Durkheim: his Life and Work*, London, Allen Lane.

MacClancy, Jeremy (1986), 'Unconventional character and disciplinary convention: John Layard, Jungian and anthropologist', in G. Stocking (ed.), *Malinowski, Rivers, Benedict and Others: Essays on Culture and Personality, History of Anthropology*, vol. 4, Madison, Wisconsin, University of Wisconsin Press.

Mach, Ernst (1898), *Popular Scientific Lectures*, La Salle, Illinois, Open Court.

McIlvaine, J. S. (1867), 'Malthusianism', *The Biblical Repertory and Princeton Review*, XXXIX, pp. 103–28.

McIlvaine, J. S. (1923), 'The life and works of Lewis H. Morgan, LL.D.: an address at his funeral', *Rochester Historical Society Publication Fund*, Series 2, pp. 47–60.

McLennan, Donald (1885), *The Patriarchal Theory* ('based on the papers of the late John Ferguson McLennan'), London, Macmillan.

McLennan, J. M. (1865), *Primitive Marriage: an Inquiry into the Origin of the Form of Capture in Marriage Ceremonies*, Edinburgh, Black.

McLennan, J. M. (1868), 'Totemism', in *Chambers' Encyclopaedia*, London, Chambers.

McLennan, J. M. (1869–70), 'The worship of animals and plants', *The Fortnightly Review*, 6, pp. 407–582; 7, pp. 194–216.

McLennan, J. M. (1876), *Studies in Ancient History*, London, Quaritch.

Maine, H (1861), *Ancient Law*, London, John Murray.

Maine, H. (1871), *Village Communities in the East and West*, London, John Murray.

Maine, H. (1875), *Lectures on the Early History of Institutions*, London, John Murray.

Maine, H. (1883), *Dissertations on Early Law and Custom*, London, John Murray.

Maine, H. (1885), *Popular Government*, London, John Murray.

Malinowski, Bronislaw (1913), *The Family Among the Australian Aborigines*, London, University of London Press.

Malinowski, Bronislaw (1927), *The Father in Primitive Psychology*, London, Routledge & Kegan Paul.

Malinowski, Bronislaw (1929), *The Sexual Life of Savages*, London, Routledge & Kegan Paul.

Malinowski, Bronislaw (1930), 'Kinship', *Man*, 30, pp. 19–29.

Malinowski, Bronislaw (1935), *Coral Gardens and Their Magic*, London, Allen & Unwin.

Malthus, Thomas (1798), *An Essay on the Principle of Population*, London, Johnson.

Mannhardt, Wilhelm (1875), *Der Baumkultus der Germanen und ihrer Nachbarstämme*, Berlin, Bornträger.

Marett, R. R. (1936), *Tylor*, London, Chapman & Hall.

Marett, R. R. and Penniman, T. K. (eds) (1932), *Spencer's Scientific Correspondence with Sir J. G. Frazer*, Oxford, Clarendon Press.

Mark, Joan (1980), *Four Anthropologists: An American Science in its Early Years*, New York, Science History Publications.

Marwick M. (1965), *Sorcery in its Social Setting*, Manchester, Manchester University Press.

Mauss, Marcel (1954), *The Gift: Forms and Functions of Exchange in Archaic Societies*, London, Cohen & West (original French publication, 1925).

Maybury-Lewis, D. (1965), 'Durkheim on relationship systems', *Journal for the Scientific Study of Religion*, IV, 2, pp. 253–60.

Mayr, Ernst (1959), 'Agassiz, Darwin and evolution', *Harvard Library Bulletin*, XIII, 2, pp. 165–94.

Mayr, Ernst (1982), *The Growth of Biological Thought*, Cambridge, Mass., Belknap Press.

Medawar, Peter (1982), *Pluto's Republic*, Oxford, Oxford University Press.

Meek, Ronald L. (1975), *Social Science and the Ignoble Savage*, Cambridge, Cambridge University Press.

Meggitt, M. J. (1965), *The Lineage System of the Mae-Enga of New Guinea*, London, Oliver & Boyd.

Meillassoux, Claude (1981), *Maidens, Meal and Money: Capitalism and the Domestic Community*, Cambridge, Cambridge University Press.

Meinhard, H. (1975), 'The patrilineal principle in early Teutonic kinship', in J. Beattie and R. Lienhardt (eds), *Studies in Social Anthropology*, Oxford, Clarendon Press.

Middleton, John and Tait, David (eds) (1958), *Tribes without Rulers*, London, Routledge & Kegan Paul.

Mill, James (1817), *The History of British India* (3 vols), London, Baldwin.

Mill, J. S. (1871), 'Mr Maine on village communities', *Fortnightly Review*, IX, pp. 543–56.

Moore, James R. (1979), *The Post-Darwinian Controversies: A Study of the Protestant Struggle to Come to Terms with Darwin in Great Britain and America 1870–1900*, Cambridge, Cambridge University Press.

Morgan, Lewis H. (1851), *League of the Ho-de-no-sau-nee, or Iroquois*, Rochester, NY, Sage & Bros.

Morgan, Lewis H. (1868a), *The American Beaver and his Works*, Philadelphia, J. Lippincott.

Morgan, Lewis H. (1868b), 'A conjectural solution of the origin of the classificatory system of relationship', *Proceedings of the American Academy of Arts and Sciences*, VII, pp. 436–77.

Morgan, Lewis H. (1871), *Systems of Consanguinity and Affinity of the Human Family*, Smithsonian Contributions to Knowledge, 218, Washington, DC, Smithsonian Institute.

Morgan, Lewis H. (1877), *Ancient Society: Researches in the Lines of Human Progress from Savagery through Barbarism to Civilization*, New York, Holt.

Müller, Max (1861), *Lectures on the Science of Language*, London, Longman.

Mulvaney, D. J. and Calaby, J. H. (1984), '*So Much That is New': Baldwin Spencer, A Biography*, Melbourne, Melbourne University Press.

Murdock, G. P. (1949), *Social Structure*, New York, Macmillan.

Needham, Rodney (1962), *Structure and Sentiment*, Chicago, University of Chicago Press.

Needham, Rodney (1971), Introduction and 'Remarks on the analysis of kinship and marriage' in Rodney Needham (ed.), *Rethinking Kinship and Marriage*, London, Tavistock, pp. xiii–cxvii, and 1–3.

Needham, Rodney (ed.) (1973), *Right and Left*, Chicago, University of Chicago Press.

Needham, Rodney (1974), *Remarks and Inventions*, London, Tavistock.

Pace, David (1983), *Levi-Strauss, The Bearer of Ashes*, London, Routledge & Kegan Paul.

Parry, Jonathan P. (1979), *Caste and Kinship in Kangra*, London, Routledge & Kegan Paul.

Pederson, H. (1959), *The Discovery of Language: Linguistic Science in the Nineteenth Century*, Bloomington, Indiana University Press.

Peel, J. D. Y. (1971), *Herbert Spencer: The Evolution of a Sociologist*, London, Heinemann.

Peel, J. D. Y. (ed.) (1972), *Herbert Spencer on Social Evolution*, Chicago, University of Chicago Press.

Pouillon, Jean (1985), 'Levi-Strauss', in Adam Kuper and Jessica Kuper (eds), *The Social Science Encyclopedia*, London, Routledge & Kegan Paul.

Quiggin, A. Hingston (1942), *Haddon the Head-Hunter*, Cambridge, Cambridge University Press.

Radcliffe-Brown, A. R. (1910), 'Marriage and descent in North Australia', *Man*, 32, 55–7.

Radcliffe-Brown, A. R. (1912), 'Marriage and descent in North and Central Australia', *Man*, 64, pp. 123–4.

Radcliffe-Brown, A. R. (1913), 'Three tribes of Western Australia', *Journal of the Royal Anthropological Institute*, 43, pp. 143–94.

Radcliffe-Brown, A. R. (1914a), 'The definition of totemism', *Anthropos*, 9, 622–30.

Radcliffe-Brown, A. R. (1914b), Review of *The Family among the Australian Aborigines* by B. Malinowski, *Man*, XIV, 16, pp. 31–2.

Radcliffe-Brown, A. R. (1918), 'Notes on the social organization of Australian tribes: Part I, *Journal of the Royal Anthropological Institute*, 48, pp. 222–53.

Radcliffe-Brown, A. R. (1923), 'Notes on the social organization of Australian tribes: Part II', *Journal of the Royal Anthropological Institute*, 53, pp. 424–47.

Radcliffe-Brown, A. R. (1927), 'The regulation of marriage in Ambrym', *Journal of the Royal Anthropological Institute*, 57, pp. 343–8.

Radcliffe-Brown, A. R. (1929), 'A further note on Ambrym', *Man*, 29, pp. 50–3.

Radcliffe-Brown, A. R. (1931), *The Social Organization of the Australian Tribes*, Sydney, Oceania Monographs no. 1; originally published in *Oceania*, 1, 1–4, pp. 34–63, 206–46, 322–41 and 426–56 (1930–1).

Radcliffe-Brown, A. R. (1935), 'Patrilineal and matrilineal succession', *Iowa Law Review*, 20, 286–303.

Radcliffe-Brown, A. R. (1953), 'Dravidian kinship terminology', *Man*, 53, p. 112.

Radcliffe-Brown, A. R. and Forde, D (eds) (1950), *African Systems of Kinship and Marriage*, London, Oxford University Press for the International African Institute.

Radin, Paul (1958), 'Robert H. Lowie: 1883–1957', *American Anthropologist*, 60, pp. 356–75.

Ratzel, F. (1885–90), *Völkerkunde*, 3 vols, Leipzig, Bibliographisches Institut.

Resek, Carl (1960), *Lewis Henry Morgan: American Scholar*, Chicago, University of Chicago Press.

Rey, Pierre-Philippe (1975), 'The lineage mode of production', *Critique of Anthropology*, 3, pp. 27–9.

Rey, Pierre-Philippe (1979), 'Class contradiction in lineage societies', *Critique of Anthropology*, 4, pp. 41–60.

Richards, A. I. (1941), 'A problem of anthropological approach', *Bantu Studies*, 15, 1, pp. 45–52.

Richards, F. J. (1914), 'Cross-cousin marriage in South India', *Man*, XIV, pp. 194–8.

Rivers, W. H. R. (1904), 'Kinship' and 'The regulation of marriage', in *Reports of the Cambridge Anthropological Expedition to Torres Straits*, vol. V, Cambridge, Cambridge University Press.

Rivers, W. H. R. (1906), *The Todas*, London, Macmillan.

Rivers, W. H. R. (1907), 'On the origin of the classificatory system of relationships', Balfour et al. *Anthropological Essays Presented to Edward Burnett Tylor*, Oxford, Clarendon Press.

Rivers, W. H. R. (1910), 'The genealogical method of anthropological inquiry', *Sociological Review*, 3, pp. 1–12.

Rivers, W. H. R. (1911), 'The ethnological analysis of culture', opening presidential address to Section H of the British Association for the Advancement of Science' *Nature*, 87, pp. 356–60.

Rivers, W. H. R. (1914a), *Kinship and Social Organization*, London, Constable.

Rivers, W. H. R. (1914b), *The History of Melanesian Society* (2 vols), Cambridge, Cambridge University Press.

Rivers, W. H. R. (1914c), 'Is Australian culture simple or complex', *Reports of the British Association for the Advancement of Science.*

Rivers, W. H. R. (1915), 'Descent and ceremonial in Ambrym', *Journal of the Royal Anthropological Institute*, 45, pp. 229–33.

Rivers, W. H. R. (1924), *Social Organization* (ed. W. J. Perry), London, Kegan Paul.

Rivière, Peter (1970), Introduction to *Primitive Marriage* by John McLennan, Chicago, University of Chicago Press.

Robertson Smith, W. (1880), 'Animal worship and the animal tribes among the Arabs and in the Old Testament', *The Journal of Philology*, 9, pp. 75–100.

Robertson Smith, W. (1885), *Kinship and Marriage in Early Arabia*, Cambridge, Cambridge University Press.

Robertson Smith, W. (1889), *Lectures on the Religion of the Semites*, Edinburgh, A. & C. Black.

Rohner, Ronald P. (ed.) (1969), *The Ethnography of Franz Boas*, Chicago, University of Chicago Press.

Ruijter, A. de (1978), 'The Leiden school of anthropology in historical perspective', in G. A. Moeyer, D. S. Moyer and P. E. de Josselin de Jong (eds), *The Nature of Structure*, ICA Publications no. 45, Institute of Cultural and Social Studies, Leiden University.

Sahlins, M. D (1965), 'On the ideology and composition of descent groups', *Man*, 65, pp. 104–7.

Savigny, F. K. (1834–5), *Die Geschichte des Römischen Rechts in Mittelalter* (7 vols), Heidelberg, Mohr.

Scheffler, Harold W. (1970), 'Ambrym revisited: a preliminary report', *Southewestern Journal of Anthropology*, 26, pp. 52–65.

Schneider, David M. (1968), 'Rivers and Kroeber in the study of kinship', in W. H. R. Rivers, *Kinship and Social Organization*, London School of Economics Monographs on Social Anthropology, London, Athlone Press, pp. 7–16.

Schneider, David M. (1984), *A Critique of the Study of Kinship*, Ann Arbor, Michigan, University of Michigan Press.

Service, Elman R. (1985), *A Century of Controversy: Ethnological Issues from 1860 to 1960*, London, Academic Press.

Slobodin, Richard (1978), *W. H. R. Rivers*, New York, Columbia University Press.

Smith, H., Shelton, R. T., Hardy and Loetscher, L. A. (eds) (1963), *American Christianity: An Historical Interpretation with Representative Documents*, New York, Scribner.

Smith, M. (1985), 'Four Germans jurists', *Political Science Quarterly*, X, 4, pp. 664–92.

Southall, A. (1953), *Alur Society: A Study in Processes and Types of Domination*, Cambridge, Heffers.

Speck, F. G. (1915a), 'The family hunting band as the basis of Algonkian social organization', *American Anthropologist*, 17, pp. 289–305.

Speck, F. G. (1915b), *Family Hunting and Social Life of Various Algonkian Bands of the Ottawa Valley*, Ottawa, Geological Survey, Canada, Memoir 70, no. 8, Anthropological series.

Spencer, Baldwin (1928), *Wanderings in Wild Australia*, 2 vols, London, Macmillan.

Spencer, Baldwin and Gillen, F. J. (1904), *The Northern Tribes of Central Australia*, London, Macmillan.

Speth, William W. (1978), 'The anthropogeographic theory of Franz Boas', *Anthropos*, 73, pp. 1–31.

Srinivas, M. N. (1975), 'The Indian village: myth and reality', in J. Beattie and R. Lienhardt (eds), *Studies in Social Anthropology*, Oxford, Clarendon Press.

Stanton, William (1960), *The Leopard's Spots: Scientific Attitudes toward Race in America 1815–1859*, Chicago, University of Chicago Press.

Stein, Peter (1980), *Legal Evolution: The Story of an Idea*, Cambridge, Cambridge University Press.

Stern, Bernard J. (ed.) (1930), 'Selections from the letters of Lorimer Fison and A. W. Howitt to Lewis Henry Morgan', *American Anthropologist*, 32, pp. 257–453.

Stern, Bernard J. (1931), *Lewis Henry Morgan: Social Evolutionist*, Chicago, University of Chicago Press.

Stevens, D. (1975), 'Adam Smith and the Colonial disturbances', in Andrew Skinner and Thomas Wilson (eds), *Essays on Adam Smith*, Oxford, Clarendon Press.

Steward, Julian H. (1955), *Theory of Culture Change*, Urbana, Illinois, University of Illinois Press.

Stocking, George W. (1968), *Race, Culture, and Evolution: Essays in the History of Anthropology*, New York, The Free Press.

Stocking, George W. (ed.) (1974), *A Franz Boas Reader: The Shaping of American Anthropology, 1883–1911*, Chicago, University of Chicago Press.

Stocking, George W. (1983), 'The ethnographer's magic: fieldwork in British anthropology from Tylor to Malinowski', in G. Stocking (ed.), *Observers Observed: Essays in Ethnographic Fieldwork*, Madison, Wisconsin, University of Wisconsin Press.

Stokes, E. (1959), *The English Utilitarians and India*, Oxford, Clarendon Press.

Stokes, W, (1892), *Life and Speeches of Sir Henry Maine*, London, John Murray.

Swanton, John R. (1904), 'The development of the clan system and of secret societies among the Northwestern tribes', *American Anthropologist*, 6, pp. 477–85.

Swanton, John R. (1905), 'The social organization of American tribes', *American Anthropologist*, 7, pp. 663–73.

Swanton, John R. (1906), 'A reconstruction of the theory of social organization', B. Laufer (ed.), *Anthropological Papers Written in Honor of Franz Boas*, New York, Stechert, pp. 166–78.

Tanner, J. M. (1959), 'Boas's contributions to knowledge of human growth and form', in Goldschmidt (1959), pp. 76–111.

Thompson, D'Arcy Wentworth (1917), *On Growth and Form*, Cambridge, Cambridge University Press.

Tooker, E. (1983), 'The structure of the Iroquois League: Lewis H. Morgan's research and observations', *Ethnohistory*, 30, 3, pp. 141–54.

Tylor, E. B. (1865), *Researches into the Early History of Mankind and the Development of Civilization*, London, John Murray.

Tylor, E. B. (1866), 'The religion of savages,' *The Fortnightly Review*, 6, pp. 71–86.

Tylor, E. B. (1871), *Primitive Culture* (2 vols), London, John Murray.

Tylor, E. B. (1881), Obituary of McLennan, *The Academy*, XX, pp. 9–10.

Tylor, E. B. (1889), 'On a method of investigating the development of institutions; applied to laws of marriage and descent', *Journal of the Anthropological Institute*, 18, pp. 245–72.

Tylor, E. B. (1899), 'Remarks on totemism, with especial reference to some modern theories respecting it', *Journal of the Anthropological Institute* (ns), 1, pp. 138–48.

Urry, James (1982), 'From zoology to ethnology: A. C. Haddon's conversion to anthropology', *Canberra Anthropology*, 5, 2, pp. 58–85.

Urry, James (1985), 'W. E. Armstrong and social anthropology at Cambridge, 1922–1926', *Man*, 20, pp. 412–33.

Vinogradoff, P. (1892), *Villainage in England*, Oxford, Clarendon Press.

Vinogradoff, P. (1904), *The Teaching of Sir Henry Maine*, London, Frowde.

Vogt, W. P. (1976), 'The use of studying primitives: a note on the Durkheimians, 1890–1940', *History and Theory*, 15, pp. 33–44.

Warner, W. L. (1937), *A Black Civilization: A Study of an Australian Tribe*, New York, Harper.

Westermarck, Edward (1891), *The History of Human Marriage*, London, Macmillan.

Westermarck, Edward (1927), *Memories of My Life*, London, Allen & Unwin.

White, Isobel (1981), 'Mrs Bates and Mr Brown: An examination of Rodney Needham's allegations', *Oceania*, 52, pp. 193–210.

White, Leslie A. (ed.) (1937), *Extracts from the European Travel Journal of Lewis Henry Morgan*, Rochester Historical Society Publications, XVI, pp. 219–389.

White, Leslie A. (1957), 'How Morgan came to write *Systems of Consanguinity and Affinity*', *Papers of the Michigan Academy of Sciences, Arts, and Letters*, XLII, pp. 257–68.

White, Leslie A. (1959), *The Evolution of Culture*, New York, McGraw-Hill.

White, Leslie A. (1964), Introduction to *Ancient Society* by Lewis Henry Morgan, Cambridge, Mass., Harvard University Press.

White, Leslie A. (1966), *The Social Organization of Ethnological Theory*, Houston, Rice University Studies, no. 52.

Wikman, K. Rob V. (ed.) (1940), *Letters from Edward B. Tylor and Alfred Russel Wallace to Edward Westermarck*, *Proceedings*, Åbo Akademi, Åbo, Finland.

Wilson, R. J. (ed) (1967), *Darwin and the American Intellectuals*, Homewood, Ill., Dorsey Press.

Wouden, F. A. E. van (1935), *Sociale Structuurtypen in de Groote Oost*, Leiden, Ginsberg (translated as *Types of Social Structure in Eastern Indonesia*, The Hague, Martinus Nijhoff, 1968).

Young, M. (ed) (1979), *The Ethnography of Malinowski*, London, Routledge & Kegan Paul.

Zwernemann, Jurgen (1983), *Culture History and African Anthropology: A Century of Research in Germany and Austria*, Uppsala, Uppsala Studies in Cultural Anthropology, no. 6.

INDEX

Agassiz, Louis, 44, 45–6, 61, 67, 132
Ambrym, 178–86
animism, 7, 80–1, 82, 234
Aristotle, 27, 28, 59
Armstrong, W. E., 180, 184, 188
Atkinson, J. J., 111, 167
Austin, J., 19, 29–30
Australian aborigines, 68, 83, 90, 92–104, 106–7, 156, 157, 162, 168, 178, 180–5 passim, 213–14, 218, 221, 230, 232, 233; Malinowski on, 109–10, 174, 186, 237; Radcliffe-Brown on, 172–7, 192; system of kinship and marriage, 94–8; totemism among, 103–4
Aztec, 68, 69–70

Bachofen, J., 2, 3, 6, 35, 36, 99, 119n.
Baffin Island (Formerly Baffin Land), 127, 132
Bandelier, A., 69, 70, 74
Barnard, T. T., 181–2, 185
Barnes, J., 205–7
Bastian, A., 126, 127–8, 131, 142
Bentham, Jeremy, 17–20, 23, 29–30, 31, 32, 241
Bible, 4, 26, 44, 52, 80, 83, 84, 210–16
Boas, Franz, 8, 42, 106, 121, 125–51 passim, 152, 154, 160, 171, 186, 192, 211, 236, 237, 239, 241; biography, 125–35, 140–2, 148–9; fieldwork, 127, 132–5; on Kwakiutl, 135–40; on matriliny, 135–40; totems, 135–40, 146
Bureau of American Ethnology, 74, 130–1, 133, 139, 142, 148, 236, 237

Cambridge University, 152–8, 171–2, 178, 184–6
Childe, V. G., 235, 238
clan, 87, 89, 94, 115, 118, 119, 145, 147, 156, 158, 159, 166, 175, 186–7, 191, 192, 193, 195, 197, 202, 204; see also descent, gens, lineage
Cohen, I. Bernard, 10–13, 17, 74
Columbia University, 132, 140–2, 143–5, 171, 236
Comte, A., 3, 81
contract, 23, 27, 33, 34
cross-cousin, 62, 156, 157, 158, 162, 166–70, 173–5, 179, 188, 210–16, 232, 233; cross-cousin marriage, 173–5, 179; Lévi-Strauss's theory of, 218–24.

Darwin, Charles, 1–5, 10–11, 39, 40, 44–6, 64, 73, 77, 78, 79, 83, 92, 100, 107, 111, 114, 131, 140, 143, 164, 167, 236, 237; theory of evolution, 2–3
Deacon, Bernard, 172, 182–5
Descartes, R., 10, 120

descent, 6, 7, 9, 100n., 110, 135–40, 145, 146–7, 158, 242–3;
descent theory, 146–7, 190–209
diffusion, 1, 78, 128, 138, 142, 162–5, 169–70, 237
Dumont, Louis, 228–9
Durkheim, E., 2, 4, 8, 77n., 110, 121, 125, 173, 177, 186, 192, 193, 210, 217, 234, 237, 240, 241; biography and theories, 112–20

Elliot Smith, G., 101, 163n., 181, 188
Encyclopaedia Britannica, 35, 83–5, 88, 89
Engels, F., 8, 9, 42, 72, 73–4, 75, 113, 205, 209, 235, 240, 241
Evans-Pritchard, E. E., 190, 191, 194–201, 202, 203, 206, 208, 209, 225, 233, 234, 235, 236, 237
evolutionary theories, 1, 2, 8, 9, 38–9, 41, 44–6, 77, 79, 83, 121; the Boasian critique, 143–4, 147; German reaction to, 129–30; Larmarckian theories, 2, 3, 28, 69, 108, 114, 129, 132, 164; Rivers' conversion from, 162–5, 166, 169; see also Darwin
exogamy, 37, 60, 62, 68, 82, 84, 94, 158–9, 215, 216, 220; Durkheim on, 117–18; Frazer on, 105–7; Freud on, 110–2, Tylor on, 98–100, 104, 105–7; see also incest, marriage

family, 3, 5, 9, 26, 28, 38, 67, 73, 191, 197, 203–4, 222–3, 237, 240, 241; Durkheim on, 113–20; Malinowski on, 109–10
Fison, Lorimer, 68, 74, 92–100, 101, 102, 103, 105, 106, 114, 155, 156, 173, 174, 177, 179, 212, 232
Fortes, Meyer, 12n., 190, 191, 201–4, 207, 208, 209, 225, 233, 234, 235, 237
Frazer, J. G., 4, 6, 92, 101, 102, 104, 154, 155, 210, 210–16, 218, 219, 220, 221, 222, 223, 232, 243; Folklore in the Old Testament, 210–16; The Golden Bough, 90, 121; on totemism, 85, 88–91, 105–7, 110
Freeman, E. A., 3, 22
Freud, S., 8, 110–12, 121, 126, 146, 187, 234, 240
Fustel de Coulanges, N.-D., 2, 6, 40n., 118

Gallatin, Albert, 50, 51, 83
Galton, F., 2, 98
gens (see clan), 27, 47–8, 60, 67, 68, 73, 83, 135, 137, 147
Gifford, E. W., 192, 200
Gillen, G., 93, 101–4, 173
Gluckman, Max, 196, 198, 204
Goldenweiser, A., 106–7, 120, 121, 140, 146, 236

Graebner, F., 120, 150, 163, 164
Gray, Asa, 44, 61
Grey, George, 83, 93n.
Grimm, J., 22, 35
Grote, George, 47–8, 60, 67, 68, 70, 74
group marriage, 94–5, 103, 158, 159, 173–4, 232

Haddon, A. C., 152, 153, 155, 157, 172, 180, 188
Haeckel, Ernst, 129, 130, 140, 143
Haven, Samuel, 50–1, 55
Henry, Joseph, 58, 60
Héritier, F., 229–30
Hocart, A., 156, 164, 228
Holmes, W. H., 132, 142, 148–9
Howitt, A. W., 92–103, 105, 114, 155, 167, 168, 173, 174
Huxley, T. H., 2, 64, 78, 79, 154

incest, 106, 156, 216; Darwin on, 117–18; Freud on, 110–12; *see also* exogamy
Indian Empire, 4, 17–35 *passim*; Maine on, 33–5
Indo-European languages, 22, 32, 39, 51, 53
infanticide 36–8
Iroquois, 47–9, 56, 68, 69, 70, 114

Jakobson, Roman, 148, 210, 211, 220
Jhering, R., 20–1, 30
Josselin de Jong, J. P. B., 216–17, 226, 228

Kachin, 205, 213, 224–6, 234, 235
Kemble, J. M., 22, 28–9
kinship terminologies, 6, 7, 74, 76, 94, 97, 106, 156, 157, 159–62, 174, 175, 178, 185, 191, 215, 232, 236, 241; classificatory and descriptive, 56–64; Iroquois, 48, 49, 55; Kroeber on, 145–6, 160–2; Malinowski on, 187–8, 237; Morgan on, 48, 49, 55–62; 'relationship terminologies', 159–62, 165, 181; Rivers on, 160–2, 165
Kohler, Josef, 3, 155, 161–2
Kroeber, Alfred, 140, 141, 145–6, 148, 149, 150, 151, 188, 223, 236, 239; on kinship terminology, 145–6, 160–2; on Zuni, 146–7, 148
Kuhn, Thomas, 10–11
Kwakiutl, 130, 133–40, 144, 150

Lamarckian theory on evolution, 2, 3, 28, 69, 108, 114, 129, 132, 164; theory outlined, 3
Lang, Andrew, 81, 82, 111, 159, 167
law, 3; German, 21; Hindu, 32–3; legal fictions, 29–30; Natural, 23; Roman, 3, 4, 6, 12–14, 21
Layard, John, 153, 172, 180–1, 182
Leach, E. R., 13n., 205, 207–9, 218, 224–6, 227
Leiden University, 216–17, 226

Lévi-Strauss, C., 11–13, 17, 75, 138, 151, 209, 216, 217, 218, 226, 233–4, 235, 241; biography: 210–11; theory of kinship and marriage (initial exposition), 218–24, (criticisms and developments), 224–30
lineages, 109–209, 225, 230, 233, 234
London School of Economics, 109, 160, 172, 188, 190, 236, 237
Lowie, Robert, 133, 140, 145, 148, 188, 211, 223, 236, 239
Lubbock, J., 2, 3, 39, 41, 64, 65, 66, 68, 72, 75, 81, 108, 117; theory of, 78–9
Lyell, Charles, 4, 10–11, 39, 49

Macaulay, T. B., 3, 19–20, 34
Mach, Ernst, 11, 140, 143
McIlvaine, J. S., 43–4, 46, 51, 55, 58–9
McLennan, J. M., 2, 3, 6, 40, 41, 42, 60, 61, 62, 64, 65, 68, 74, 75, 76, 84, 88, 89, 90, 91, 93n., 94, 97, 99, 100, 108, 111, 117, 119n., 120, 156, 158, 160, 228; biography, 35; theory of marriage, 35–9; theory of totemism, 82–3, 88, 107
magic, 5, 77, 106, 237
Maine, Henry, 1–5, 9, 17–41, 42, 46, 60, 64, 67, 72, 76, 111, 186, 193, 231, 233, 235, 237, 240, 241; *Ancient Law*, 22–33; biography, 17–18, 34–5; on India, 33–5
Malinowski, Bronislaw, 8, 133, 172, 174, 180, 186–9, 190, 191, 193, 197, 198, 199, 203, 204, 207, 209, 215, 223, 226, 233, 236, 237, 239; biography, 109; on the family in Australia, 109–10; on Trobriand Islands, 186–8
Malthus, Thomas, 10–11, 36, 40, 100
Mark, 22, 28–9, 41
marriage, 3, 6, 49, 60, 65, 73, 85, 94; 'anomalous' marriages, 167–70, 181, 185; cross-cousin marriage, 173–5, 179; group marriage, 94–5, 103, 158, 159, 173–4, 232
Marx, Karl, 4, 72, 73
Marxist ideas, 9, 229, 235, 238, 239, 240
Mason, Otis T., 131, 141
matriarchy, 6, 35–9, 64, 73, 76, 84, 86, 94, 99, 135–40, 232
matriliny, 68, 83
Mauss, Marcel, 112, 193, 210, 217, 219, 220, 223, 225
Melanesia, 106, 163, 171, 172, 177, 178, 180; Ambrym, 78–86; *History of Melanesian Society*, 165–70, 178, 185; Trobriand Islands, 186–8
Mill, James, 19–20, 28, 33
Morgan, Lewis Henry, 2, 3, 6, 9, 39, 40, 41, 42–76 *passim*, 92, 93, 94, 95, 97, 99, 100, 108, 114, 117, 119n., 125, 130, 135, 137, 143, 144, 145–6, 149, 152, 156, 158, 159, 160, 162, 171, 179, 186, 193, 209, 222, 232, 233,

Morgan, Lewis Henry—*contd.*
235, 236, 237, 238, 239, 241, 243;
Ancient Society, 65–72; biography,
47, 49–50, 55–6; *League of the
Iroquois*, 47–9; kinship
terminologies, 48, 49, 55–62; *Systems
of Consanguinity and Affinity of the
Human Family*, 58–64
Muller, Max, 4, 22, 51–2, 53, 55, 56,
74, 75, 79, 81
Murdock, G. P., 238, 239

Needham, Rodney, 186n., 226–9
New Guinea, 205–7, 213
Nuer, 190, 194–201, 203, 207, 208, 236,
239

Oxford University, 188, 189, 190–1,
196, 233

paternity, 37–8, 40, 109, 110, 191
patriarchal theory, 25, 76, 86, 94, 96,
99, 135–40, 232
philology, 4, 17, 22, 25, 46, 51, 74, 76,
79, 241
polyandry, 37, 60, 61, 62, 68, 94
Powell, John, 130, 131, 141, 142
promiscuity, primitive, 60, 108, 156,
159
property, 3, 5, 7, 32, 38, 60, 63–4, 67,
71, 74, 76
Putnam, F. W., 132, 133, 142, 144

Radcliffe-Brown, A. R., 121, 171, 178,
180, 183–9 *passim*, 190, 191–2, 193,
198, 216, 218, 223, 229, 230, 233,
235, 237, 239, 241; on the Australian
aborigines, 172–7
Ratzel, F., 128, 133
relationship terminologies, *see* kinship
terminologies
religion, 3, 5, 7, 9, 65, 77, 79–81; *see also*
animism, Bible, sacrifice
Richards, A. I., 196, 207
Rivers, W. H. R., 109, 120, 152–70, 171,
172, 177–82, 186, 187, 188, 191, 215–
16, 221, 222, 232–3, 235, 237, 241,
243; converted to diffusionism, 162–
65; *History of Melanesian Society*,
165–70; on relationship systems,
159–62
Robertson Smith, W., 4, 82, 90, 91, 100,
107, 110, 117, 120, 193n., 234;
biography, 83–5; theory of totemism,
83–8, 103–4, 107, 110, 117, 120,
193n., 234
Rousseau, Jean-Jacques, 17, 25, 231,
241

sacrifice, 80–1, 86–8
Sanskrit, 22, 43, 49, 51

Sapir, E., 140, 149
Savigny, F. K., 20–2, 30
Schneider, David, 241–3
sexual jealousy, 40–1, 111
Smithsonian Institution, 43, 50, 58, 61,
130–2, 139, 140, 144, 148, 150, 236
Speck, F. G., 146, 148, 236
Spencer, B., 89, 92, 93, 101–4, 143, 152,
173
Spencer, H., 2, 3, 6, 81, 114, 115, 117,
153
state, 3, 5, 9, 26, 28, 73–4, 76, 87, 96,
147, 177, 225, 232, 233, 235, 240,
241
Stephen, J. F., 18, 31
Steward, Julian, 235, 238
Stubbs, William, 3, 22
Swanton, J., 121, 144–5

taboo, 87–8, 89; Durkheim on, 118;
Freud on, 110–12
Tallensi, 190, 201–4, 206, 207, 208
Tamil, 51, 55, 56, 58, 59
Tonnies, 4, 116
Torres Straits, 154–5, 158, 160
totemism, 82–122, 155, 156, 159, 162;
Australian, 103–4; Boas on, 135–40,
146; Durkheim on, 117–20; Frazer
on, 85, 88–91; Freud on, 110–12;
Goldenweiser on, 146; Lévi-Strauss
on, 217; McLennan's theory of, 82–
3, 107; Radcliffe-Brown and Rivers
on, 177; Tylor on, 104, 106–7
transformations, 10–13, 17, 231–6, 243
Trobriand Islands, 172, 186–8, 203, 237
Turanian, 51, 52, 55, 56, 58
Tylor, E. B., 2, 3, 6, 35, 39, 41, 64, 65,
66, 68, 75, 76, 77, 86, 89, 108, 133,
139, 142, 155, 156, 159, 162, 174,
179, 212–13, 214, 216, 217, 232, 234,
238, 243; biography, 78–82;
definition of culture, 81; on
exogamy, 98–100, 105–7; on
totemism, 104, 106–8

Utilitarian ideas, 3, 44; on India, 17–20;
see also Austin, Bentham, Mill

Virchow, Rudolf, 126, 128, 129, 131,
140, 150, 236
village community, 28–9, 33, *see also*
Mark

Waitz, T., 127, 128
Wallace, A. R., 79, 108, 237
Wellhausen, J., 81, 83, 84
Westermarck, Edward, 8, 110, 116, 159,
186, 188, 237; biography, 107–9
White, Leslie, 149, 235, 237
Wouden, F. A. E. van, 217, 218